IMAGES
of America

AROUND TRONA AND SEARLES VALLEY

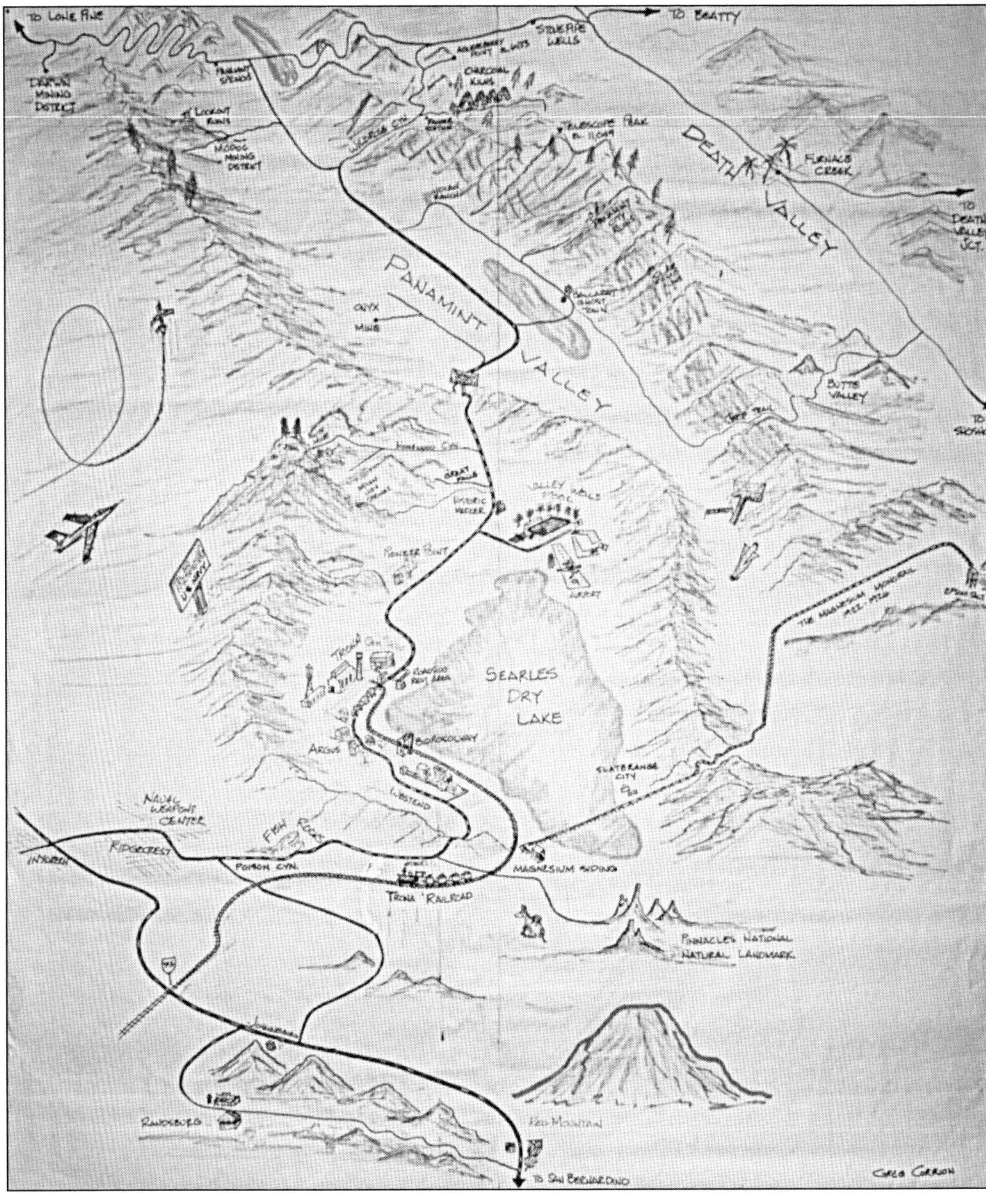

Greg Corrion, a native of Trona and 56-year resident, drew this map of Searles Valley for the Old Guest House Museum so visitors could see the locations of places of interest.

On the Cover: This 1959 photograph shows the Trona Plant of American Potash and Chemical Corporation as the backdrop to Austin Hall, with the Argus Range and Trona Peak in the background. For more than 50 years Austin Hall was the heart of Trona, housing many of the businesses in Searles Valley.

IMAGES
of America

Around Trona and Searles Valley

James L. Fairchild, Russell L. Kaldenberg,
and the Searles Valley Historical Society

ARCADIA
PUBLISHING

ISBN 978-1-4671-3399-9

Published by Arcadia Publishing
Charleston, South Carolina

Printed in the United States of America

Library of Congress Control Number: 2015935024

For all general information, please contact Arcadia Publishing:
Telephone 843-853-2070
Fax 843-853-0044
E-mail sales@arcadiapublishing.com
For customer service and orders:
Toll-Free 1-888-313-2665

Visit us on the Internet at www.arcadiapublishing.com

To Margaret "Lit" Brush for her tireless work to save the history of Trona as well as the history of all of Searles Valley and Panamint Valley.

Contents

ACKNOWLEDGMENTS

The real genius behind this book is the Searles Valley Historical Society, whose members had the foresight to collect and preserve a vast store of historical documents, photographs, and artifacts of Trona, Searles Valley, and Panamint Valley. These historical materials provide the foundation for this book.

Margaret "Lit" Brush, president of the Searles Valley Historical Society, curator of the Old Guest House Museum, and 86-year resident of Searles Valley, deserves special thanks for her help in locating obscure photographs, fact checking, and editing all of our text. Thanks also to Bonnie Fairchild for her tireless hours retrieving photographs and information, Judyth Reed for editing suggestions, and Zee Malas for assisting with the photographs.

All photographs are owned by the Searles Valley Historical Society except for those few identified in captions; photographs from the Settle-Dearborn collections are identified as (SD). We thank them for their generosity.

We also appreciate our original editor with Arcadia Publishing, Alyssa Jones, for all of her encouragement, and Matt Todd for his guidance.

Introduction

Searles Valley is an arid closed basin lying 43 miles east of the south end of the Sierra Nevada Mountains in California. It is bounded on the east and northeast by the Slate Range, on the west by the Argus Range and Spangler Hills, and on the south by the Lava Mountains. Searles (dry) Lake occupies the north-central part of the valley. During those parts of the late Pliocene and Pleistocene periods, precipitation and runoff from the east side of the Sierra Nevada into the Owens River were much greater than at present, and a chain of as many as five large lakes was created, of which Searles Lake was third. In Searles Valley, maximum-depth lakes rose to the 2,280-foot contour, the level of the spillway at the south end of the Slate Range that led overflowing waters to Panamint Valley. That spillway is about 660 feet above the present dry lake surface.

Deposits in the Searles Lake Formation contain numerous fossil snails and clams, especially in Poison Canyon and Salt Wells Valley. These regions were near the main source of inflowing freshwater at the times Searles Valley contained large lakes, and the genera and species of snails and clams all indicate low-salinity environments. The same species of snail has also been found in Panamint Valley to the east, indicating that when Searles Lake contained freshwater, it also overflowed into Panamint Valley. Only one vertebrate fossil has been found, a fish found at a depth of 68 feet in mud that was deposited between 24,000 and 10,500 years ago.

The 14 economically important saline mineral beds in Searles Lake are the products of 150,000 years of wet, glacial epochs separated by brief hot dry periods. When it was wet, the Owens River drained into Searles Valley, carrying over 40 chemical elements in its water. Some of these elements were leached from the rocks in the Sierra Nevada Mountains through glacial erosion, and other elements were the result of extensive volcanism in the Owens and Long Valleys and as far north as the Mono Craters. All dissolved elements were at very low concentrations in the river water. However, over many thousands of years and with a river flow averaging 290,000 gallons every minute, and two-and-a-half to four times that flow during glacial periods, many billions of tons of dissolved materials have been carried by the river's water. During periods when the river flow was low to moderate, Searles Lake was the terminus lake for the river, so all of the dissolved elements accumulated in Searles Lake's water. During periods of desiccation, these materials were deposited as saline mineral beds.

Searles Lake has remained mostly dry since its most recent desiccation 10,500 years ago, except for a period centered at about 3,500 years ago when the lake surface rose to an elevation of about 1,800 feet, 180 feet above the present dry surface. This last desiccation was when the topmost mineral bed, the 50- to 80-foot thick Upper Salt, was deposited.

Archeological sites occur at several locations in Searles Valley, including at the high-water shoreline, which may mean they are more than 10,000 years old. Other sites date from less than 500 years ago.

Gold and silver miners built the first settlements in Searles Valley, although none were more than a collection of a few shacks or roofed dugouts. These were near their mines, first in the

Slate Range and later in the Argus Range. None of their settlements were built to last, and all are now gone, most with little evidence they ever existed. Some of the early settlements and associated mills were burned by Indians, some were salvaged to be moved to other sites, and the rest succumbed to the elements, including flash floods, sun and wind, and vandals. Even the iron machines in their mills and their water pipes are now gone, collected to supply critical materials during World War II. The only exception is the Ruth Mine site in Homewood Canyon, although even there much of the small settlement that once existed is gone.

In 1873, John Searles and his San Bernardino Borax Mining Company started mining borax that was found in the surface mud along the western edge of a dry lake that covers 50 square miles of the floor of Searles Valley. Their first borax mill was burned by Indians in the spring of 1878, but Searles quickly rebuilt his mill at a new site called Borax. This mill was the start of continuous habitation in Searles Valley by nonnative peoples, which has now lasted for more than 137 years.

In 1912, potash was found in the brine in Searles Lake. With the outbreak of World War I, potash became a critical nutrient for the crops needed to feed our country. Two factories were built to process the brine to recover potash, but they had only marginal success. The year 1921 was pivotal for Searles Valley. One of the early potash factories had shut down in February, never to restart. The other factory shut down in May and remained closed the rest of the year. However, the scientists and engineers working for American Trona Corporation persevered and invented ways to make the idle plant one of the most profitable businesses in the country.

Later, scientists learned that the dry lake would yield several other important and valuable mineral commodities, including borax, soda ash, and sodium sulfate, and there was an almost infinite supply of raw ore for these products. With this knowledge, the town started by John Searles was expanded several times as mining expanded. These new miners renamed the town Trona, taking this name from a highly abundant soda-ash mineral found in the dry lake.

Initially, Trona was the commercial hub for the Panamint and Indian Wells Valleys as well as Searles Valley. The nearest town of consequence was Randsburg, 40 miles to the southwest. During World War II, the Department of the Navy established a research facility at China Lake in Indian Wells Valley, which led to the creation of the city of Ridgecrest. As Ridgecrest grew, so did its business community, and this gradually siphoned away the businesses from Searles Valley. Today, little remains of the once thriving Trona business community, although about 1,800 people still call Trona home.

One

Native People

In early times, the Searles Valley area was occupied by both Kawaiisu and Panamint Shoshone, who spoke a Uto-Aztecan language. Julian Steward claimed, "The inhabitants of the southern end of Panamint Valley, the Argus Mountains, the region around Trona, were called Mugunuwu" and were mixed with Shoshone (the Owa'dzi) from the central part of Panamint Valley (known as Uwa'gatu). Anthropologist Maurice Zigmond's studies on the Kawaiisu indicate that Searles Valley was visited seasonally. The Indians gathered salt for their own use and trade with those in the Lake Isabella area.

All of the historically known Indian people encountered by the early explorers in the area appear to have been Panamint Shoshone and not Kawaiisu. These people practiced a lifestyle of hunting and gathering. For sustenance they relied on rabbits, packrats, chuckwalla lizards, bighorn sheep, mesquite, and anything else they could gather.

"Indian" Joe Peterson, also known as Copperstain Peterson, a Panamint Shoshone, raised fruit, nuts, and vegetables at Ishhoe in the Argus Mountains (Tuntapun). The Shoshone name was recorded by Tom Wilson, a Panamint Shoshone who was raised in Bruce Canyon. Peterson's spring was deemed to be a winter village. It has variously been called Sweetwater Creek, Grass Valley, Peterson Creek, Searles Gardens, and Indian Joe Springs, and was situated about six miles northwest of Trona (Omakatun, or Toona). Around 1873, John Searles took over the gardens from the Shoshone families who had used it. He planted more trees, raised crops, and built a house. When Searles died in 1897, Joe Peterson, his father "Old Pete," and his sister Mabel returned and raised produce for the miners in the vicinity. Peterson had the only Indian allotment in the area, having received 160 acres under Farming and Grazing Lease Allotment No. 0970. He stayed there until his death in 1917.

Other Indians living in the area were located at Indian Ranch (Hautta), in Panamint Valley, Stone Corral in Pleasant Canyon (Kwe'-Dao-Po-Na-Noon), in the Panamint Mountains (Ky-e-guta), or at the Indian village in Darwin (Yatananti). Several came into Trona to work, shop, and to sell their Panamint baskets.

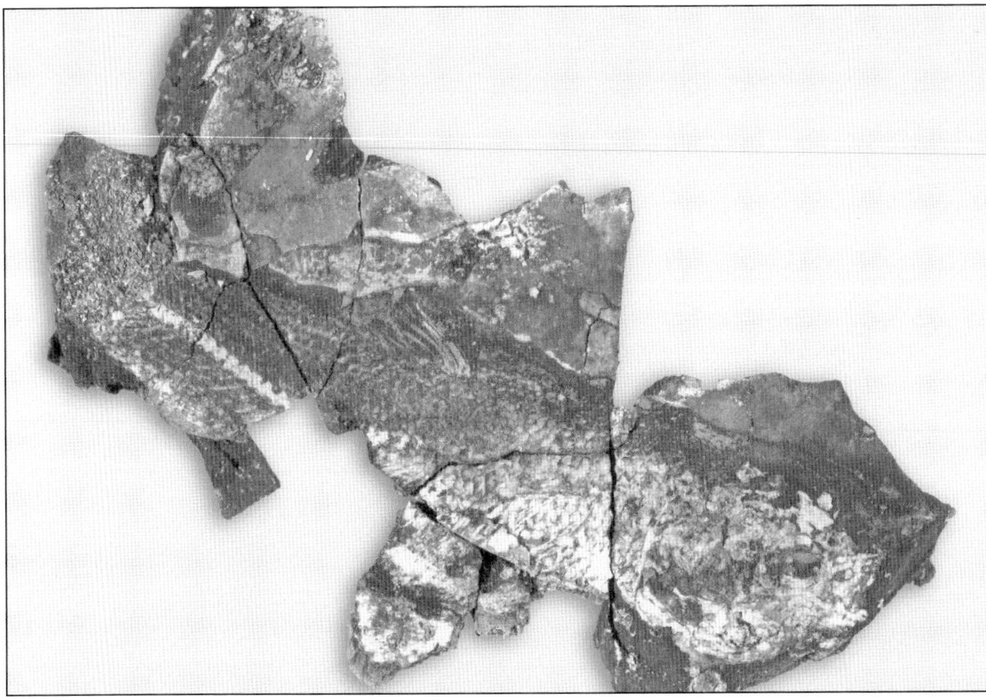

As late as 2,000 years ago, the lake contained water, but its elevation began dropping about 10,000 years ago and became what it is today, dry, about 800 years ago. The fish imprint pictured here in 1951 is probably a Sacramento perch. It was found in a bore hole in 1934 at a depth of 68 feet below the surface. Upon exposure to the air, the fossil disintegrated.

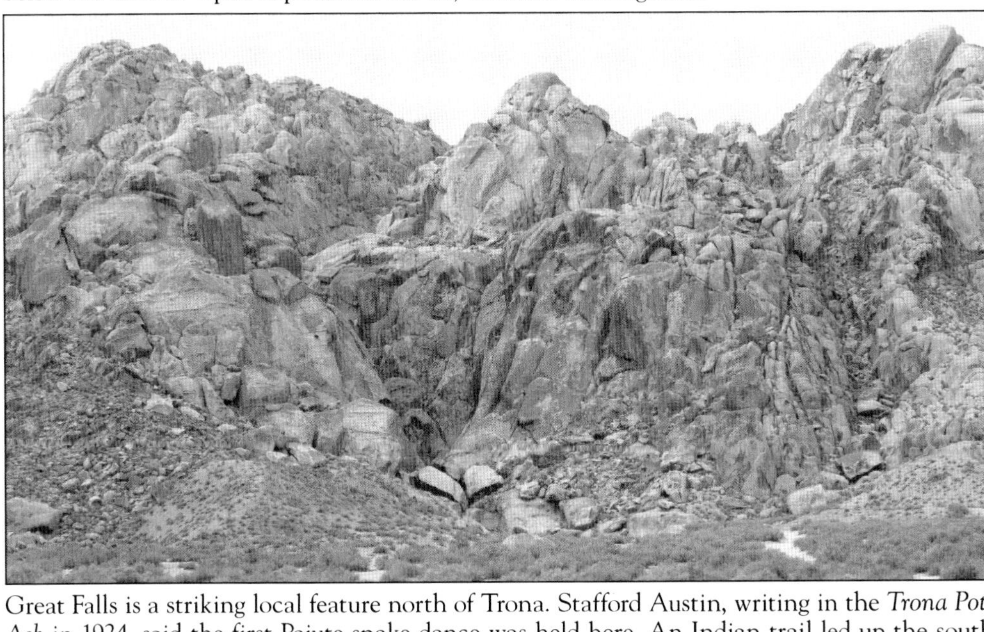

Great Falls is a striking local feature north of Trona. Stafford Austin, writing in the *Trona Pot-Ash* in 1924, said the first Paiute snake dance was held here. An Indian trail led up the south face of the canyon into Great Falls Basin and passed by stone *arrastras*. Water from the many springs was piped through 1.5-inch pipes to Searles Valley. The area was the location of many Trona picnics.

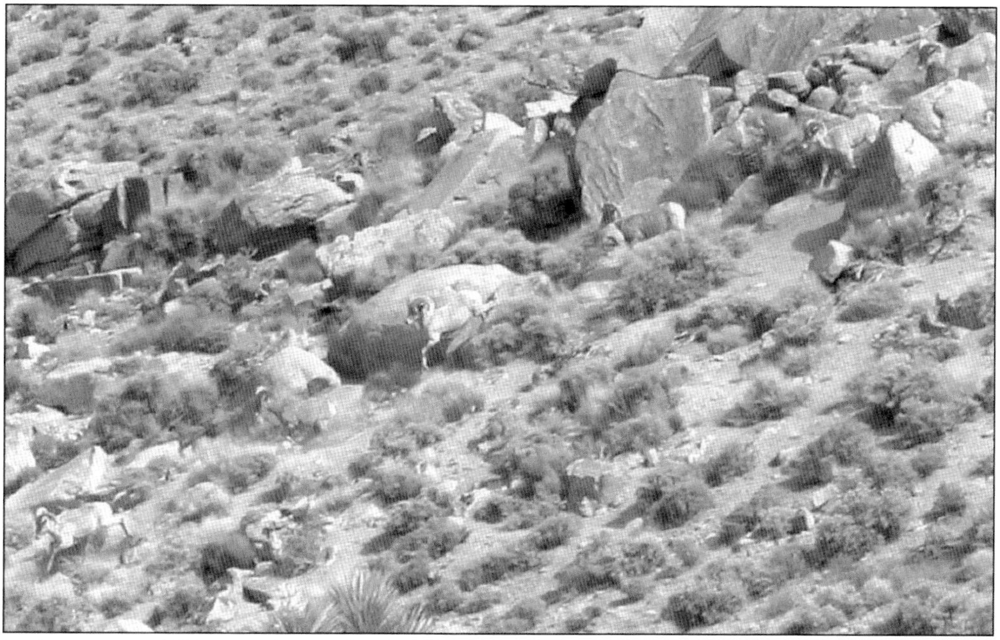

Bighorn sheep (Wa-soo-pi) provided food for the aboriginal occupants as well as for the miners. By 1960, they were locally extinct. They have been successfully reintroduced and are found in all of the surrounding mountains, including the south end of Searles Valley. Bighorn sheep are also one of the dominant images in Native American rock art found in the area and may have been a spiritual image associated with the afterlife.

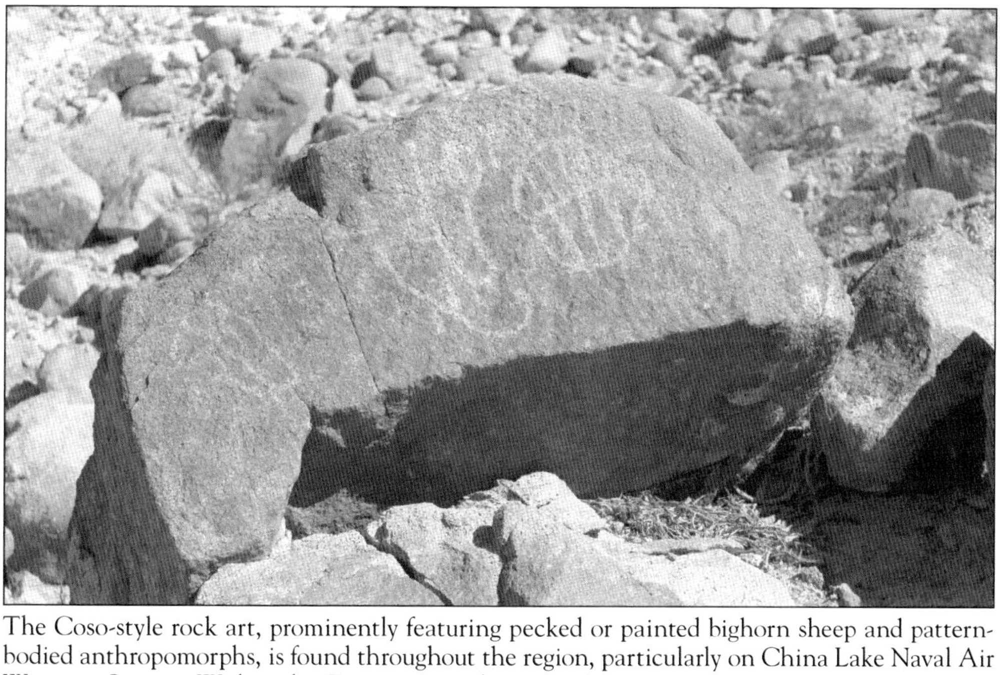

The Coso-style rock art, prominently featuring pecked or painted bighorn sheep and pattern-bodied anthropomorphs, is found throughout the region, particularly on China Lake Naval Air Weapons Station. Within the Trona area, only one rock art site has been located. The Poison Canyon rock art site is a group of small panels on several boulders. The rock art style is called Great Basin Abstract.

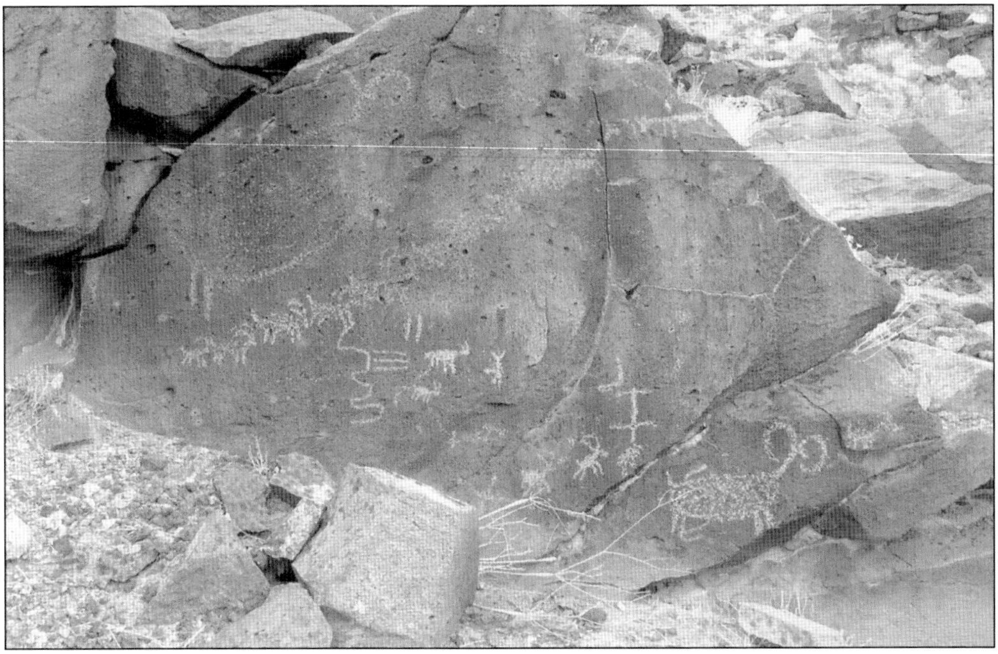

This boulder, in Wilson Canyon west of Pioneer Point in the Argus Mountains, contains representative Coso-style rock art and is the closest known Coso-style rock art site to Trona. Note the boat-shaped bighorn sheep images.

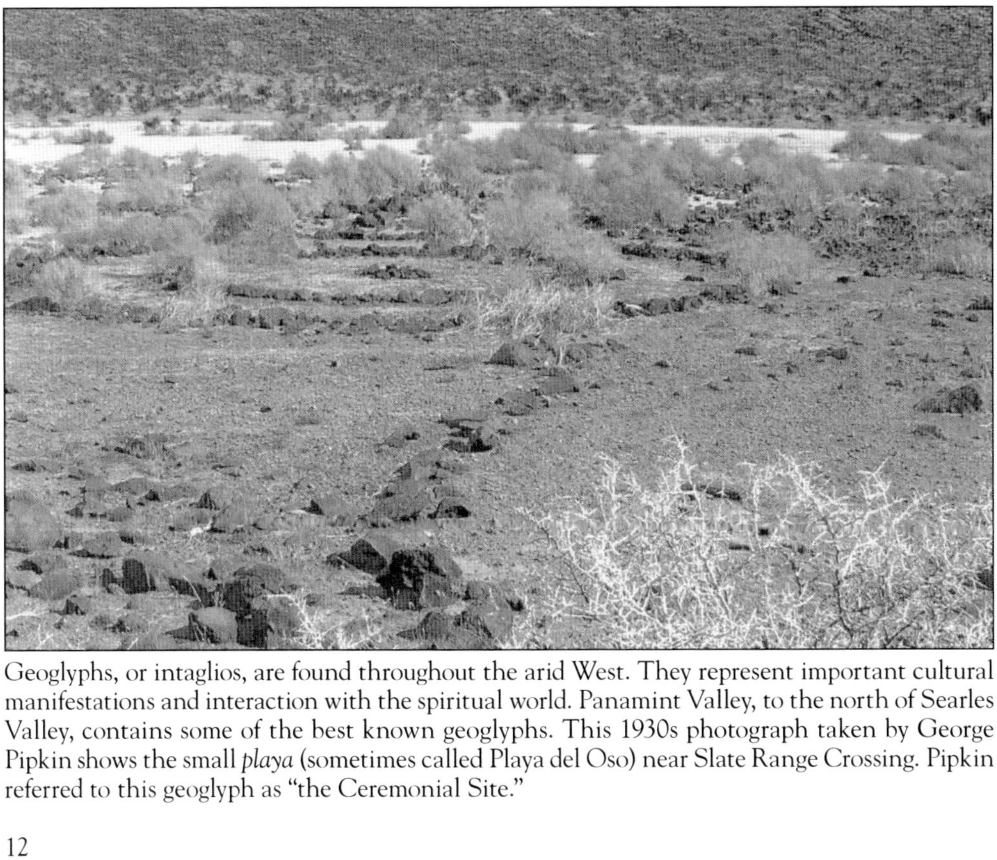

Geoglyphs, or intaglios, are found throughout the arid West. They represent important cultural manifestations and interaction with the spiritual world. Panamint Valley, to the north of Searles Valley, contains some of the best known geoglyphs. This 1930s photograph taken by George Pipkin shows the small *playa* (sometimes called Playa del Oso) near Slate Range Crossing. Pipkin referred to this geoglyph as "the Ceremonial Site."

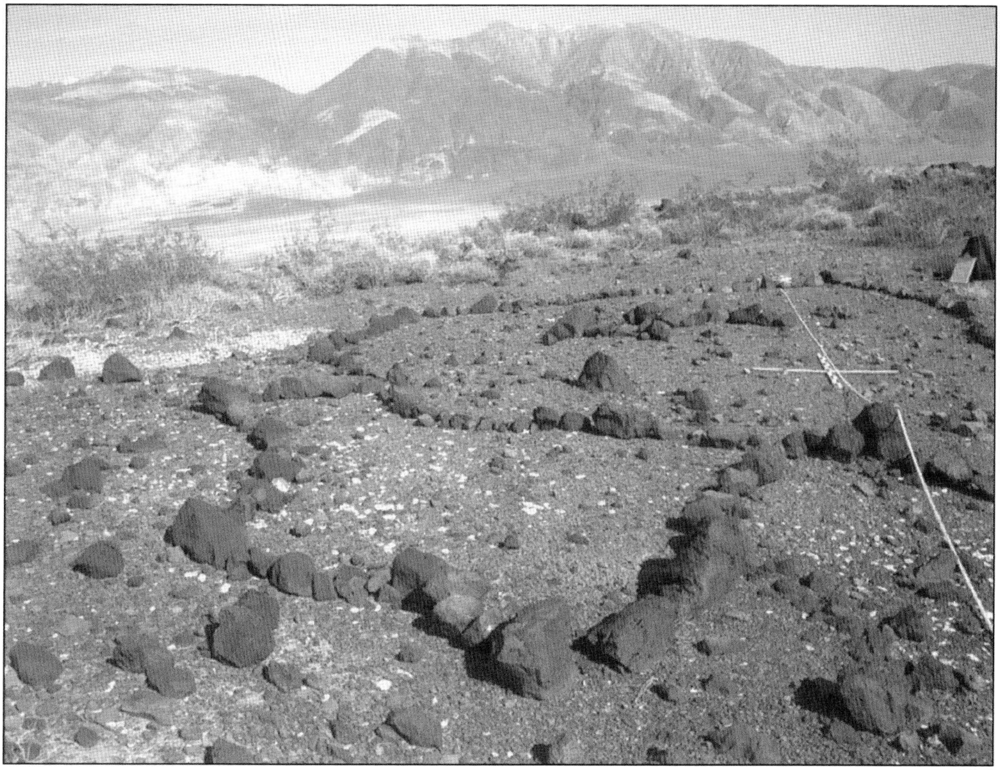

The highest known elevation for a geoglyph in California is found at over 3,000 feet in the northern portion of the Slate Range. It is a complex compartmentalized geoglyph located on well-developed desert pavement. From this site, one can overlook both Searles and Panamint Valleys.

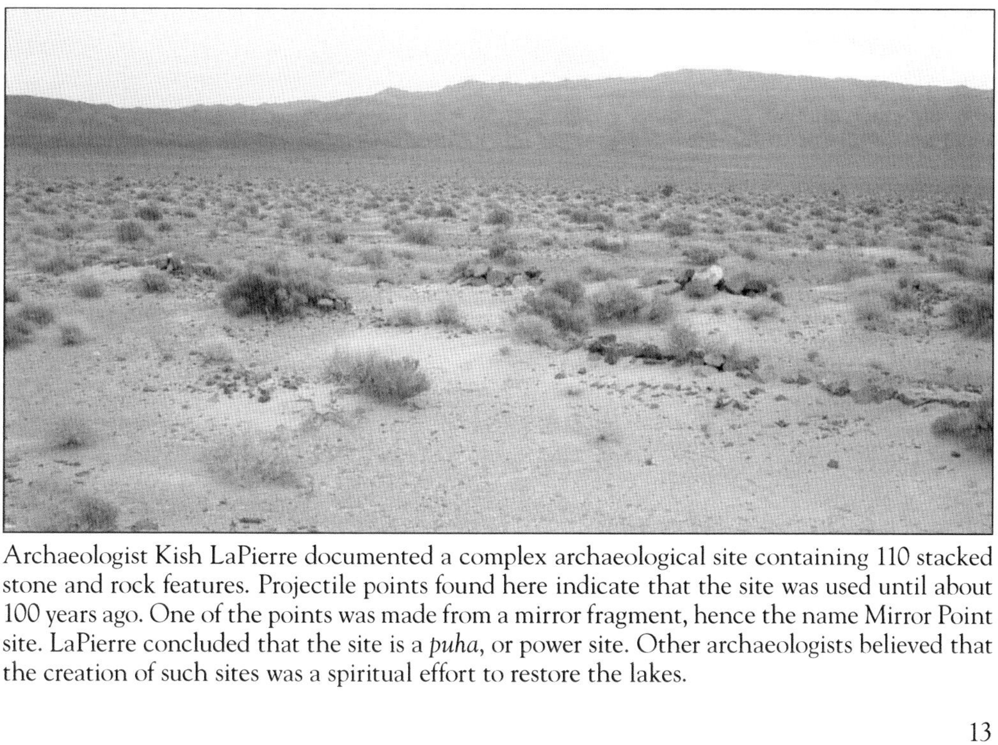

Archaeologist Kish LaPierre documented a complex archaeological site containing 110 stacked stone and rock features. Projectile points found here indicate that the site was used until about 100 years ago. One of the points was made from a mirror fragment, hence the name Mirror Point site. LaPierre concluded that the site is a *puha*, or power site. Other archaeologists believed that the creation of such sites was a spiritual effort to restore the lakes.

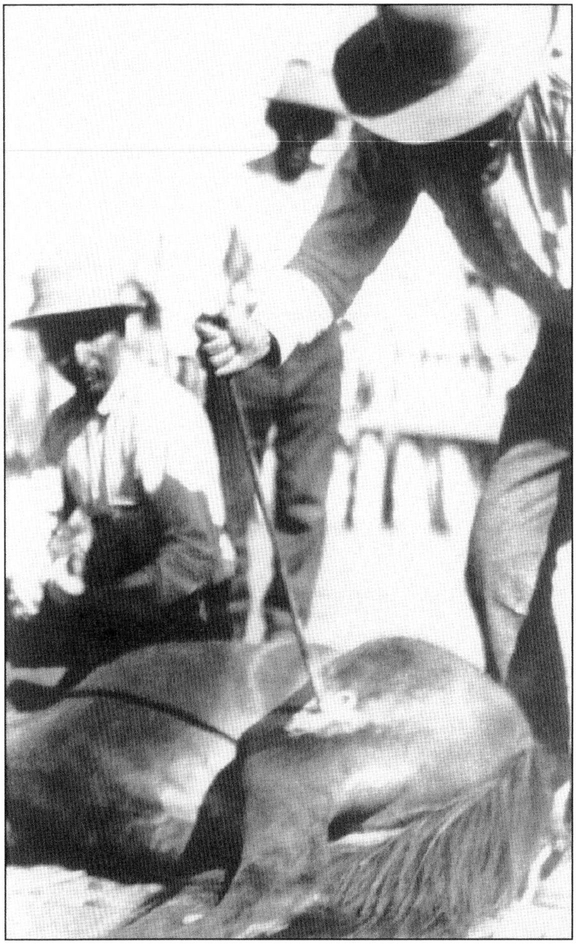

This photograph, taken in 1916, shows Shoshone men who sometimes worked for John Searles and others herding and branding cattle, horses, and mules, which roamed freely. Joe Peterson rented horses and mules to the Trona Company and Burnham Chemical Company for $2.50 each per month. After Peterson's death, George Hanson came into Trona to pick up the monthly check for Mabel Peterson and take it to her at her residence in Panamint Valley.

This 1920 photograph shows R.W. Mumford with his horse Napoleon. He is examining Joe Peterson's *wickiup* at Ishhoe in the Argus Mountains three years after Peterson's death from food poisoning. The 160 acres owned by Peterson, the only Indian allotment in the Trona area, was deeded to him in 1908. After Joe died, his sister Mabel was paid $250 per year for the water rights by the Borosolvay Chemical Corporation.

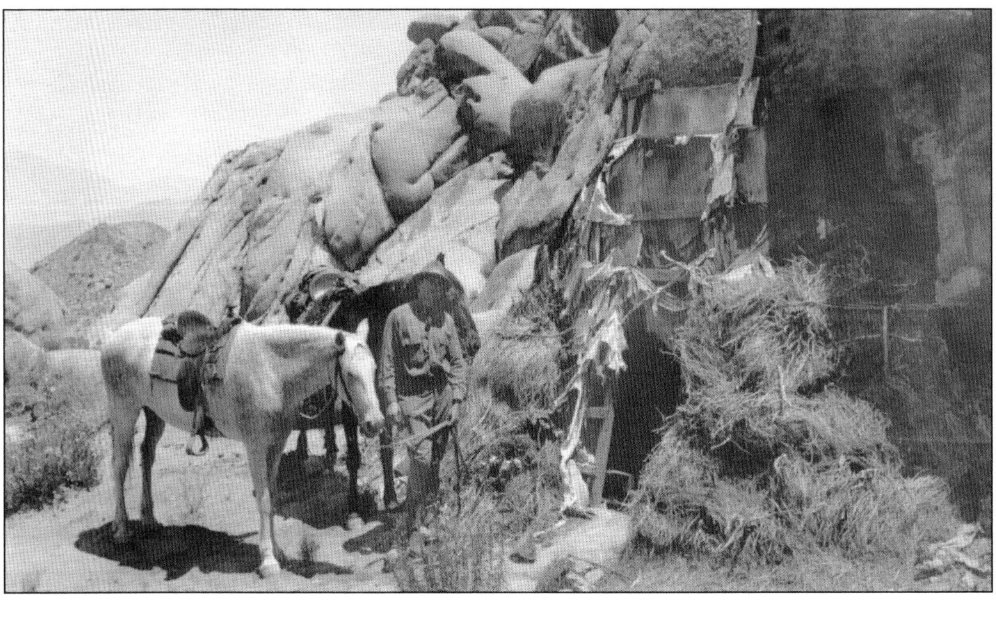

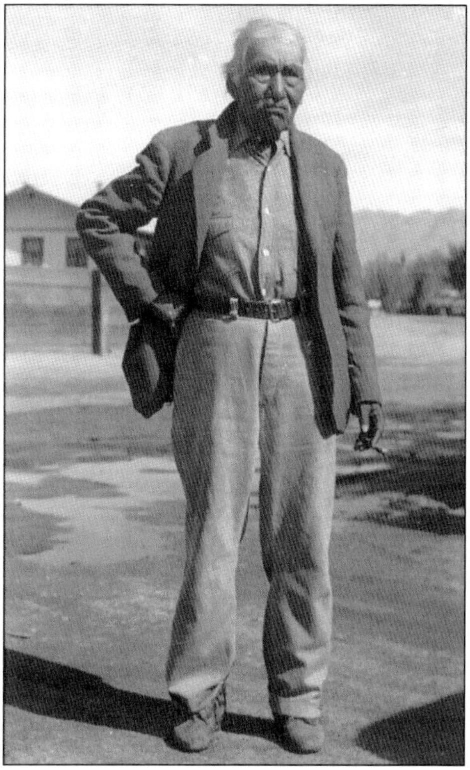

Bah-vanda-sava-nu-kee (Boy-Who-Runs-Away), George Hanson, or Indian George Inyo was very young when he saw the Manley-Bennett-Jayhawker parties traverse Death Valley, cross the Panamint Mountains and Slate Range, and enter Searles Valley around Christmas 1849. Hanson worked for John Searles during the 1870s and 1880s as a cowboy and laborer. He was literate and wrote letters to his cousin Joe Peterson. In an interview for *Desert* magazine published in February 1940, he talked about working for John Searles, whom he called "Bear Fighter" due to the scar on his face. He said he and Hungry Bill had collected salt at the dry lake before Searles developed his mining operation; George and his granddaughter Molly list their residence in the 1928 California Indian census as Trona. George was 102 when he died in 1943.

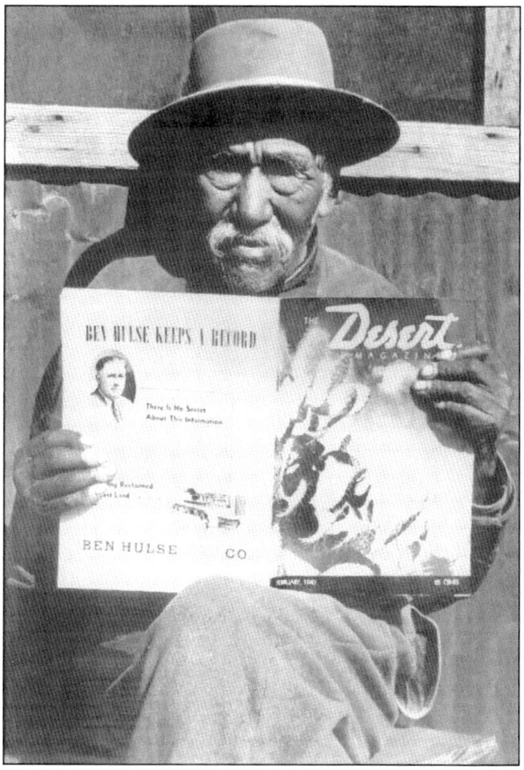

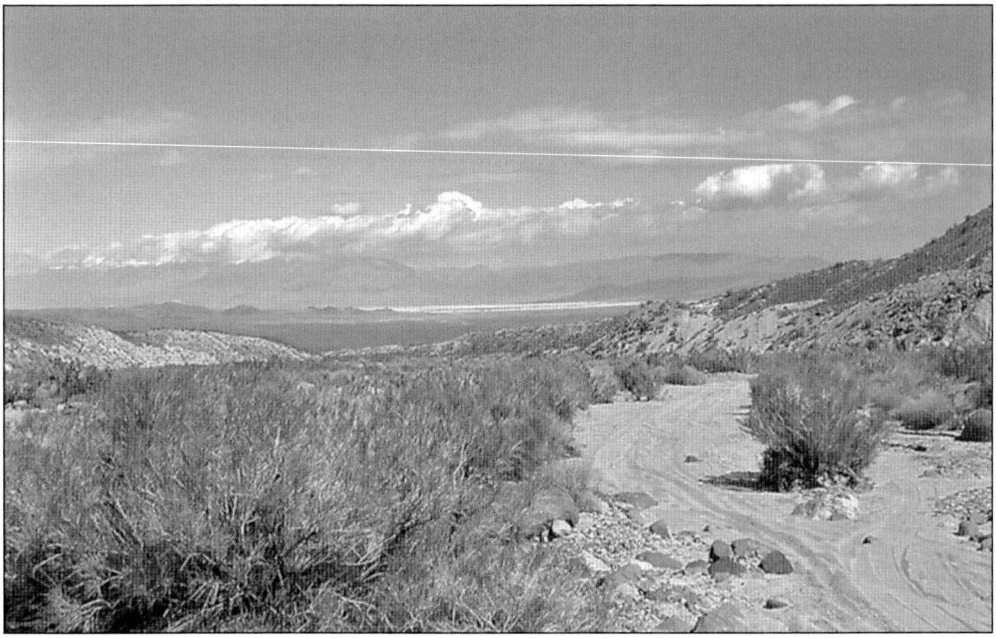

Pictured here is Bedrock Canyon, looking east into Searles Valley. It was here that one of John Searles's freight wagons was attacked by Indians. In 1859, Jacob Kuhrts and John Searles traveled from San Francisco to the Slate Range (Tin'-dab-boo) with a big mule team hauling goods. Searles and his brother, Dennis, were prospecting for gold and silver. Kuhrts hauled goods for the Searles brothers and their partners until their mining venture failed. The route Kuhrts used ran down Bedrock Canyon. On one trip, Kuhrts was driven from a spring by Indians who shot "a lot of arrows" at him, wounding one of his mules. (Courtesy of Bill Wight).

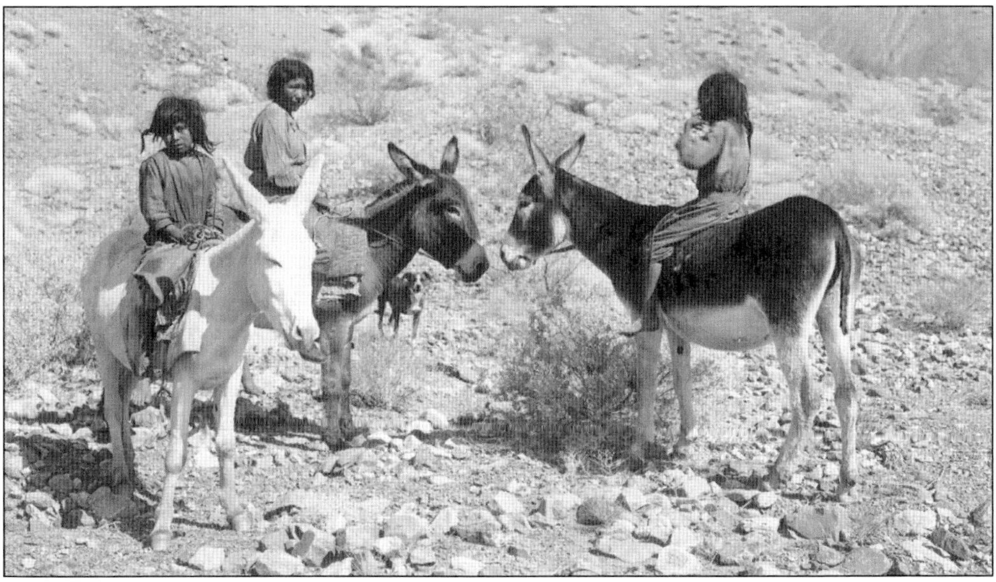

This photograph from the east side of Searles Lake, between Trona Reef and the Slate Range, dates to the early 1900s. The three young native people are unidentified. Note the dog behind the mules. John Searles and Jacob Kuhrts once tracked a group of Native Americans who had stolen some of Kuhrts's mules across the Slate Range and into Death Valley.

Two Shoshone women are standing in front of a cloth house at Borax Lake, the headquarters of John Searles. The photograph was taken in 1880. Neither woman is identified except as domestic employees. (SD).

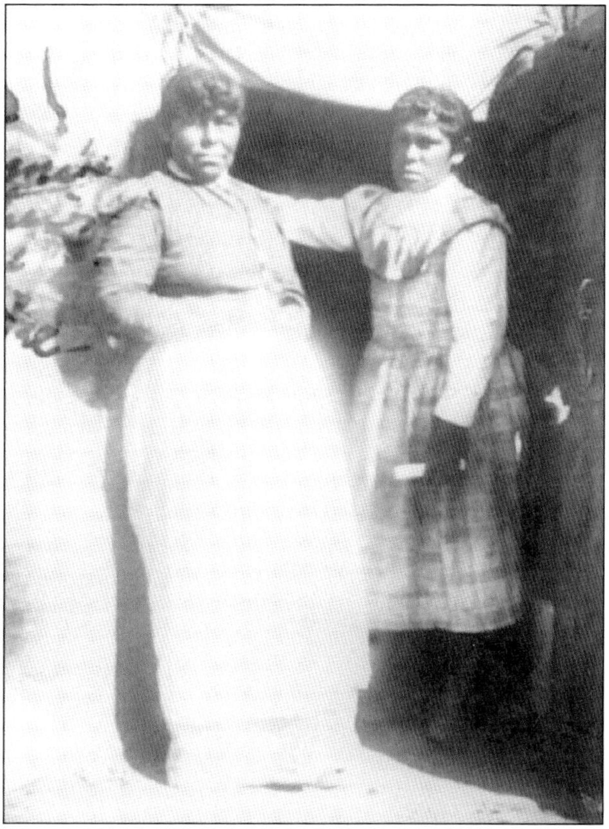

Isobel Hanson, daughter of George Hanson, is holding two of her baskets at Raven Canyon near Goat Corral Springs in 1961. She was born in Panamint Valley in 1880 and died in 1964. Her basket designs use the geology of northern Panamint Valley as an inspiration. She and her daughter Molly raised goats and sold the mohair in Trona. White ranchers complained that goats ate too much of the vegetation. Access to springs was denied by ranchers and after 1943 by the Navy.

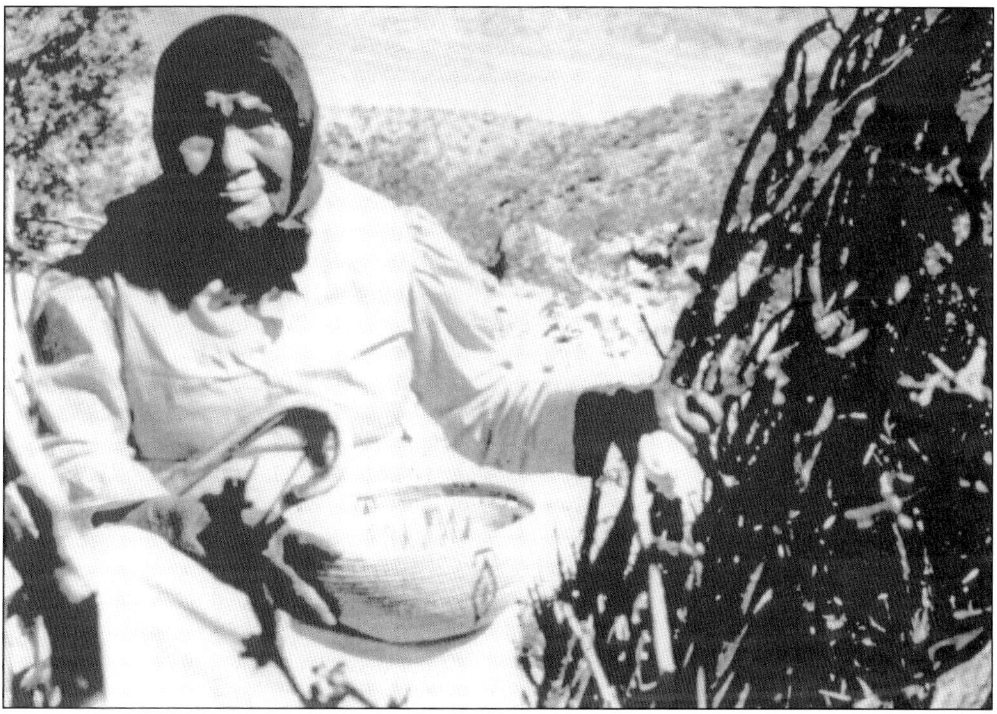

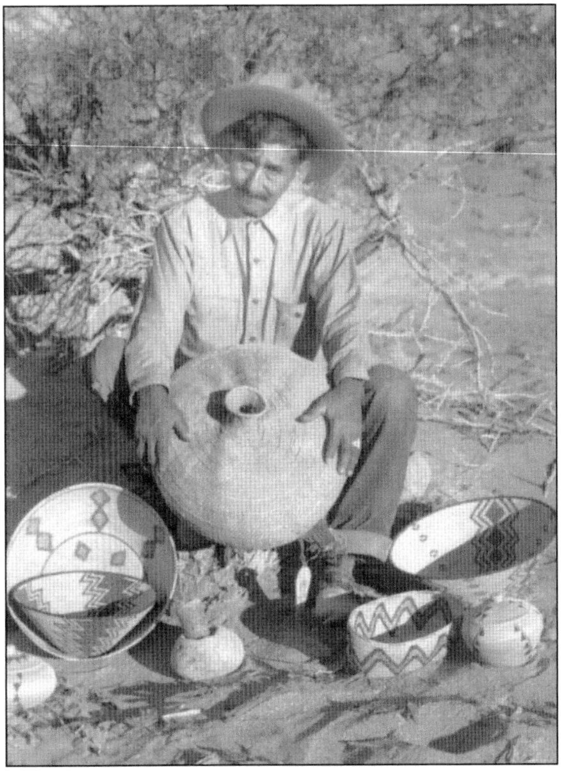

Tom Wilson displays baskets made by his wife, Susie Wilson, during the early 1900s. Panamint baskets are no longer made but were appreciated for their beauty and used domestically as well as for the tourist trade in the Death Valley region. Information suggests that Mabel Peterson's baskets were sold at an auction in Trona during the 1920s.

George Hanson is pictured here returning from Trona to his home at Hautta in Panamint Valley.

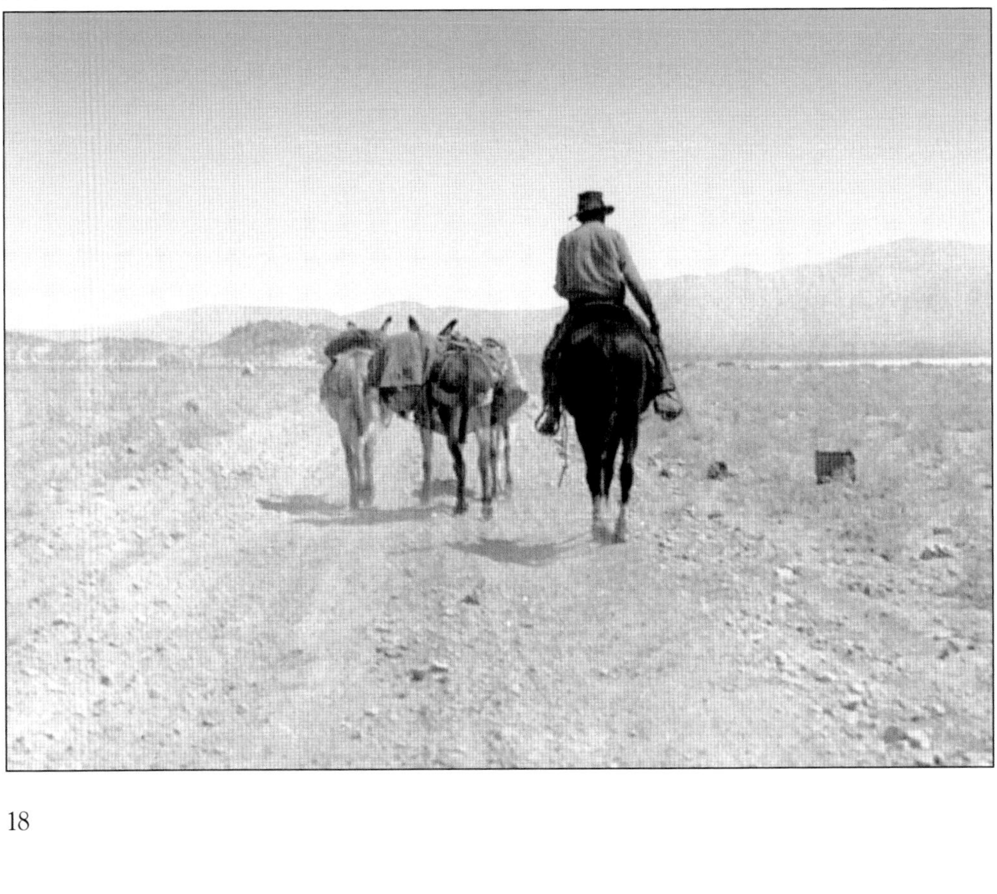

Two

Hard Rock Mining

The earliest prospectors in the Searles Valley area searched for gold and silver. In the aftermath of the Death Valley 49ers' trek from Death Valley across the Slate and Argus Mountain Ranges, prospectors trekked to the area looking for the Lost Gunsight Mine. John Searles prospected in the Slate Range during the late 1850s. His brother, Dennis, had joined Dr. Erasmus Darwin French to search for the mine; instead, they found the Coso silver deposits in 1860. Mining districts were formed in 1861, including the Slate Range and Argus Mining Districts surrounding Borax Lake. By spring of 1873, mining districts focused on borax, and the Brier and Borax Lake Mining Districts were established.

The Searles brothers mined throughout the Slate Range during the 1860s. The Albany, owned by the Searles brothers, was one of the first mines and yielded $150 per ton in gold. By February 1863, a mill had been moved to the mine.

A stage line, the Slate Range Express, brought prospectors from Los Angeles to the Slate Range. The Slate Range produced more mining companies than holes in the ground.

In April 1864, the Rochester Consolidated Gold and Silver Company shipped 200 pounds of bullion. The mill was still running that October, but it was burned by Indians in a general uprising that vacated nearly all the desert mining camps during November 1864. C.W. Tappan encountered Slate Rangers fleeing due to fear for their safety.

Mining in the Argus and Slate Ranges and throughout the Searles Valley vicinity continued until 1941, when operations were suspended by War Production Board Limitation Order L-208. In 1943, the Naval Ordnance Test Station China Lake was established. The understanding was that once the war was over, mining could resume. Instead, the withdrawal of lands continued, and mining and most other activities were prohibited. Validity examinations were conducted on the mineral content of all the mines, and all were found to be without mineral value. Today, there are no operating precious-metal mines in Searles Valley or its surrounding mountains.

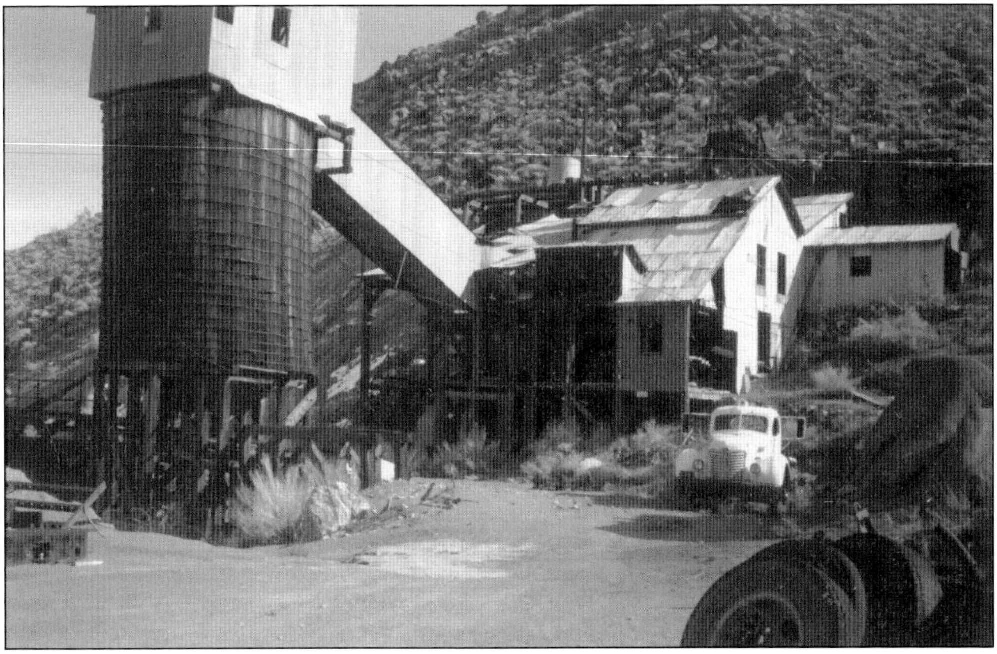

Ruth Mine (Graham-Jones) began in 1899 and is located in Homewood (originally Wibbet's) Canyon. It contained Ruth Mine School, a mess hall, a bunkhouse, and cabins. In 1938, a 40-ton cyanide plant was installed; it processed 70 tons of ore daily and employed 30 people. In 1941, a cyanide mill was built, employing 68 men. Over 10,000 tons of gold ore were processed. In 2009, the Bureau of Land Management removed the cyanide tailings.

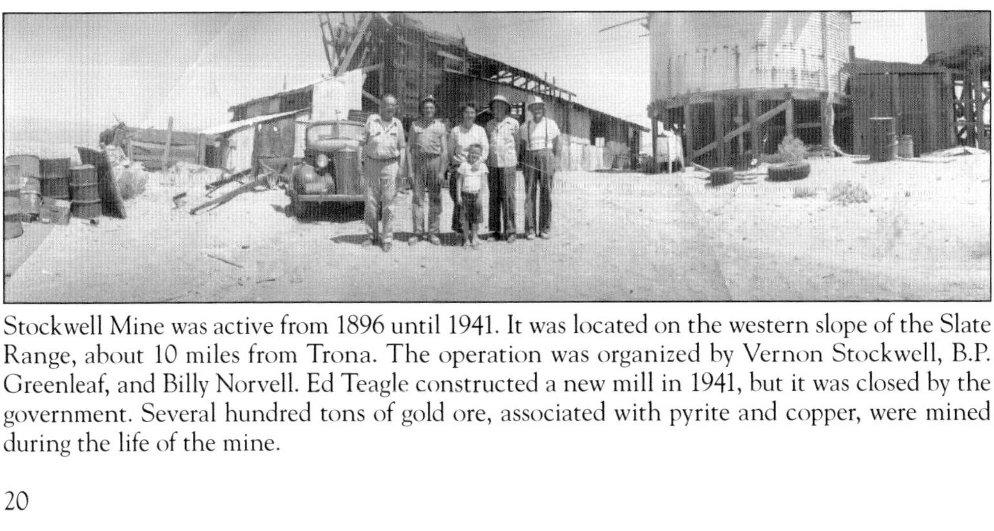

Stockwell Mine was active from 1896 until 1941. It was located on the western slope of the Slate Range, about 10 miles from Trona. The operation was organized by Vernon Stockwell, B.P. Greenleaf, and Billy Norvell. Ed Teagle constructed a new mill in 1941, but it was closed by the government. Several hundred tons of gold ore, associated with pyrite and copper, were mined during the life of the mine.

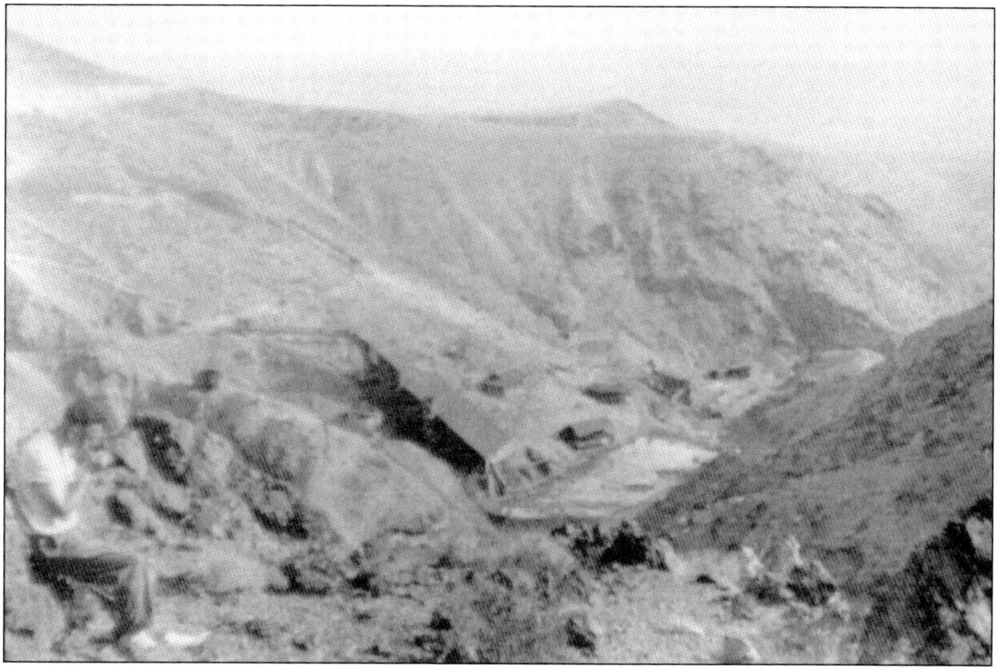

Gold Bottom Mine was also called the Copper Queen and Slate Range Mine. In 1862, the Searles brothers carved their initials on a boulder here. This may be the site of their first mine in Searles Valley and may also be the location of the community of Searlesville. It was on the west slope of the Slate Range and produced gold and silver ore. In 1937, a massive cloudburst destroyed the camp.

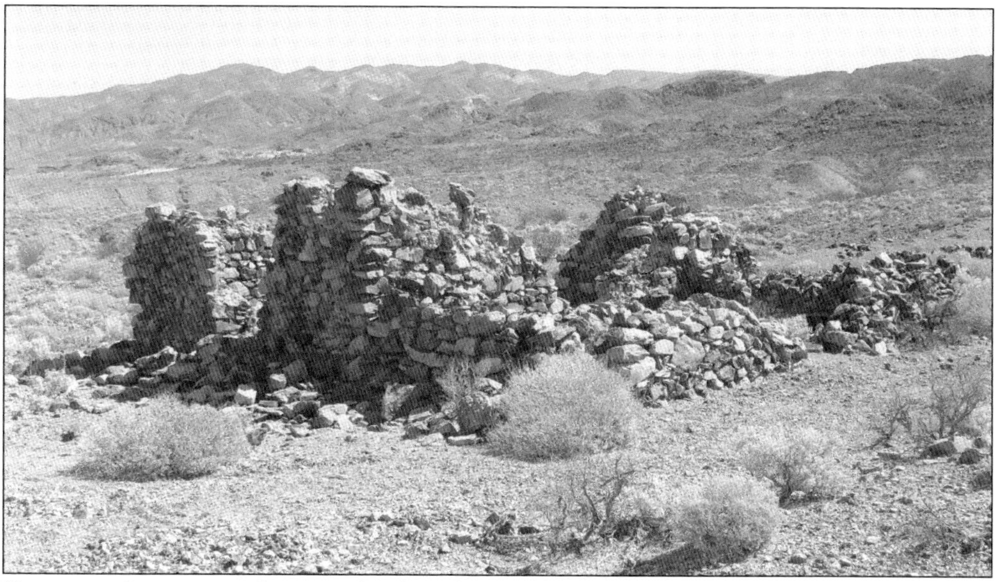

Slaterange City was on the east side of Searles Lake. It is another candidate for the community of Searlesville. It contained over a dozen rock houses, including the one pictured here, which may have been the Borax Lake Stage Station robbed by Clodoveo Chavez in March 1875. He robbed stages throughout the area as retribution for the arrest and hanging of Tiburcio Vásquez. In 1910, Wyatt Earp was arrested for claim-jumping here.

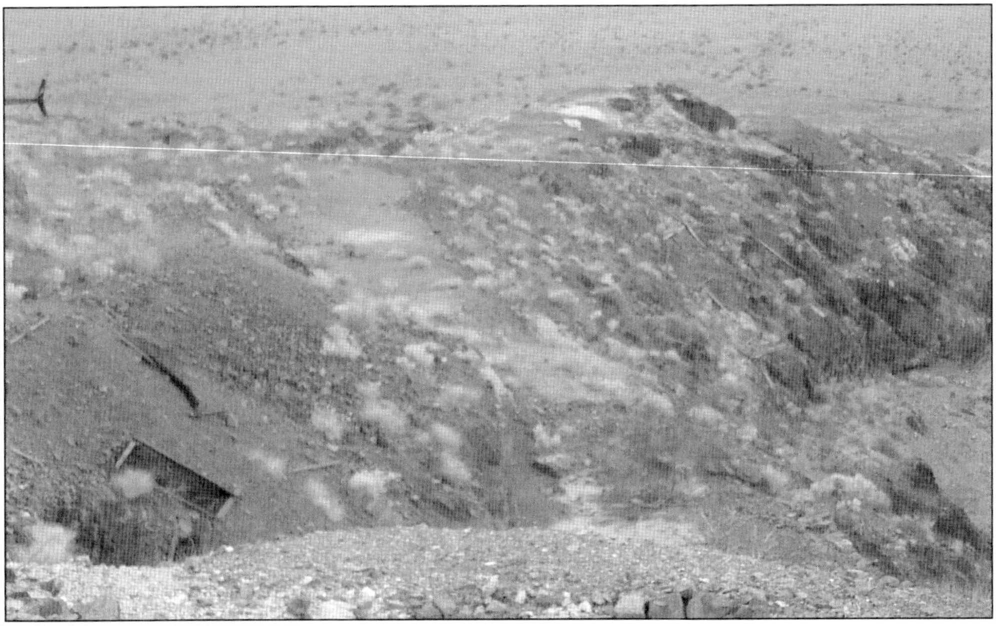

New York Mine/Dean's Mill was financed in the 1890s by George Hearst. J.C. Dean built the 20-stamp mill and crushed ore for many of the gold and silver mines in the Slate and Argus Ranges. Dean was the postmaster, and his family lived in what they called John Searles's winter house. The military ran them off the property in 1944, claiming they would pay them $150,000 for the property. They were never paid.

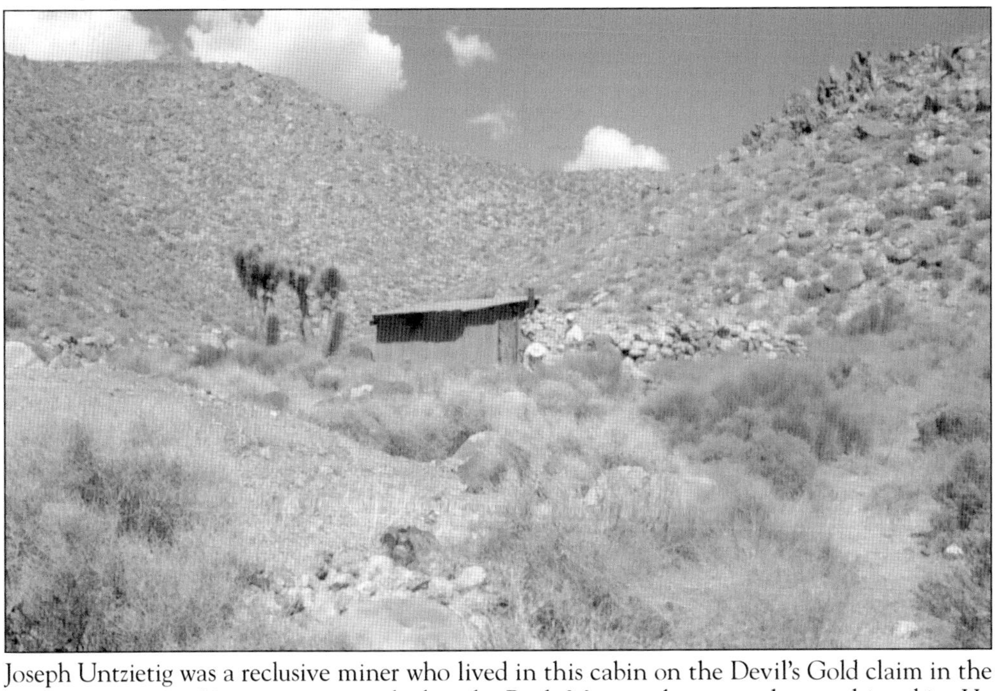

Joseph Untzietig was a reclusive miner who lived in this cabin on the Devil's Gold claim in the Argus Mountains. He sometimes worked at the Ruth Mine and processed ore at his cabin. He recorded his diary in pencil, generally in English, but some of it in German, on the metal walls of the cabin, detailing his philosophy of life. He filed five mining claims between 1936 and 1940.

Three

John and Dennis Searles and their Borax Company

Brothers John and Dennis Searles were New York gold rushers who came to California by boat over the winter of 1849–1850. For eight years, they mined, farmed, and ran cattle in the Trinity River District. Then, losing their assets in a sheriff's sale, they moved on. In 1859, John joined a freight outfit whose last stop was the Slate Range. John stayed there, joining a handful of prospectors looking for gold. Within a year, Dennis was in the same area, looking for the Lost Gunsight silver lode with Darwin French's party. On November 10, 1861, John, Dennis, Willet Dunn, and Misters Dean, Morrow, and Clarke organized the Slate Range mining district. The brothers found mining in the Slate Range costly. They had to purchase mules and wagons to haul supplies, construct a mill at their mine, and spend $50,000 for a 1,400-foot tunnel to follow a vein.

In early 1863, John learned that soda from the salt marsh west of their Slate Range mines contained enough borax to interfere with processing ore. John made samples of marsh materials, and he and Dennis took them to a San Francisco company that planned to mine borax near Clear Lake. After initial interest, the company asked for additional samples with greater variety. John returned to the marsh, but fearing claim jumpers, he took care not to be followed. On returning, interest was even greater, but the company asked for a day for assays. The next day, the brothers were told no samples had even a trace of borax; if they wanted to get rich, they should look for copper.

John and Dennis returned to mining, eventually moving to the Soledad District outside Los Angeles. In January 1873, a man named McGillivray passed through Soledad bearing samples of borax from Teel's Marsh, Nevada. When John saw those samples, he knew the Slate Range marsh could yield borax. Quickly, John, Dennis, Eben Skillings, and J.D. Creigh formed a partnership to claim land on the marsh and establish a borax-mining company. Mining at the marsh, eventually named Searles Lake, has been almost continuous since.

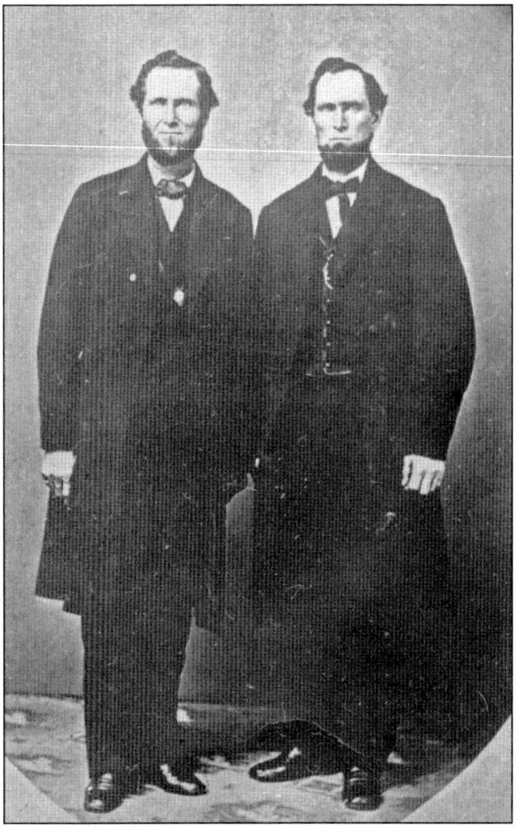

The Searles brothers, Dennis (left) and John, were leading miners in California. However, they were more than that. As a young man, John was a fine hunter but stopped hunting after being seriously mauled by a grizzly bear in 1870. John was also an Indian fighter, entrepreneur, experimental chemist, and mine superintendent. Dennis had a more political bent, serving on the grand jury in Trinity County and as organizer of the first school district in Soledad, California. (SD.)

The early miners in the Slate Range protected their claims by scribing their initials on rocks around them. In October 1862, John Searles, Willett Dunn, William Morrow, and Dennis Searles pecked their initials in Gold Bottom Canyon.

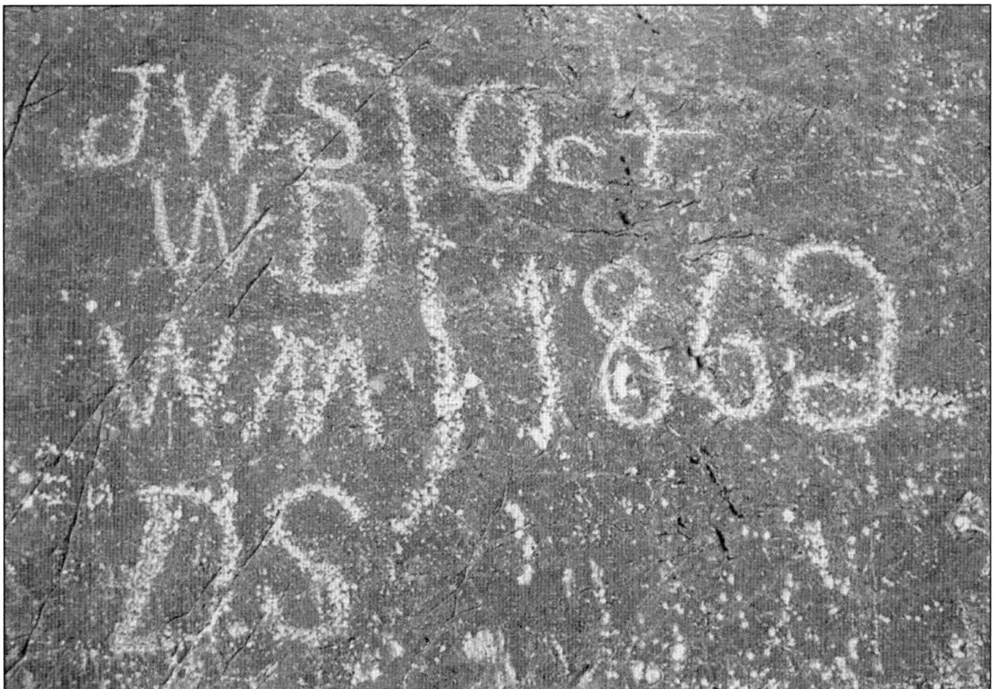

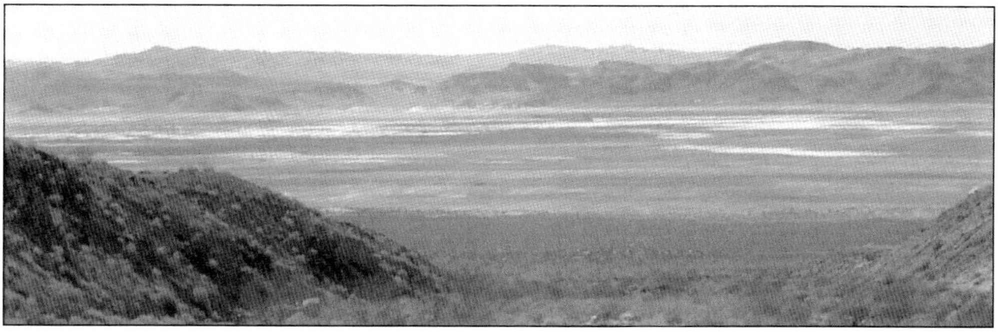

A soda-salt marsh lay at the foot of the canyon in which the Searles outfit was mining gold and silver in the Slate Range. Although borax was actually discovered here in 1863, the potential partners lied about borax being present. It was not until January 1873 that the truth became known and a new industry began.

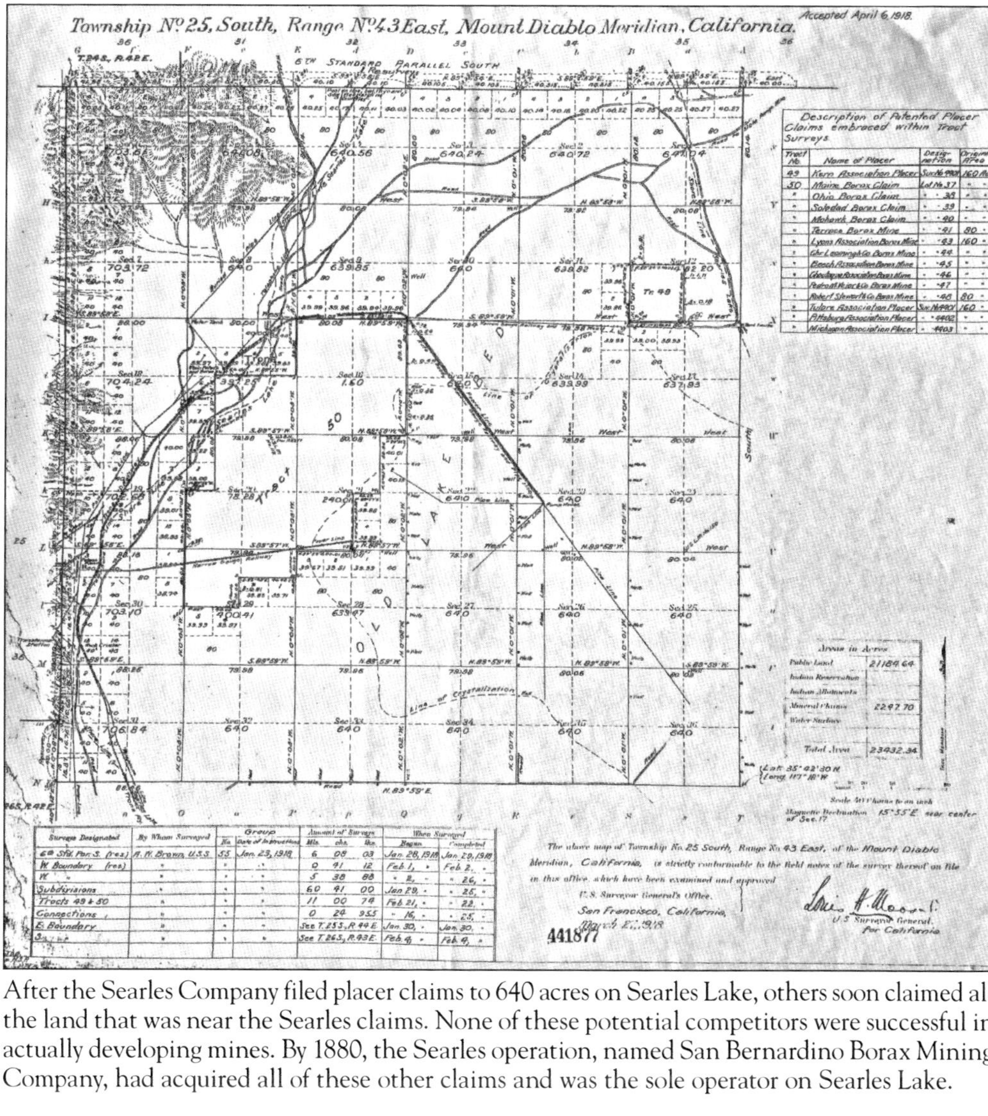

After the Searles Company filed placer claims to 640 acres on Searles Lake, others soon claimed all the land that was near the Searles claims. None of these potential competitors were successful in actually developing mines. By 1880, the Searles operation, named San Bernardino Borax Mining Company, had acquired all of these other claims and was the sole operator on Searles Lake.

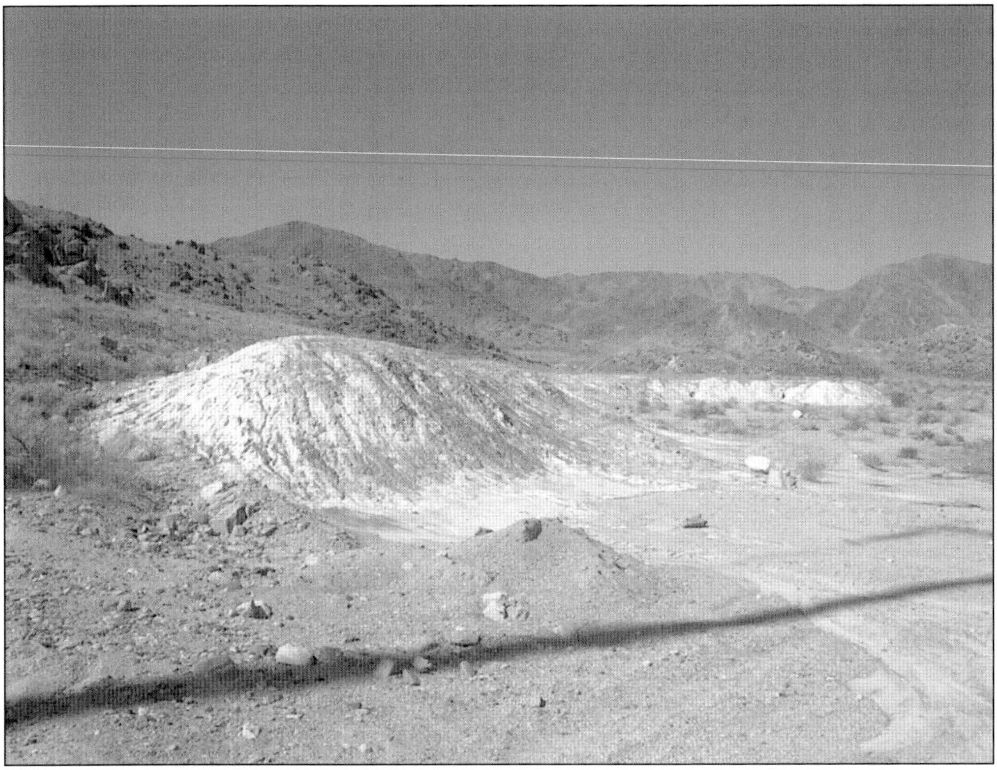

All that remains of the Searles' first borax mill are a few rock walls and two large mud-tailings piles, the waste left after the borax had been extracted. This mill was burned by Indians in the spring of 1878. The tailings piles are located on the west side of Searles Lake, about halfway between the communities of Trona and Westend.

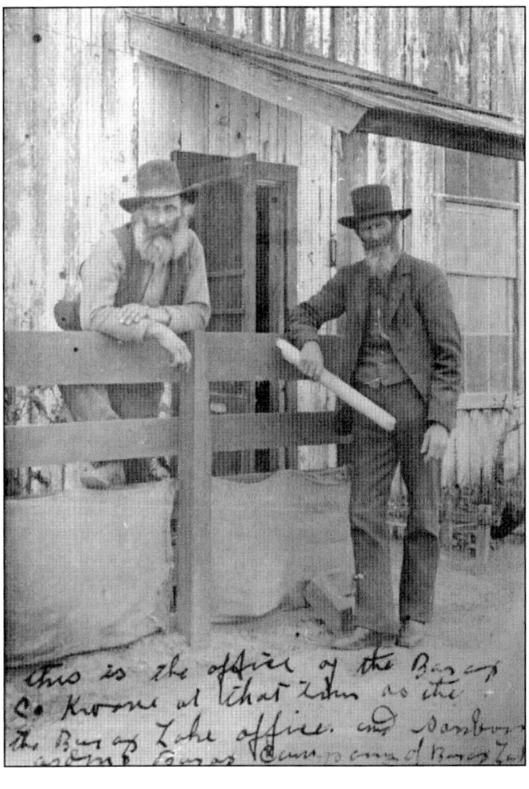

Eben Skillings (left), John Searles's brother-in-law, was one of the four original mineral claimants on Searles Lake. Skillings and John Searles (right) were also partners in the borax business at Searles Lake for many years. This 1880 photograph was taken in front of the office at Borax Lake, now known as Searles Lake. (SD.)

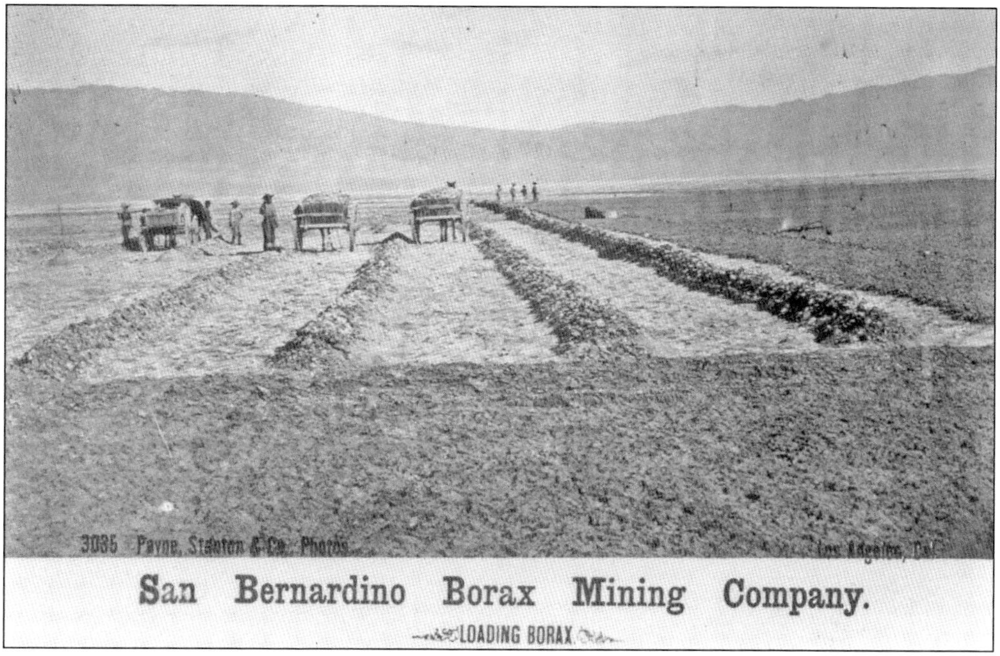

As practiced by Searles, borax mining at Searles Lake was quite simple. The borax was located in the surface crust, and mining consisted of simply raking it into windrows to dry, loading it into mule-drawn wagons, and pulling the wagons into the mill.

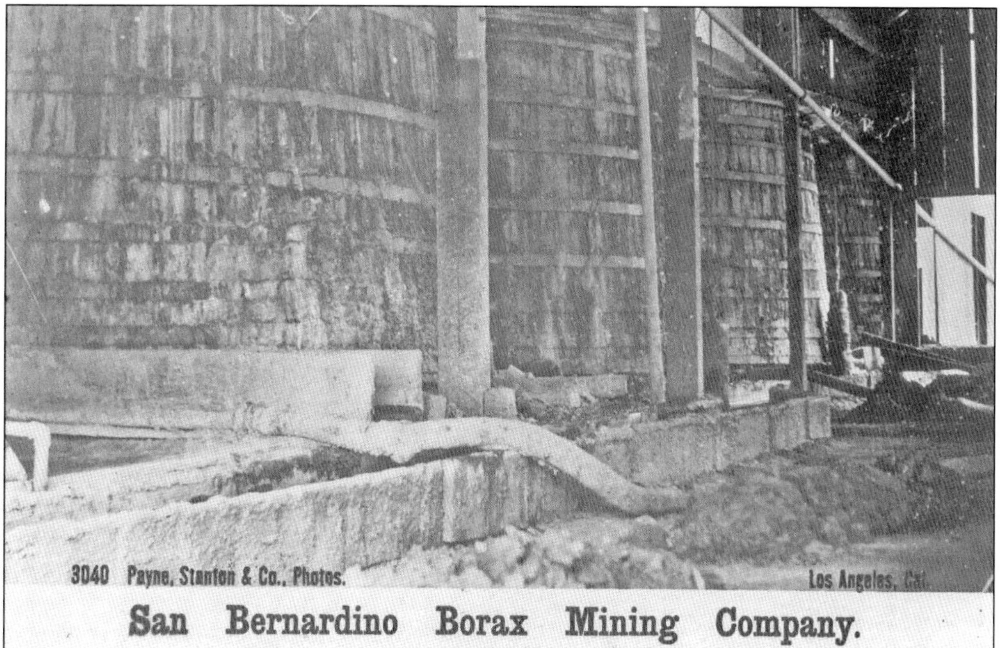

To process the crust into pure borax, measured amounts of crust and brackish water were put into a large vat into which steam was introduced and the contents heated to boiling. This dissolved the borax and any soluble impurities. The steam was then turned off, and the mud and sand would settle to the bottom of the vat.

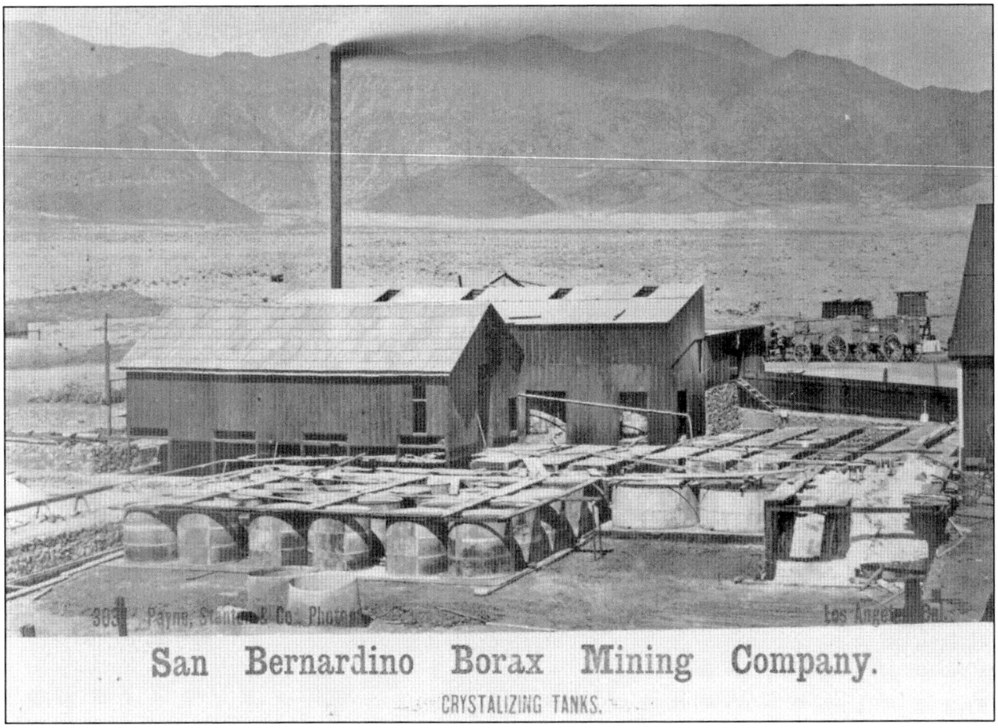

After the sand and mud had settled, producing clear hot brine, the brine was drained into small vats where it was allowed to cool for up to a week. Once cool and its burden of dissolved borax crystallized on the tank walls and bottom, the weak brine was drained away. It was a simple matter of digging out the purified borax, allowing it to air dry in a storage building, and sacking it to be carried to market.

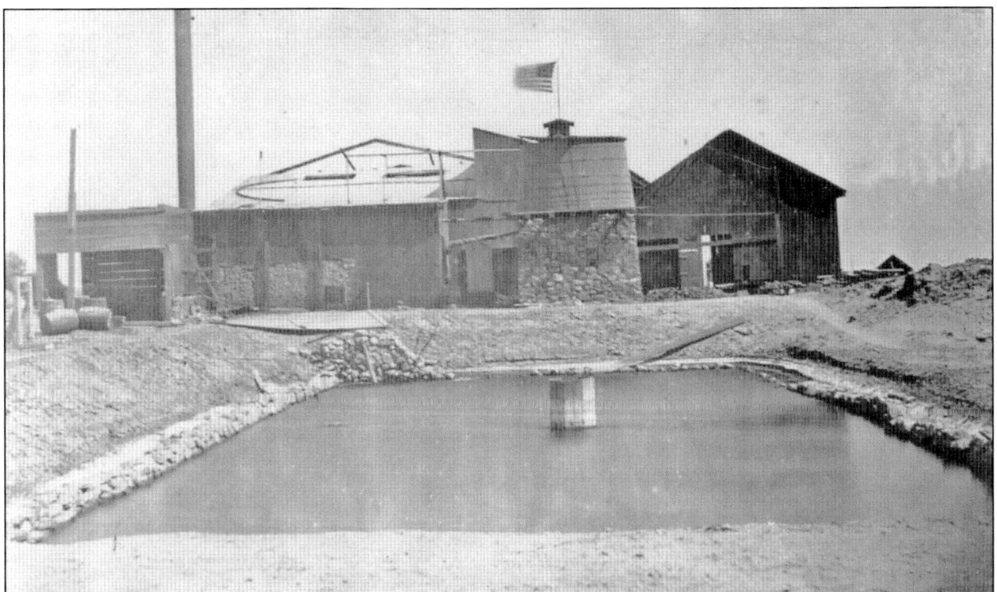

The Searles mill had a boiler to make steam to heat the mud-leach tanks. The mill also had a reservoir to hold water for leaching.

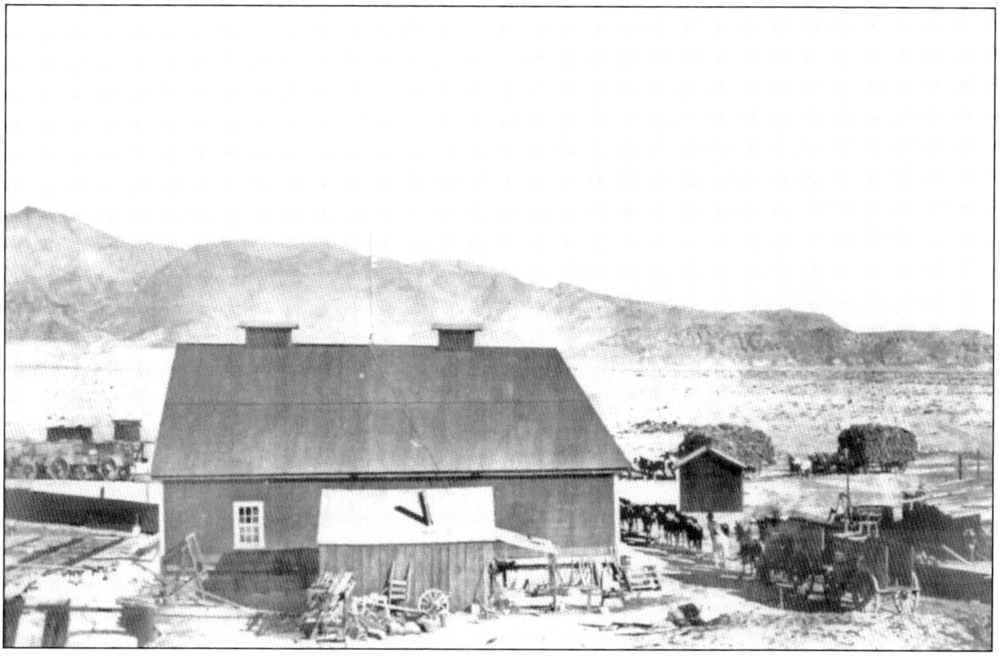

To make steam, it was necessary to build a fire to boil water. Initially, the Searles mill burned local brush, there being no wood in the area. Eventually, all the brush within 10 miles had been collected and burned. Two wagons heaped high with brush can be seen in the right rear of this photograph.

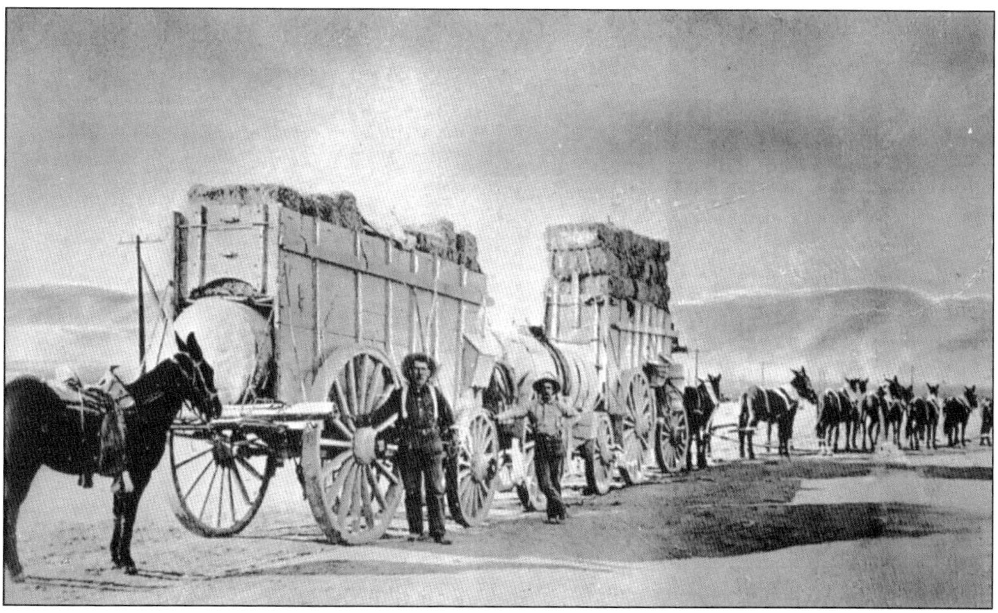

With the brush gone, Searles turned to oil to fire his boiler. This came by rail from the Ojai area to Mojave. There it was transferred to a large tank wagon that was pulled between two borax wagons when they returned to the mill after delivering a load of borax to the railroad at Mojave.

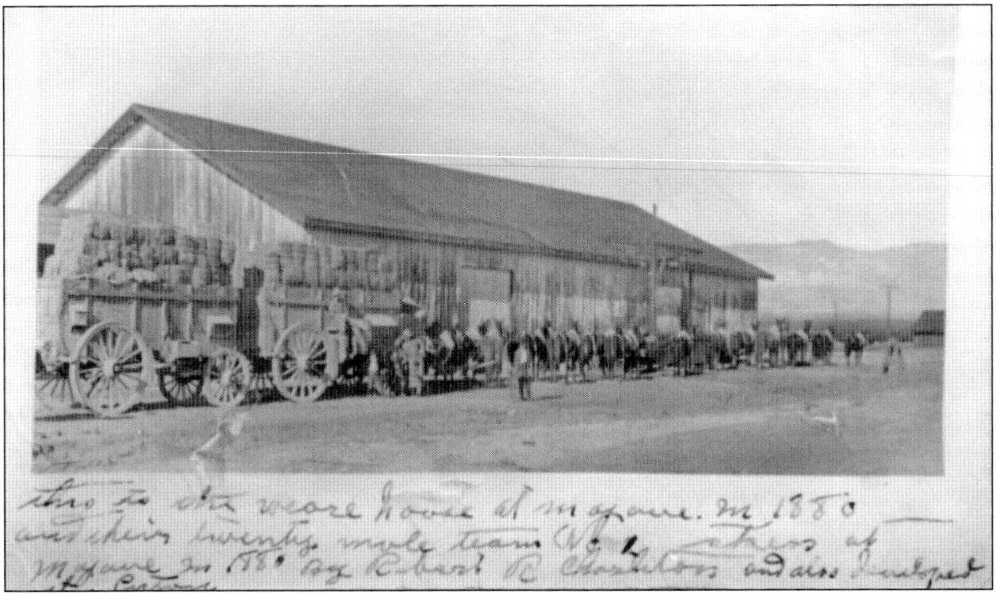

Searles maintained stables and warehouses at both Mojave and at his borax mill. This photograph shows the warehouse in Mojave with the wagons loaded with hay for animal feed to take to the stables at the borax mill. (SD.)

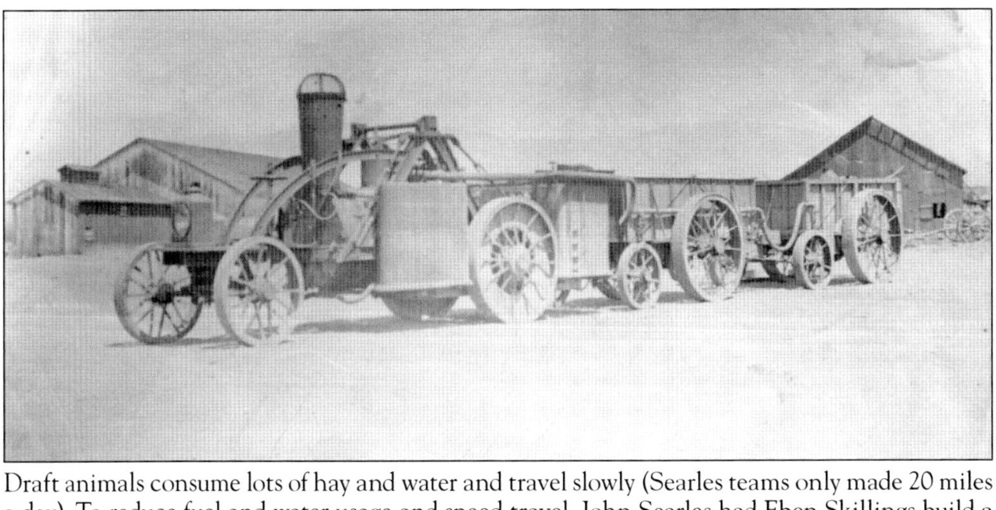

Draft animals consume lots of hay and water and travel slowly (Searles teams only made 20 miles a day). To reduce fuel and water usage and speed travel, John Searles had Eben Skillings build a steam-powered wagon train. However, it consumed as much fuel as the animals ate in hay, used as much water, and went no faster, so they abandoned the experiment. (SD.)

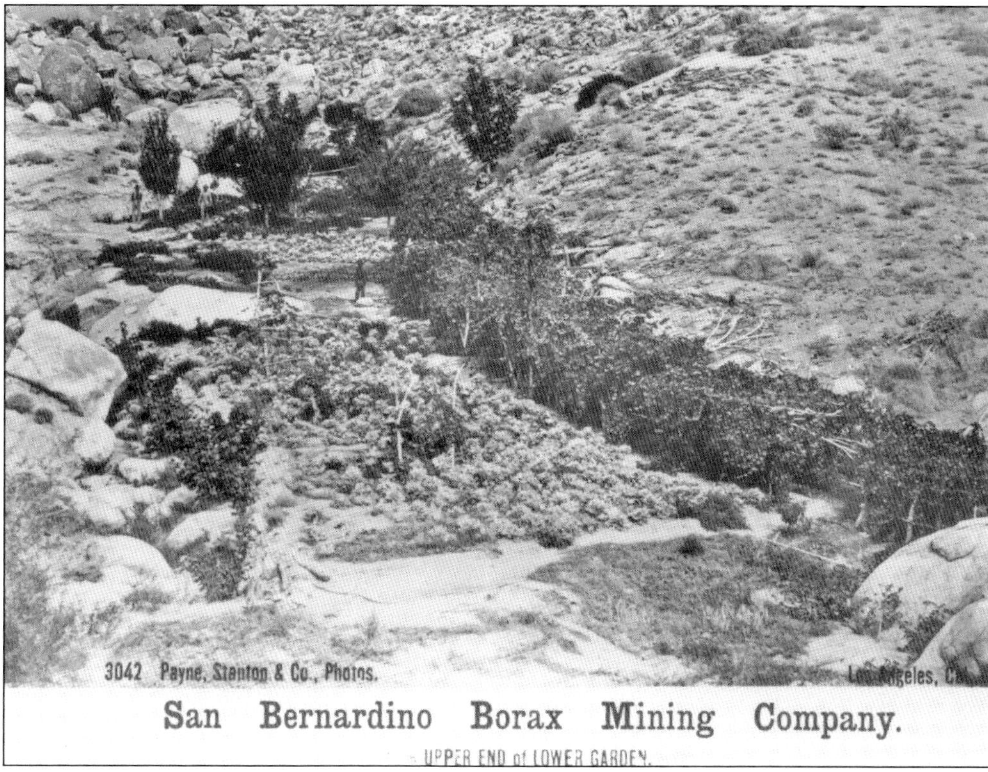

Without question, Searles Valley has a harsh desert climate with very little water, which made growing food, especially fresh vegetables and fruit, a serious problem. To provide better food for his workers, Searles developed gardens at a spring in the Argus Range, after acquiring the water rights from Indian Joe Peterson.

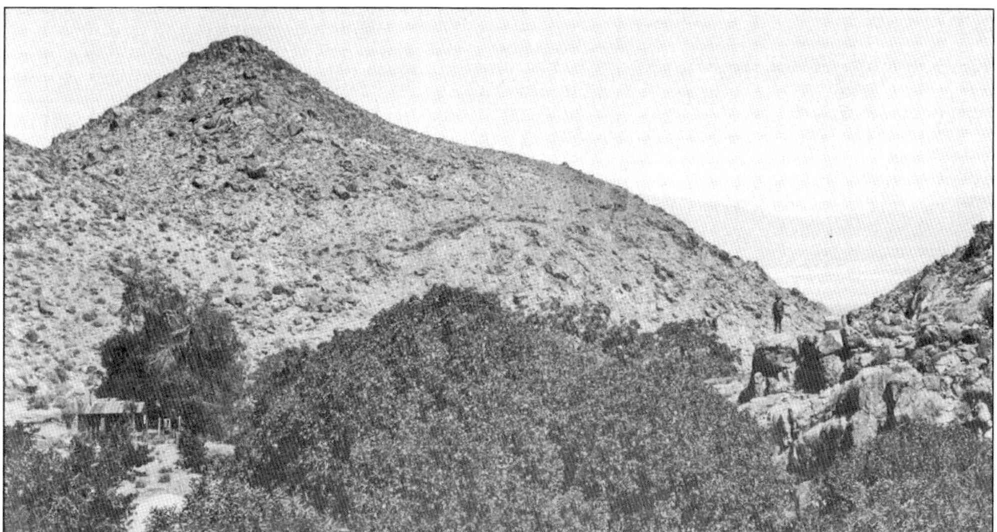

John Searles built a small house at the gardens. It can be seen in the trees at the left edge of this photograph. This was a welcome retreat on a hot summer afternoon and evening. After John Searles's death, Joe Peterson and his family lived there for many years.

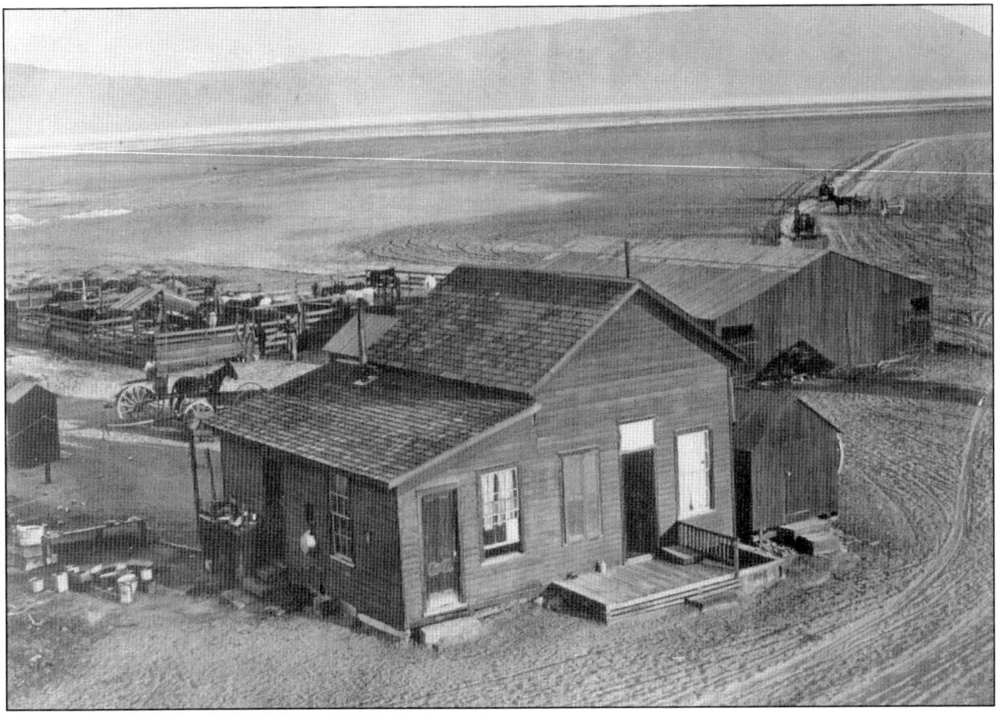

John Searles also had living quarters at the borax mill. Since cooling for buildings had not yet been invented, summer evenings must have been very warm.

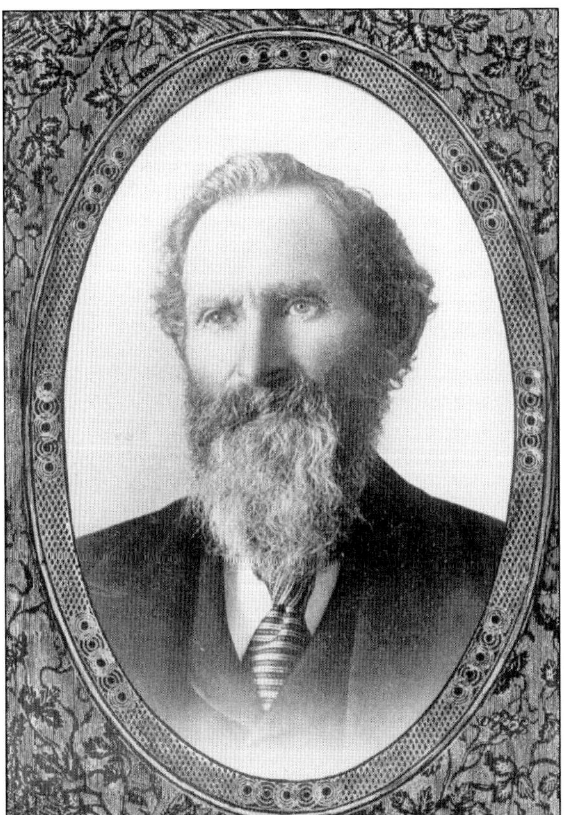

This portrait of John Searles was taken in 1885. He died on October 9, 1897, in St. Helena, California. John's brother, Dennis, died on May 3, 1880, in Newhall, California.

Four

MINING OF SEARLES LAKE AFTER JOHN SEARLES

Many companies tried mining Searles Lake, but six failed within four years. Only two processes remain profitable. Today, both the chemistry and equipment needed to mine Searles Lake are well understood, but those making initial attempts knew nothing about either.

Starting in 1873, John Searles's San Bernardino Borax Mining Company produced borax for over 20 years before weak markets forced its closure in 1896. In 1898, California Borax Company initiated a mine, but Borax Smith bought the business, ending development. In 1908, Clinton Dolbear filed placer claims on 41,200 acres, including all land not owned by Pacific Coast Borax Company. Dolbear formed the California Trona Company, purchased the Searles mill, and hoped to produce soda ash. Not understanding the chemistry and equipment needed and borrowing from Foreign Mines Development Company, his loans were foreclosed in 1911.

After John Hornsey wrote a 400-page report promising $8 million per year in profits from investing just $3 million, Foreign Mines hired him. Again, Hornsey knew little chemistry and nothing about equipment; he failed totally. The only lasting value was the Trona Railroad and a new corporate structure. American Trona then hired Charles Grimwood to produce potash and borax. Finally, 60 tons per day of potash were produced, although inefficiently and of poor quality. In May 1921, the unprofitable plant shut down for 10 months. However, work continued to solve problems, with research defining brine chemistry and engineers solving equipment problems. By 1926, twenty percent of US potash consumption came from Trona, as did half the world's borax.

In October 1916, Borosolvay Corporation started a plant like the Trona Plant and had all the same problems. However, it was contractually prohibited from producing borax, and without income from borax, the plant closed permanently on February 1, 1921.

Borax Smith lost his borax empire through bankruptcy in May 1913. Undaunted, he formed West End Chemical Company to recover borax at Searles Lake, but nothing he tried initially worked. Finally, in 1926, West End Chemical began producing borax using a process invented by Henry Hellmers.

Two entrepreneurs tried solar evaporation to separate finished products from lake brine: George Burnham in the 1920s and Occidental Petroleum in the 1960s. Both failed.

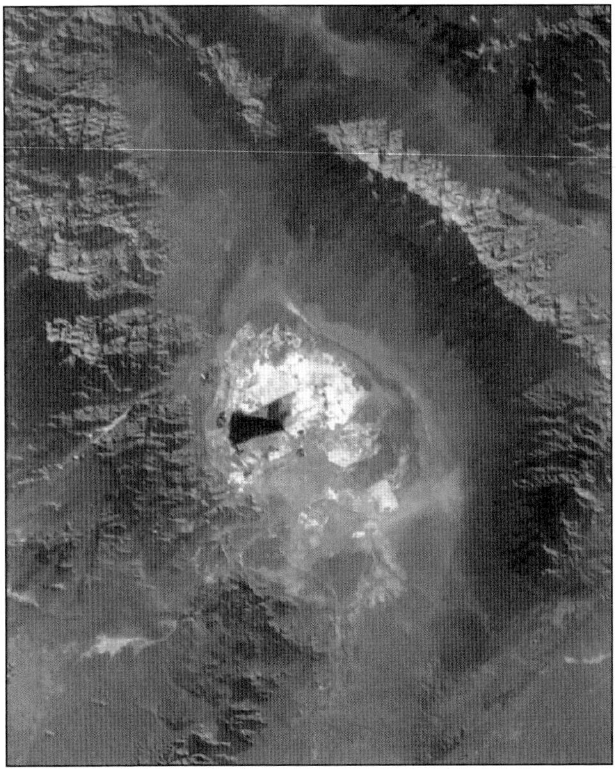

This photograph, taken from the space shuttle, shows Searles Lake in a deep valley between the Slate Range (east, right) and the Argus Range. The Owens River entered Searles Lake through Salt Wells Valley, at lower left. The dark area on the lake is brine exposed on the surface by current solution-mining activities. (Courtesy of the Earth Science and Remote Sensing Unit, NASA Johnson Space Center.)

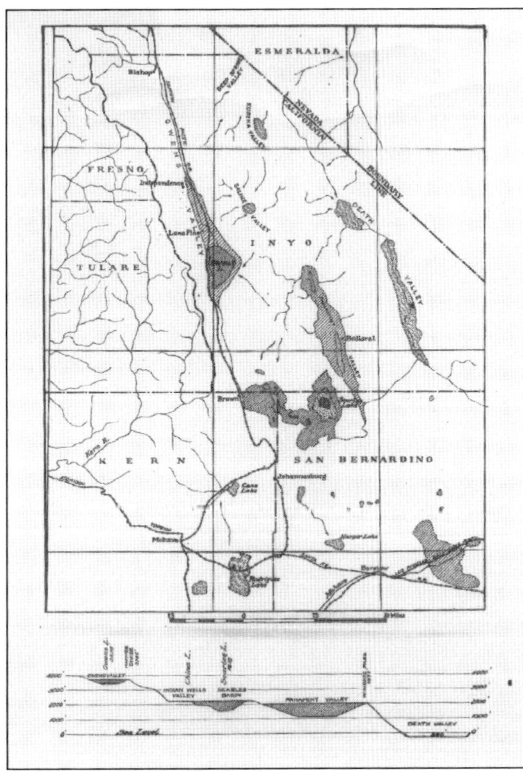

Searles Lake is the third in a chain of lakes in the Owens River drainage. For one million years, periods of high river flow alternated with dry epochs. During high river flow, Searles Lake overflowed into Panamint Valley and mud deposited on the deep lake bottom. During drier periods, the river ended at Searles Lake, and all soluble salts in the water became trapped. When the lake dried completely, these deposited as salt beds.

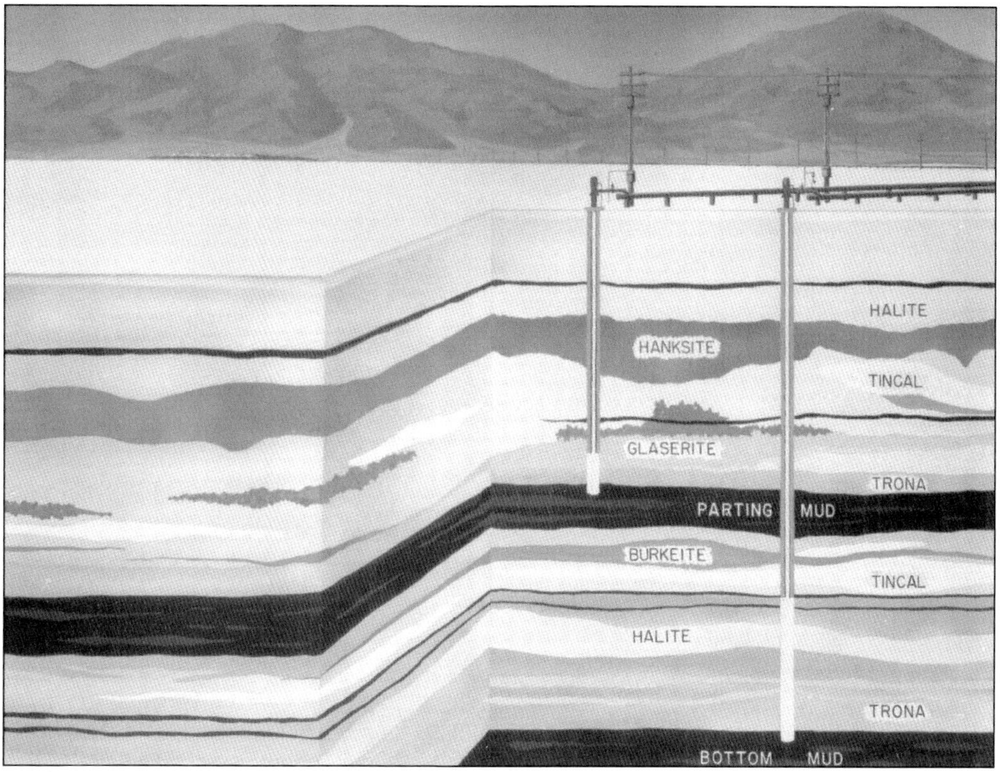

By the 1950s, the mineral deposit in Searles Lake was known to actually consist of many salt beds. Each bed covered an area of about 50 square miles and was isolated from the other beds by mud layers. The top bed, the upper salt, is 40 to 80 feet thick. Beneath this, the parting mud is 10 to 15 feet thick. The lower salt consists of six salt beds, each two to eight feet thick, separated by mud beds from one to three feet thick. All salt beds are filled with brine that is pumped to feed the mineral-extraction plants.

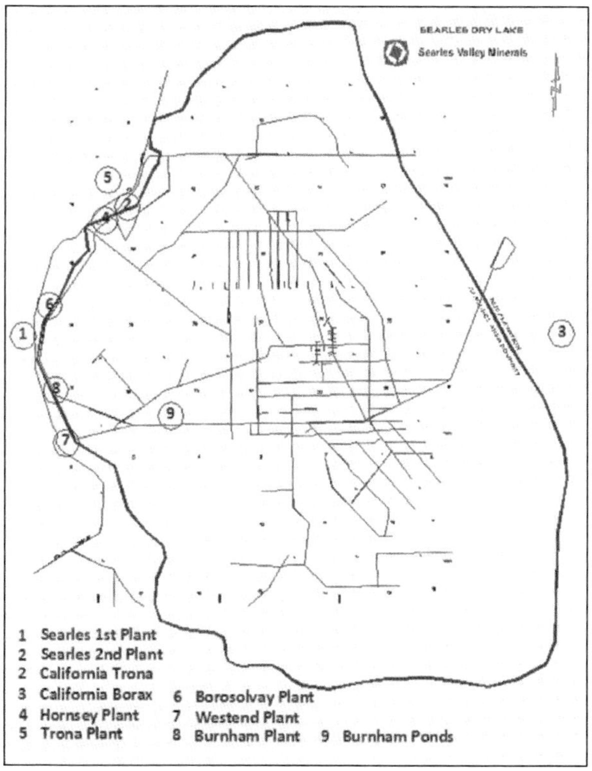

This diagram shows the location of the early attempts to mine the wealth in Searles Lake, from John Searles's two mills to the locations of George Burnham's developments from 1928 to 1931.

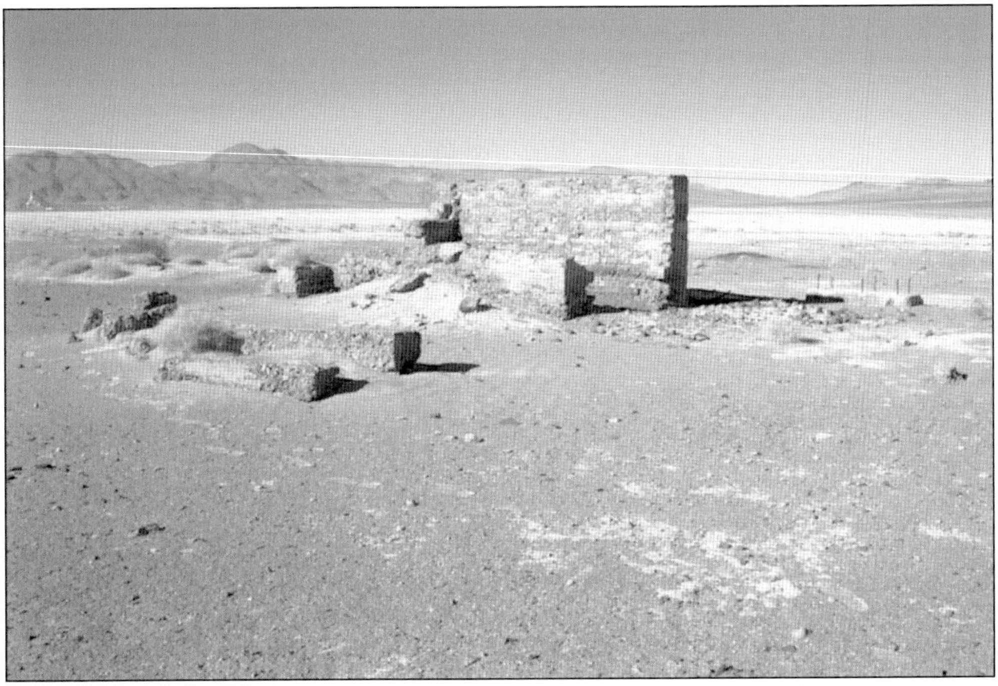

In 1898, California Borax Company began construction of a plant to produce borax, much as the Searles operation had from 1873 to 1896. The ruins of that failed attempt lie on the southeastern shore of Searles Lake. All that remains is the crumbling foundation for their boiler.

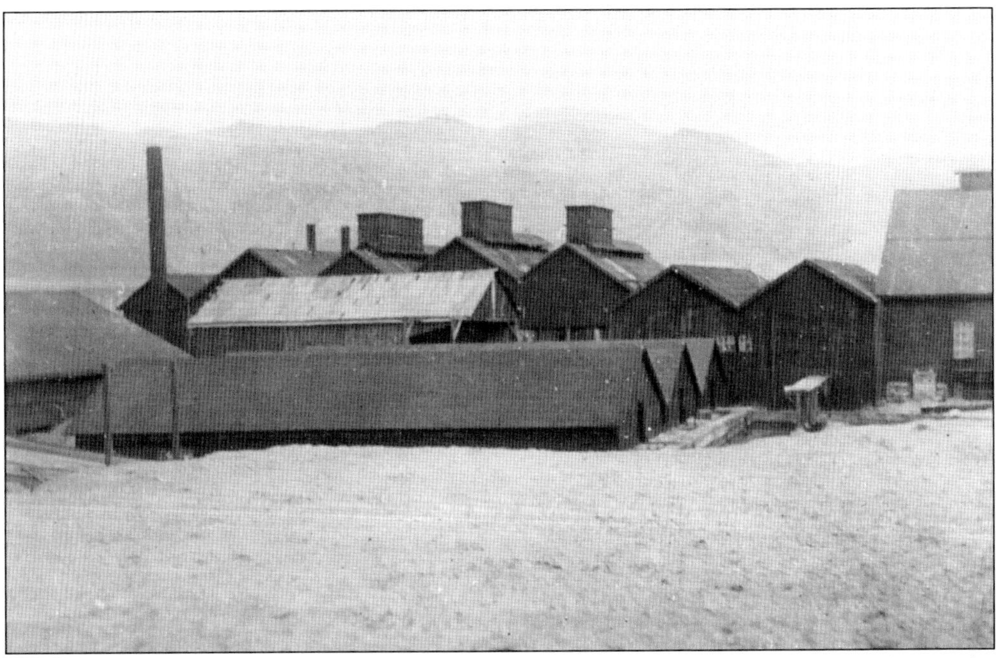

This 1904 photograph from the Settle-Dearborn Collection shows the borax mill that John Searles sold to Pacific Coast Borax Company (PCB) in 1896. In 1909, PCB sold the mill to Clinton E. Dolbear, president of California Trona Company, to use for the production of soda ash. Dolbear failed and lost his business through bankruptcy. (SD.)

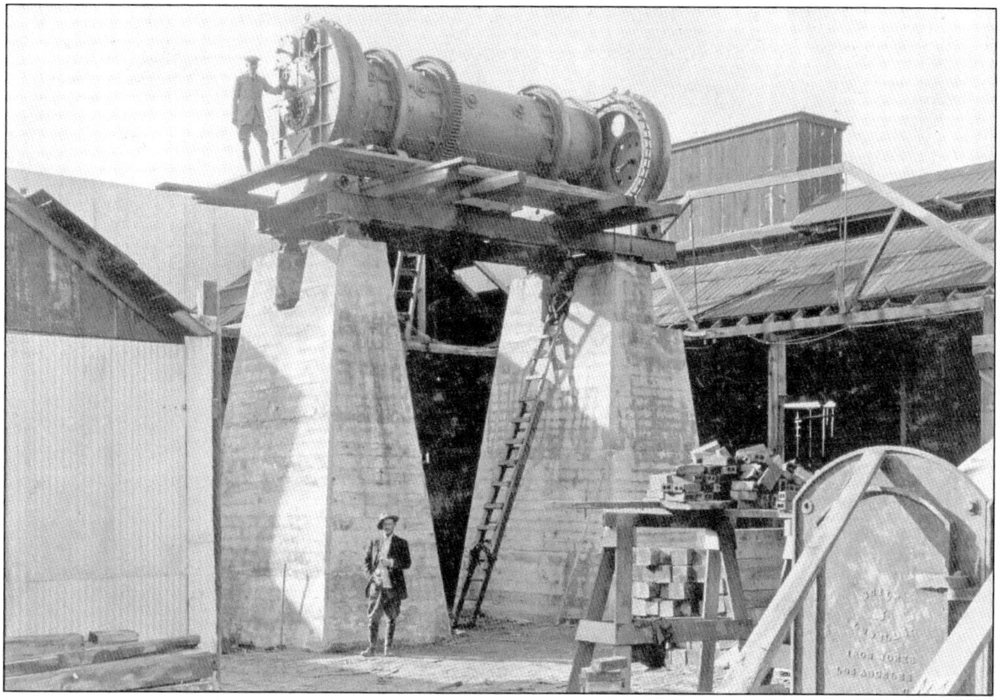

The new owners of California Trona Company hired John W. Hornsey to build a plant to recover potash, borax, and soda ash from lake brine. Hornsey's process began with a brine carbonation step where carbon dioxide would be absorbed into the brine and sodium bicarbonate precipitated. This 1913 photograph shows Hornsey's brine carbonator high on a concrete pedestal. However, this was the wrong type of reactor and failed to perform as required.

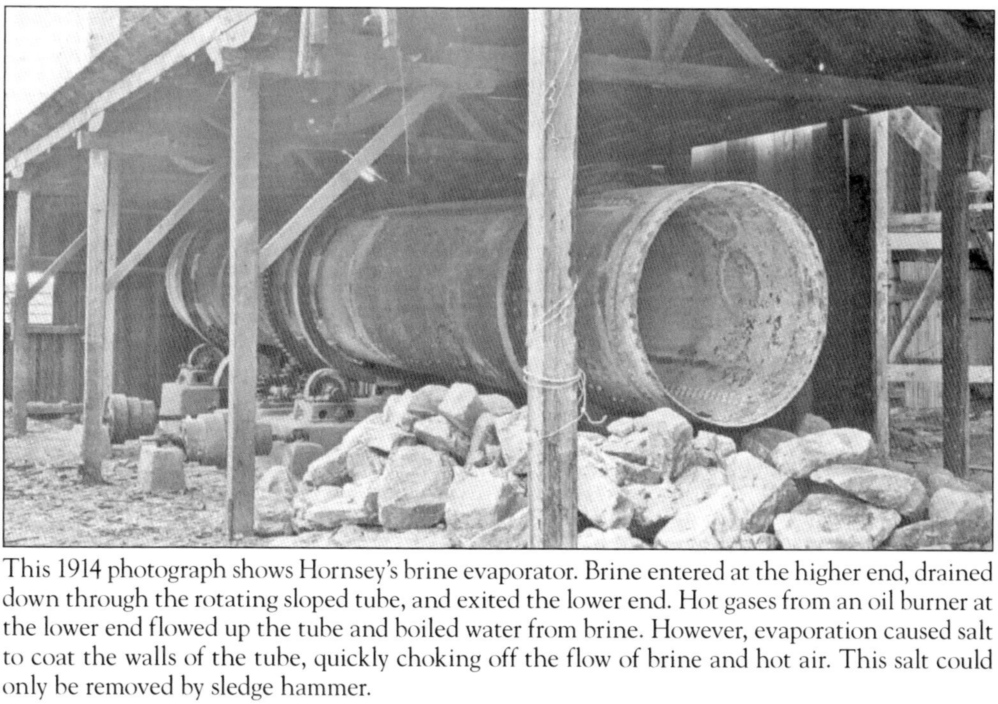

This 1914 photograph shows Hornsey's brine evaporator. Brine entered at the higher end, drained down through the rotating sloped tube, and exited the lower end. Hot gases from an oil burner at the lower end flowed up the tube and boiled water from brine. However, evaporation caused salt to coat the walls of the tube, quickly choking off the flow of brine and hot air. This salt could only be removed by sledge hammer.

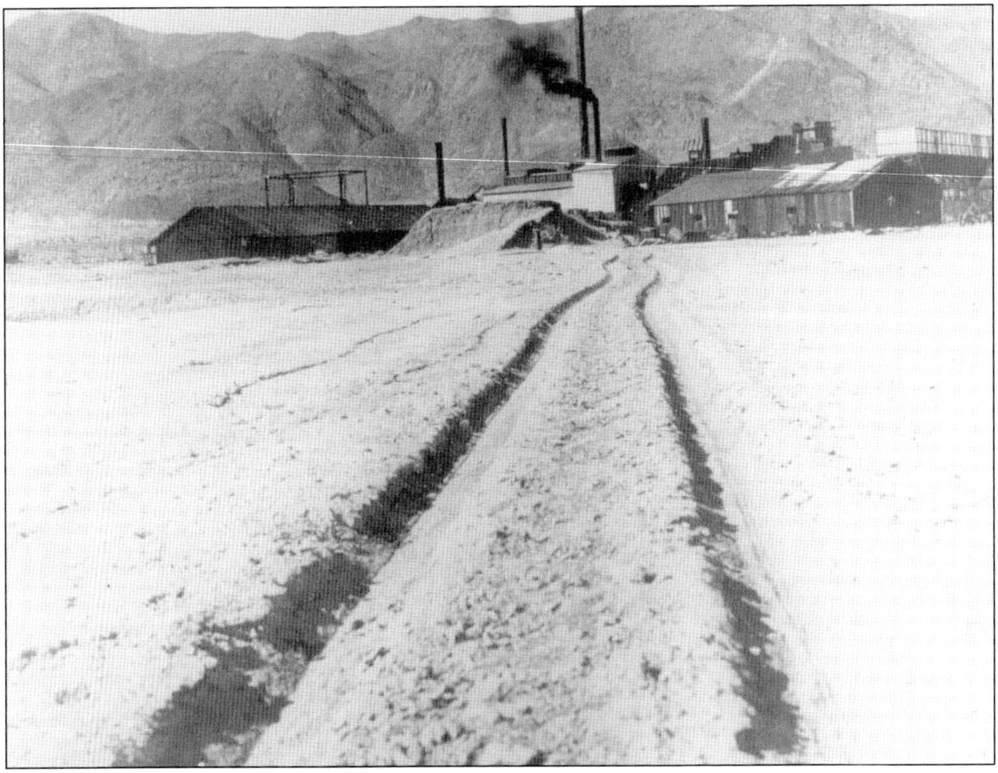

Pictured here in 1914 is the Hornsey Plant complete and an attempt to operate it being made. However, both Hornsey's process and his equipment selection were completely unworkable, and the endeavor was a complete failure.

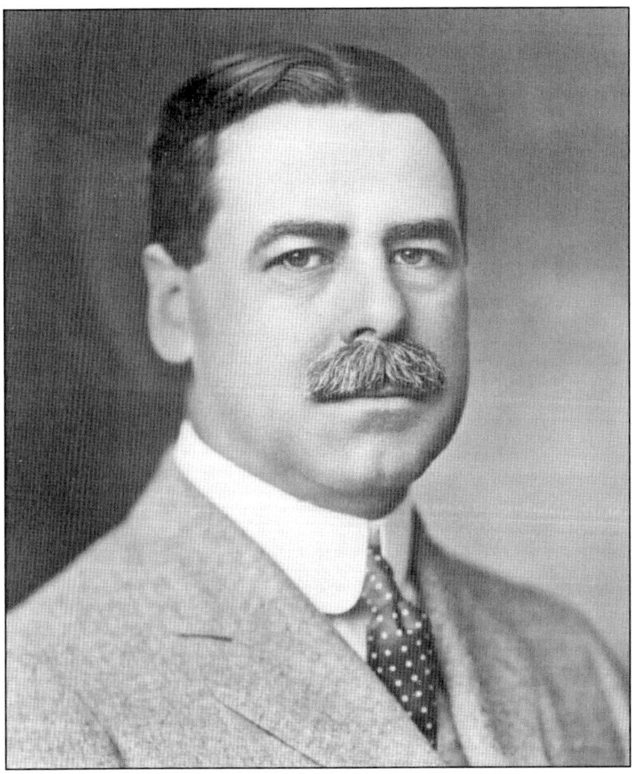

While Hornsey was failing, California Trona Company reincorporated as American Trona Corporation. With Hornsey's complete failure, American Trona hired Charles P. Grimwood to design a plant to produce potash from the brine. Grimwood had experience in the salt industry and proposed a plant nearly identical to a salt plant.

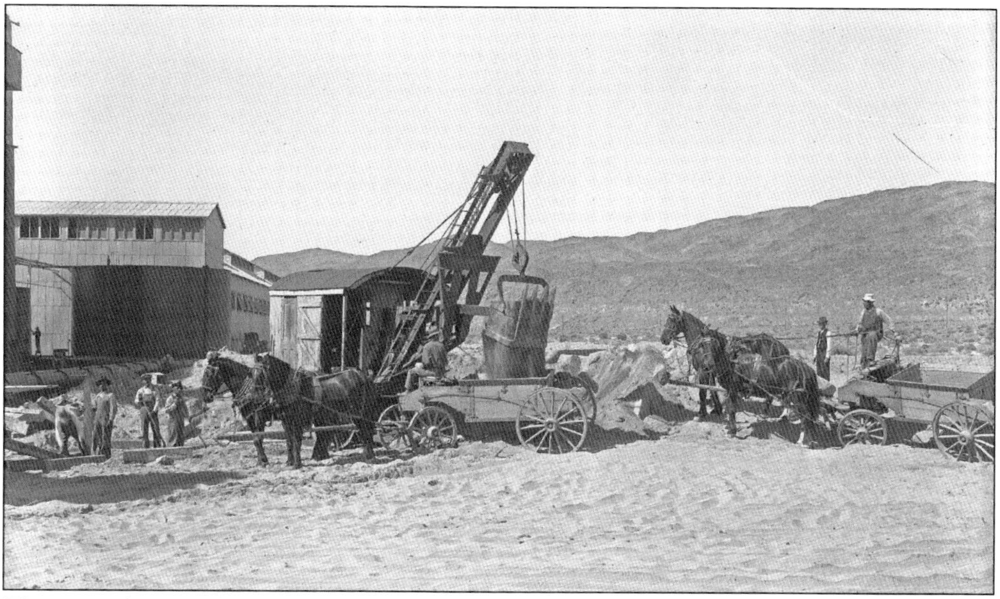

This 1917 photograph, taken during construction of the Grimwood Plant, displays the use of a power excavator to dig dirt and horse-drawn wagons to carry the dirt away. This arrangement was used because the sand was soft and thick wood beams were needed to hold up the shovel, which made moving the shovel difficult. In contrast, the horse-drawn wagons could move readily across the sand as needed.

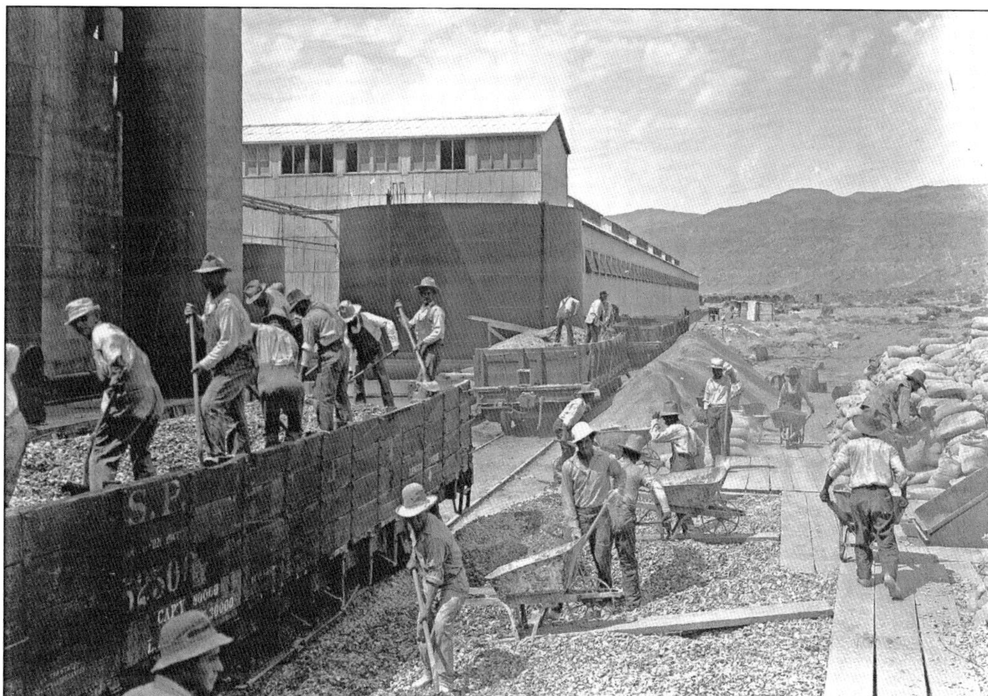

Gravel for mixing concrete was brought to the construction site in open railcars. These cars were unloaded by men using shovels, and the gravel was then shoveled into wheelbarrows and rolled to where the concrete was mixed.

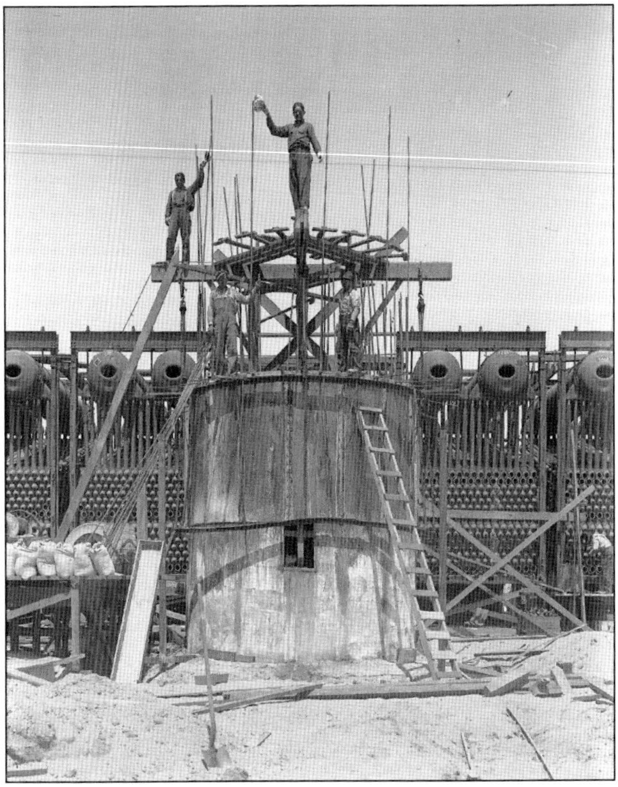

The Grimwood plant used steam to provide heat for brine evaporation. Pictured here in 1917 is the third course of a boiler stack being formed. Behind the stack, the steam boilers are being erected.

Grimwood's process was based on evaporating brine in large tanks. The evaporators were delivered to Trona by rail and came as a pile of large cast-iron pieces that had to be assembled on site. Lifting these large cast-iron pieces into place required a large crane. In 1917, the largest cranes could only operate from railroad tracks.

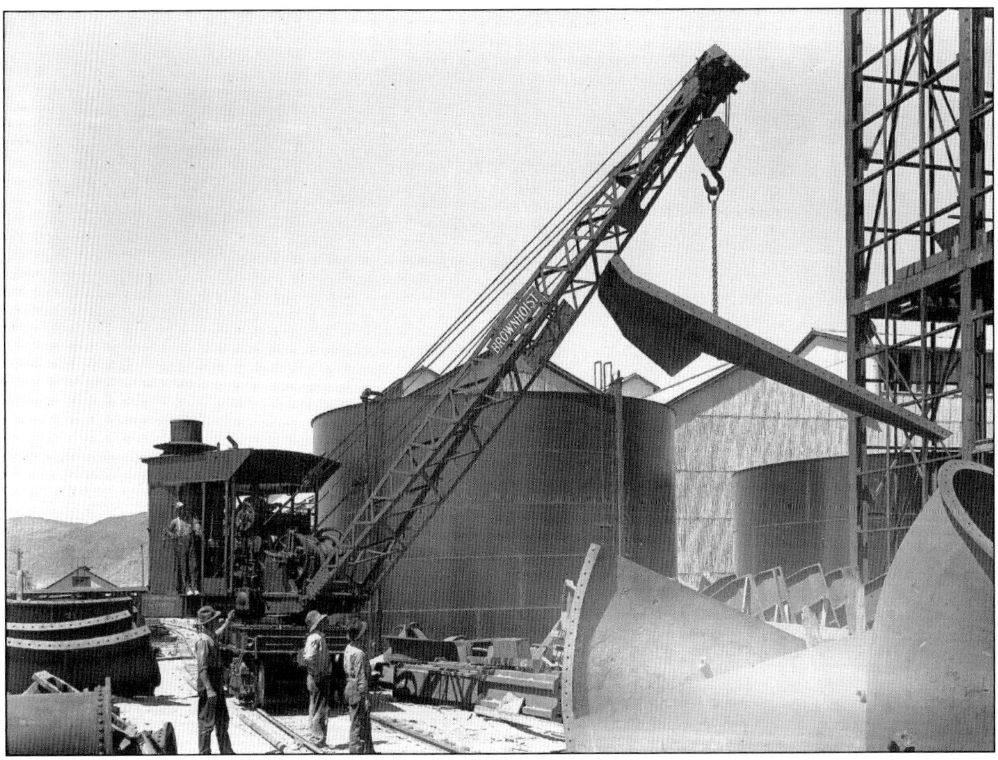

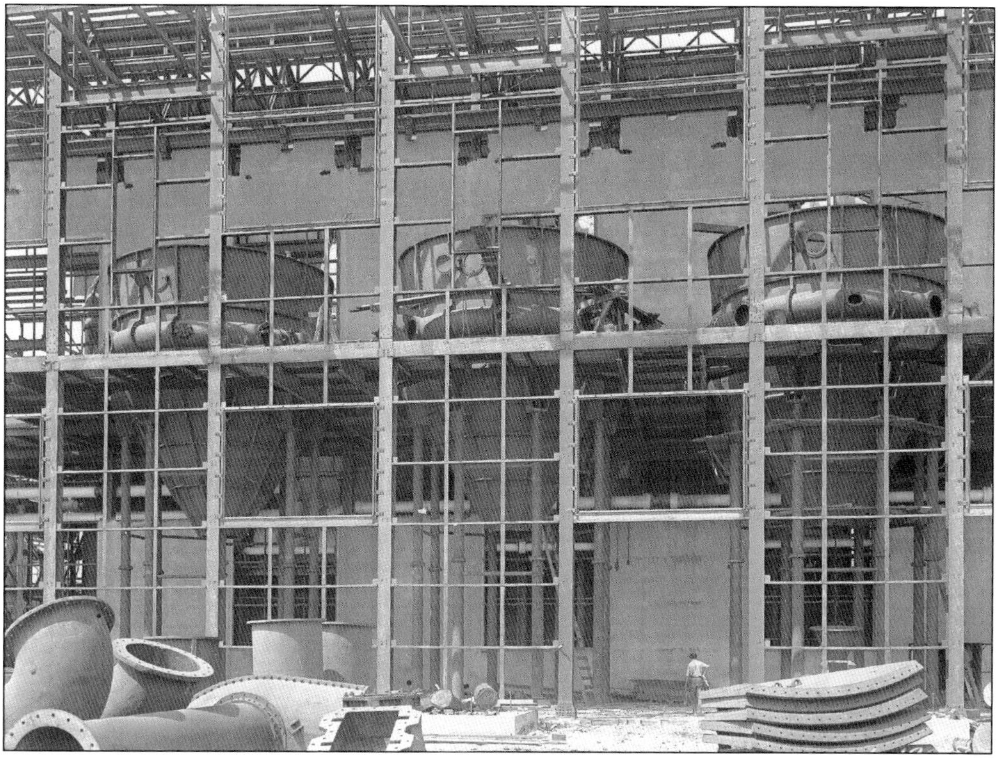

Grimwood specified that two evaporator units should be built. Each contained three evaporator tanks that were connected in series to progressively concentrate the brine. One of the evaporator units is pictured here during construction in 1917. Look for the man standing at bottom right.

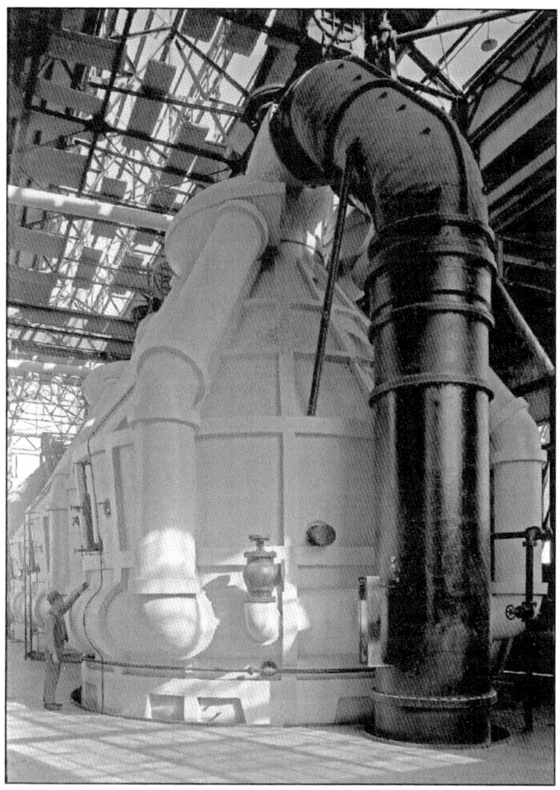

A completed evaporator unit in operation is pictured here on February 16, 1918. Notice the man standing at lower left. Each evaporator pan was 22 feet in diameter.

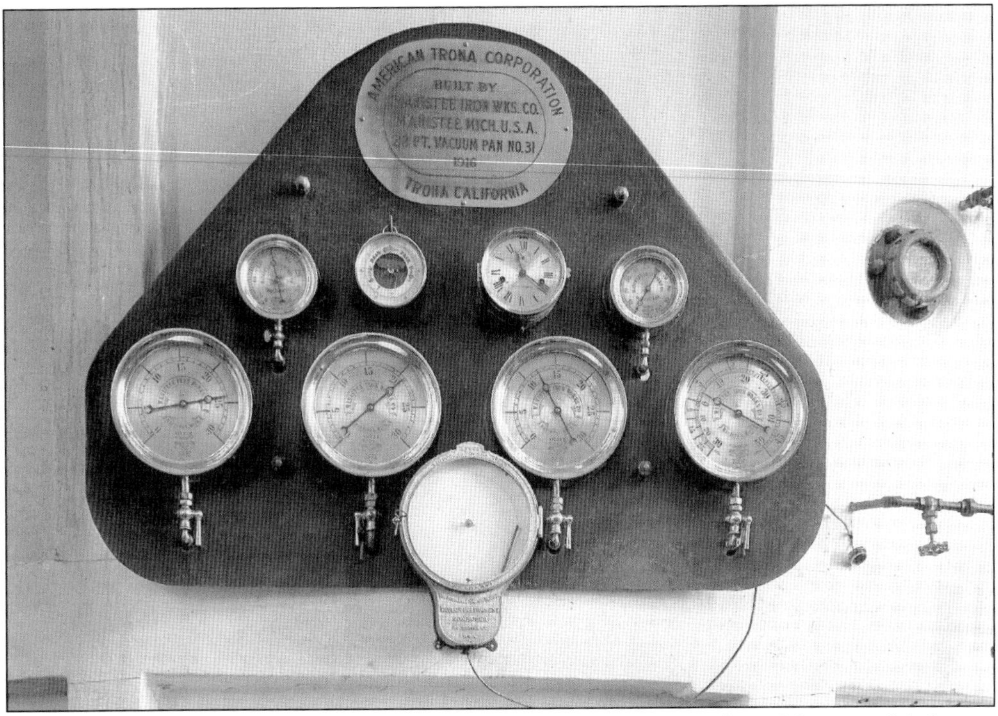

In 1916, when the evaporator was designed by the Manistee Iron Works in Manistee, Michigan, instrumentation was rudimentary, and control was largely manual. The instrument panel included a clock, barometer, pressure gauge for the steam, vacuum gauges for each evaporator body, and a Taylor recording thermometer.

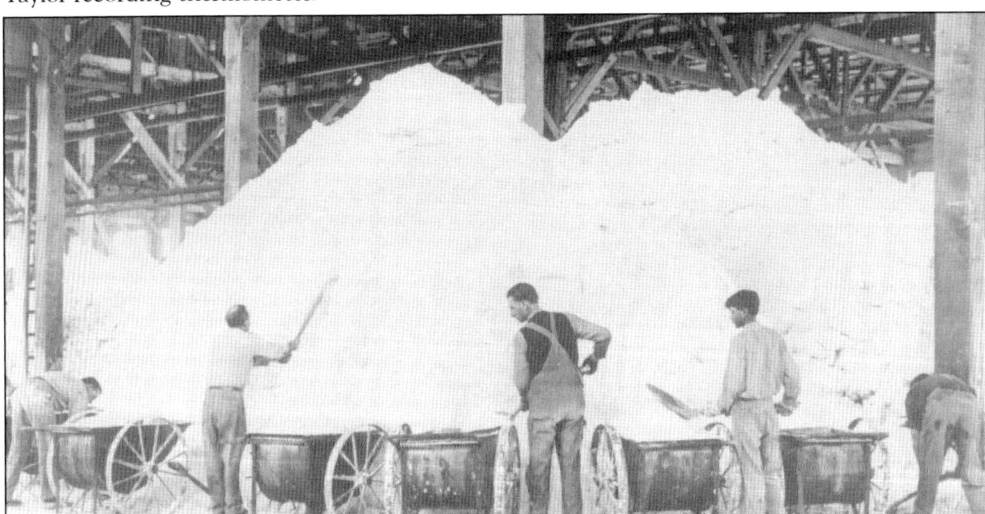

After brine had been concentrated by evaporation, it was hot and laden with potash and borax. The potash and borax were recovered by cooling the hot brine for up to eight days in 36 large vats. The product was dug from the vats by hand and conveyed to the potash storage building. Shipping the product required it to be shoveled into wheelbarrows and rolled to a crushing station before it was loaded into railcars.

Prior to loading in a railcar, the potash was dumped into an elevator, crushed, and then slid down a chute into the boxcar, where more men shoveled it away from the end of the chute.

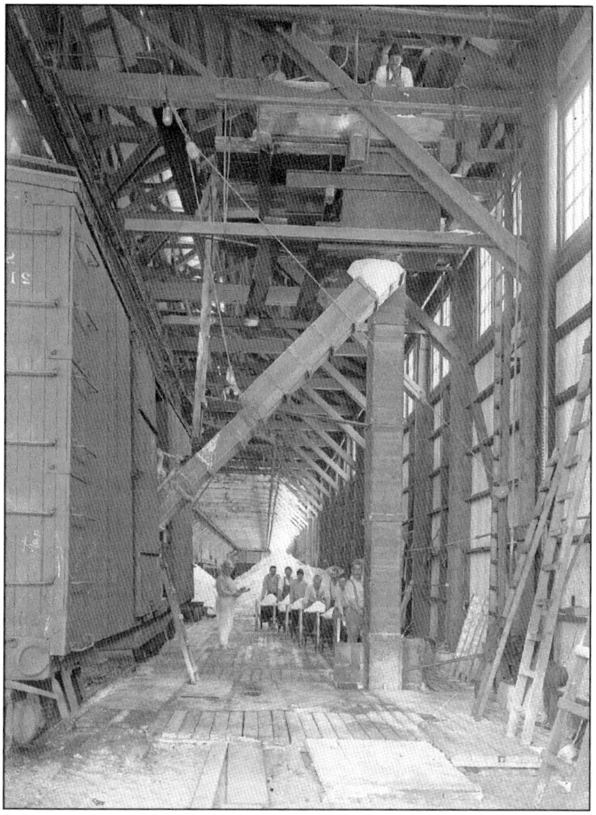

The Grimwood plant also recovered borax from the concentrated brine. This was filtered from the brine using a rotary-disk vacuum filter.

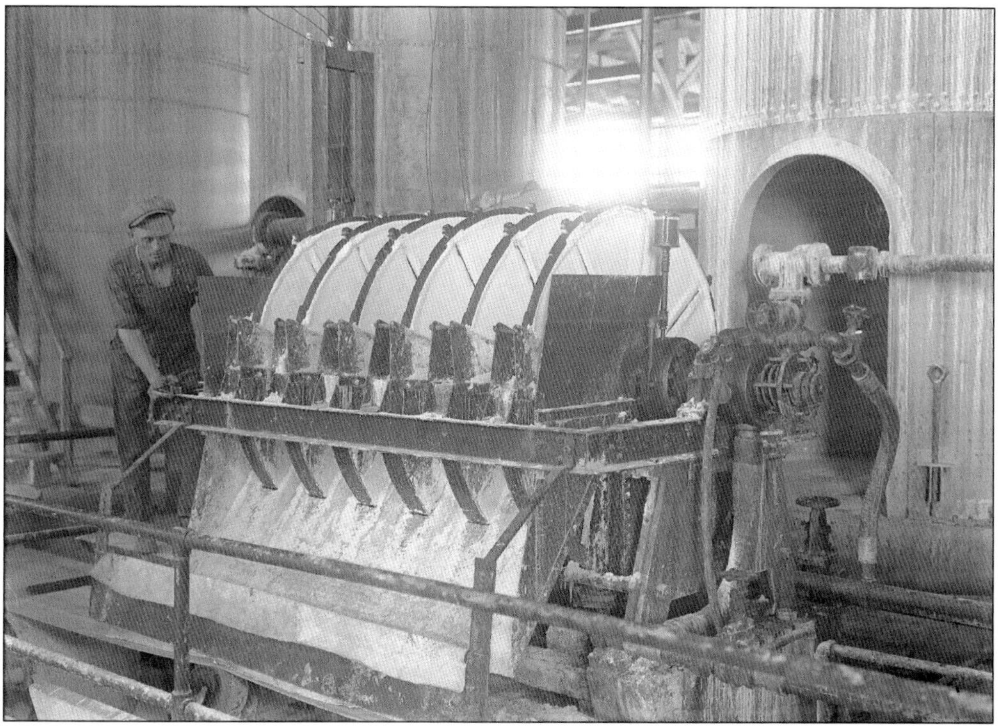

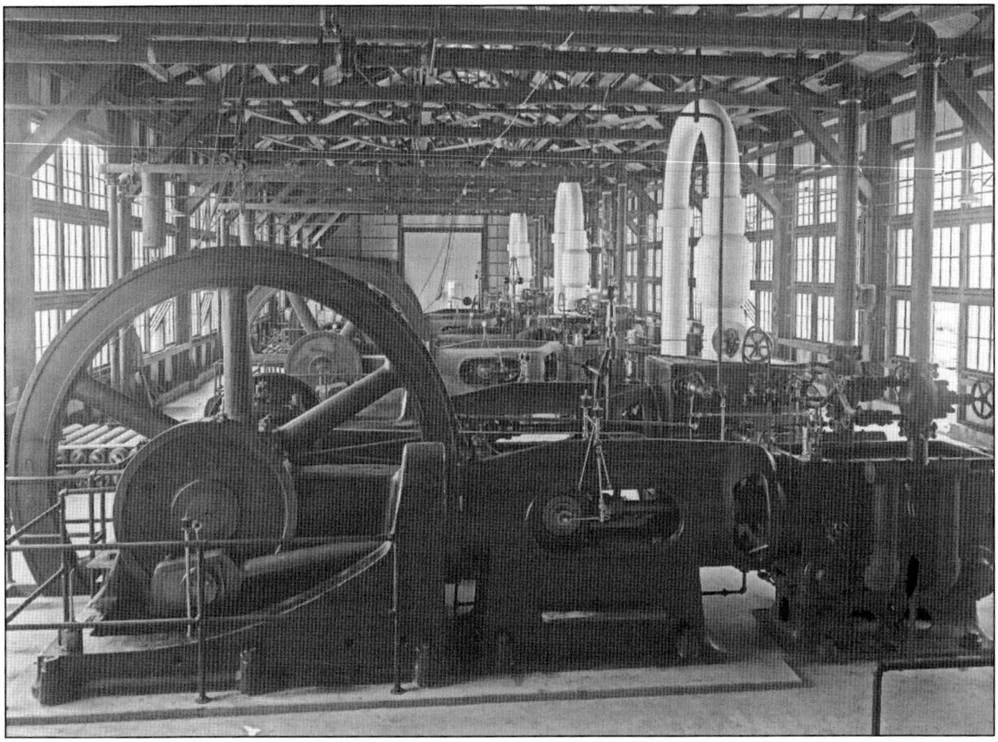

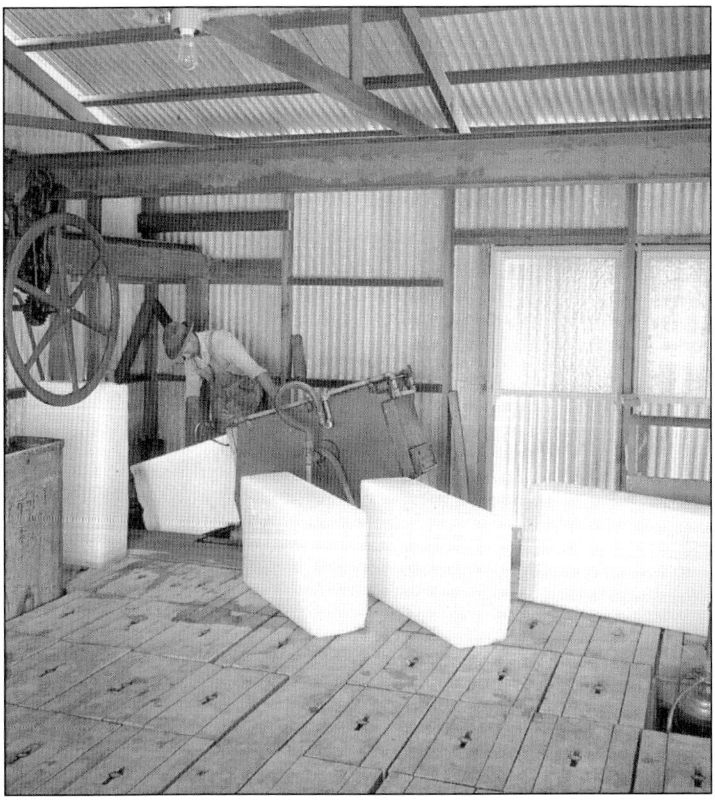

The recovery of borax required the potash-depleted brine to be refrigerated. Pictured here are three large steam-driven reciprocating compressors used to produce the refrigeration.

In 1918, small refrigerators had not yet been manufactured. American Trona Corporation operated an ice plant to produce 300-pound blocks of ice for the worker iceboxes in the plant, the butcher shop, and for home use.

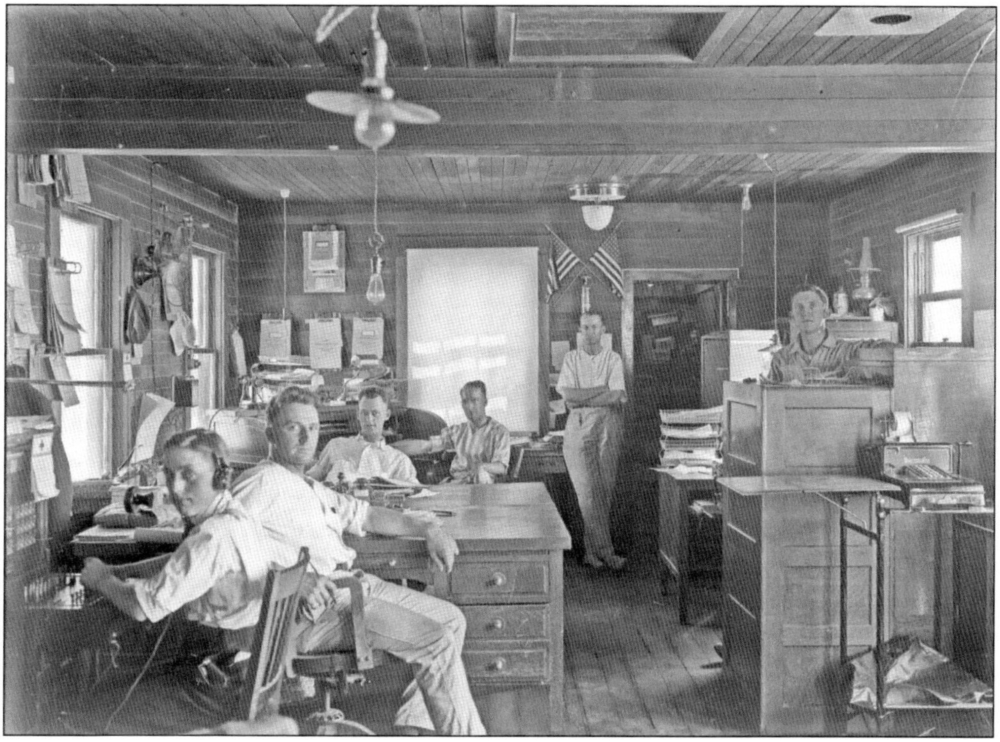

Every business had an office, including American Trona Corporation. Notice the telephone switchboard at far left. In 1918, there was just one telephone line into Trona.

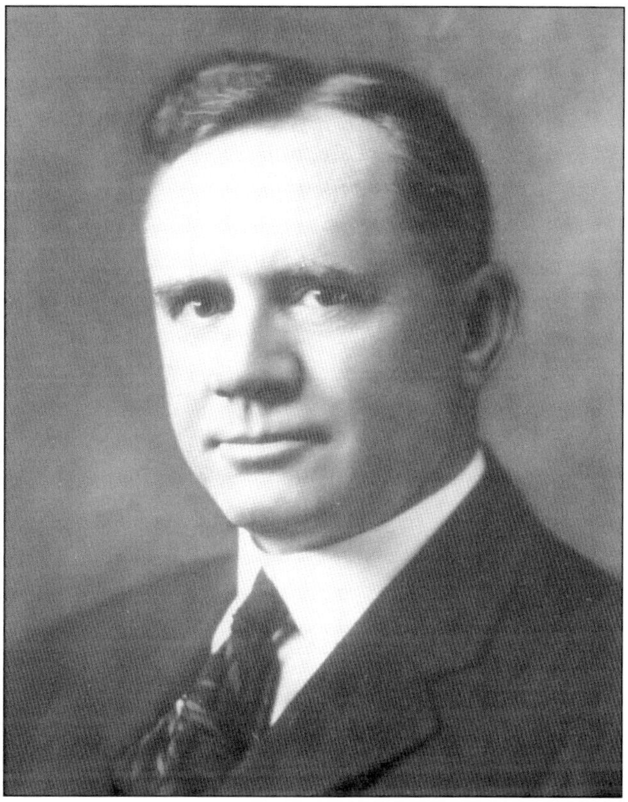

Despite producing potash and borax, Grimwood's Plant was only profitable with the high potash price caused by the World War I embargo of German potash. In May 1921, after the price for potash dropped by 90 percent, the owners shut down the Trona plant and debated permanent closure. Dr. John Edgar Teeple, pictured here, persuaded the owners that their process and equipment problems could be solved, and the plant would then be very profitable.

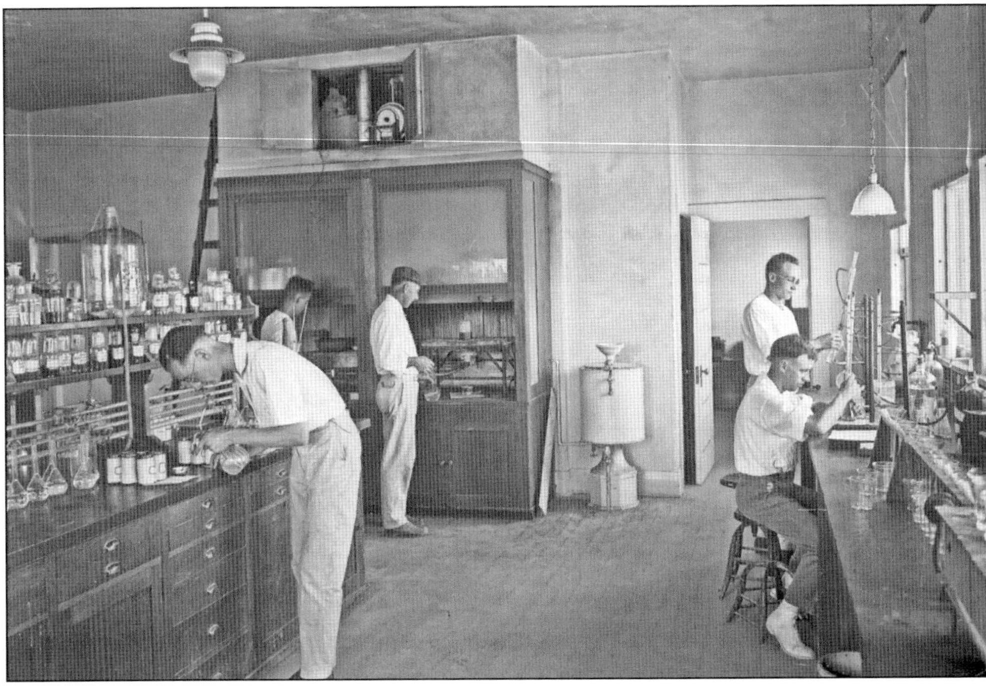

One of Dr. Teeple's actions was to perform laboratory tests to determine the chemistry of evaporating Searles Lake brine and crystallizing potash and borax. He knew that only by knowing this chemistry could he know how the plant would have to be operated.

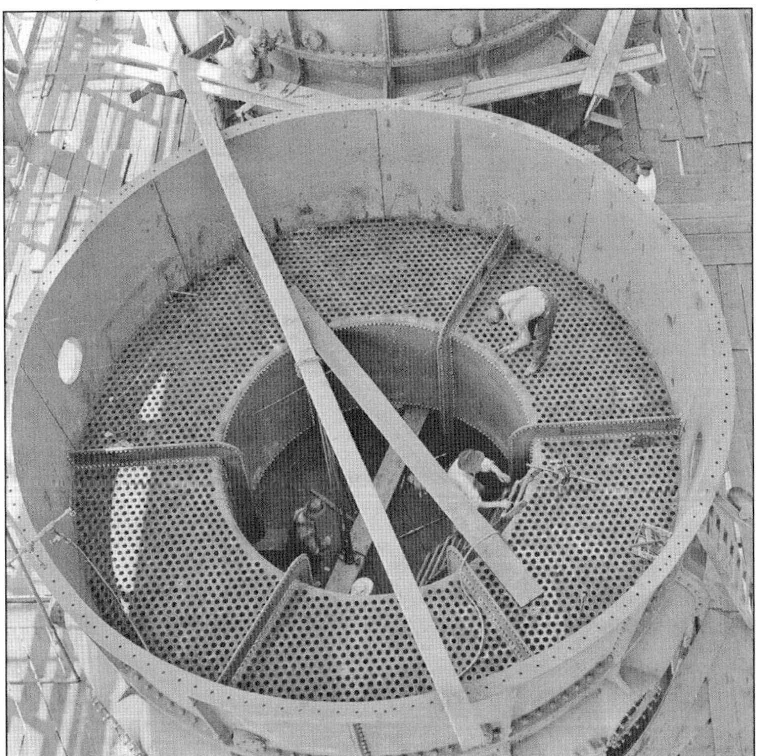

One problem the Grimwood evaporators had was that the steam-tube heaters were inside the evaporator body. Evaporating brine would coat the heating tubes with salt in just 36 hours, and this would stop evaporation of the brine. To remove the salt from the tubes, it was necessary to completely drain the evaporators, fill them with water, boil it, drain away the water, and then refill with brine to resume evaporation.

To solve this problem, Dr. Teeple's engineers invented the external heat exchanger, for which they were granted US Patent 1,810,181. Today, nearly all evaporators are designed this way when there is any possibility of forming a coating on the tubes.

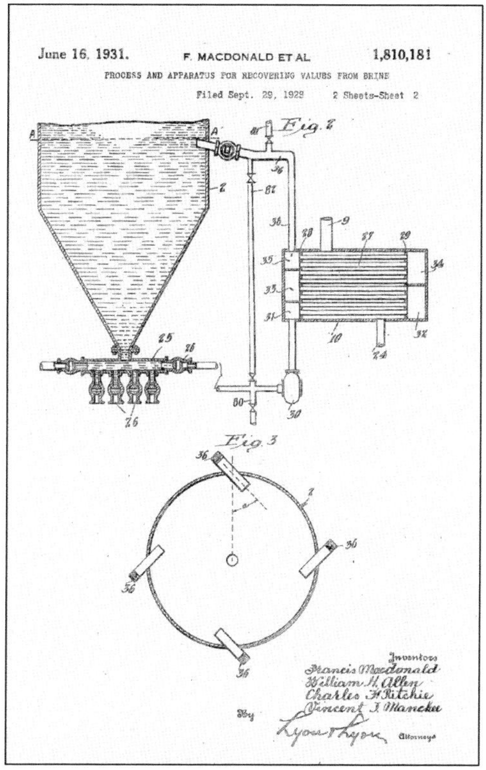

The crystallizing vats were also a serious problem. By holding the concentrated brine for eight days, both potash and borax crystallized. This caused the potash to contain about 20 percent borax, enough to make the potash more of a plant killer than the fertilizer it was intended to be. Digging the product out of the vat was also very labor intensive.

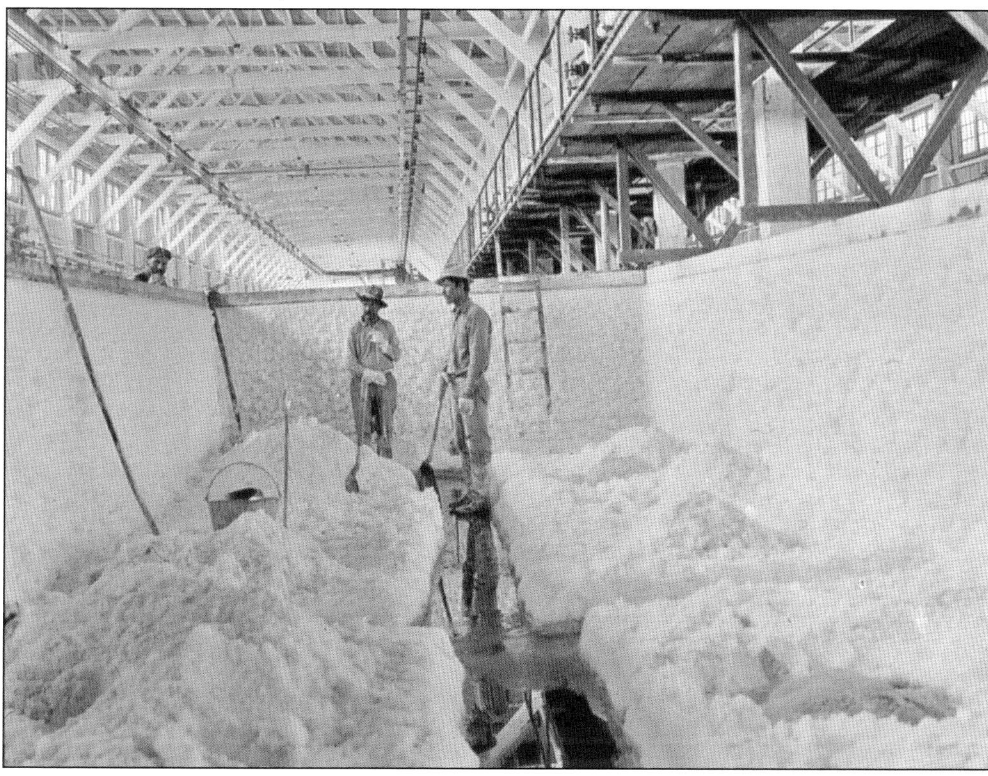

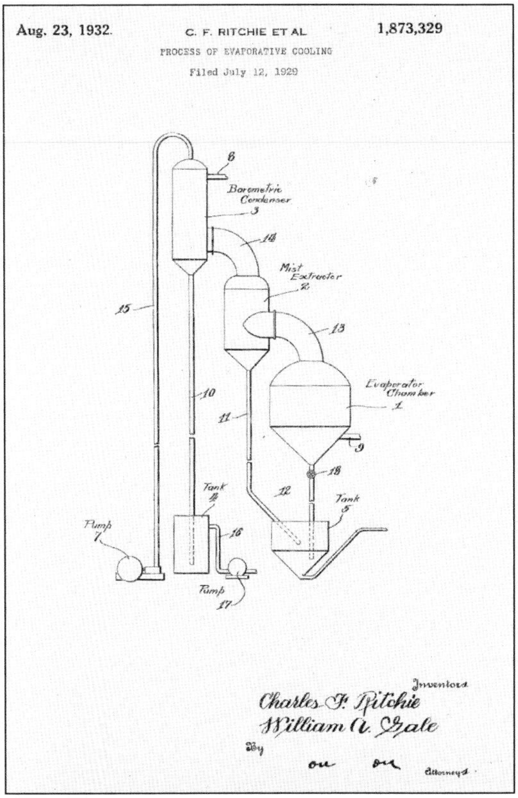

To solve this problem, Dr. Teeple's engineers invented the vacuum crystallizer. This permitted the potash to crystallize rapidly and be separated from the brine before borax had a chance to crystallize. Also, the crystallization could be done continuously. For this invention, they were granted US Patent 1,873,329. Today, nearly all cooling crystallizers follow this design.

When Searles Lake brine is evaporated to concentrate potash and borax, salt and other sodium crystals precipitate and must be removed to keep the evaporators working. Grimwood's evaporator design included bucket elevators to remove salt that settled to the bottom of the evaporator tanks. However, some of these waste salts were very fine and settled poorly. They also produced thin slurry that caused high losses of concentrated brine.

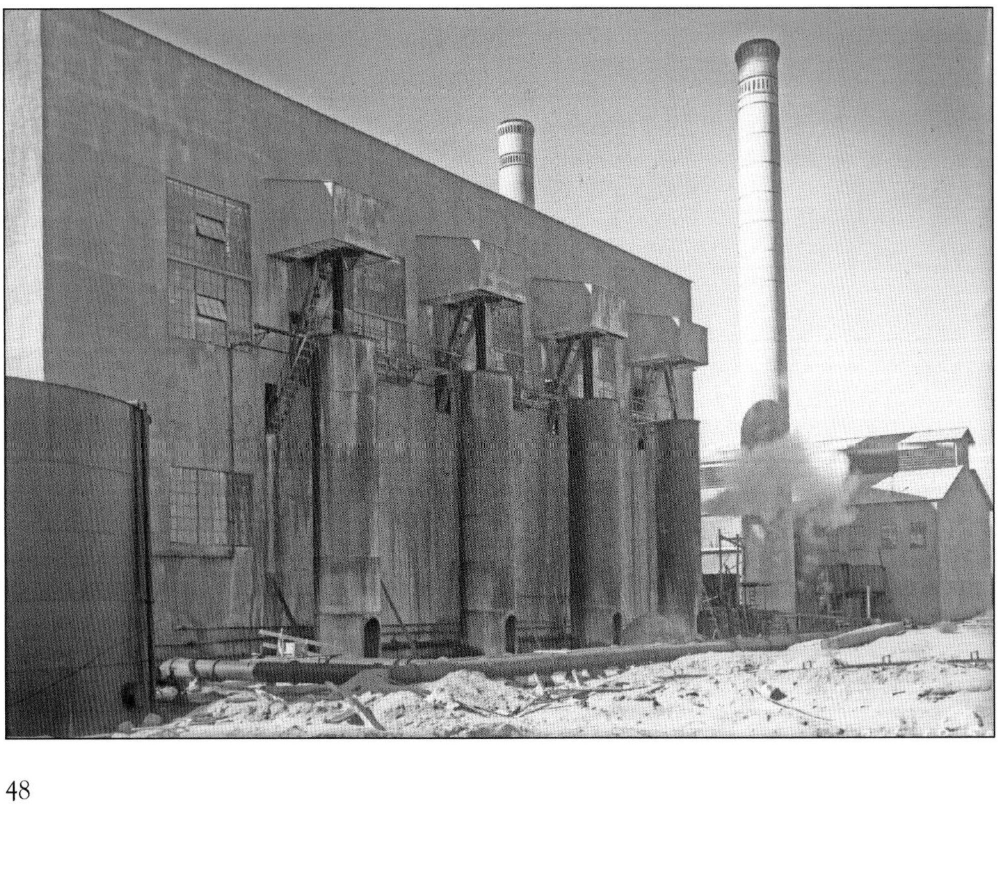

To solve this problem, Dr. Teeple's engineers invented external settling cones, arranged in a stack of three, one for each evaporator body in the evaporator unit. For this invention they were granted US Patent 1,873,251.

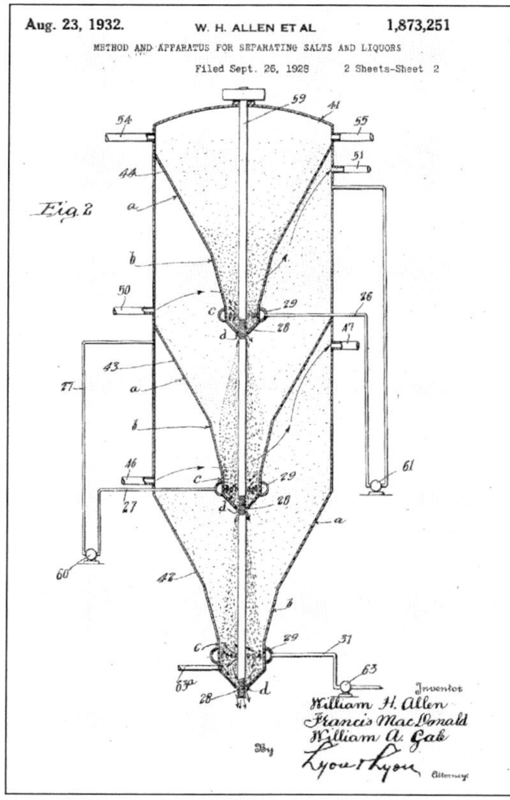

The improvements under Dr. Teeple's direction resulted in the highly efficient Trona Main Plant Cycle. By 1926, twenty percent of the potash used in the United States came from the Trona Plant, as did half the borax produced in the world. This process operated profitably for 70 years. If Dr. Teeple and his engineers had not been allowed to fix the plant's problems, Trona would have probably been just another desert ghost town by 1926.

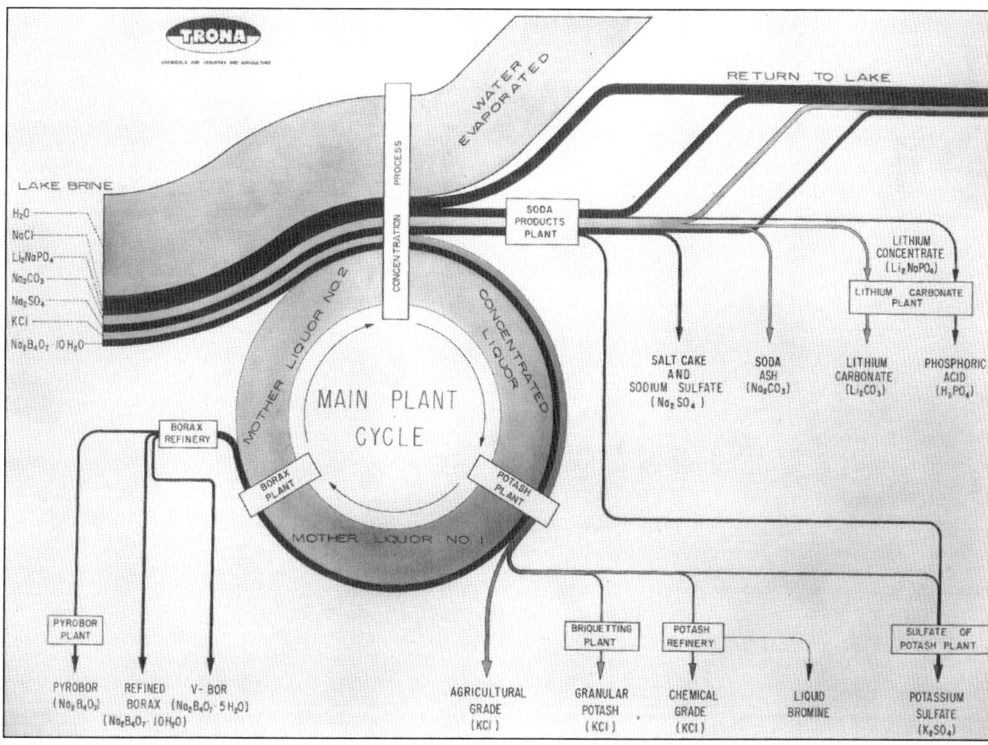

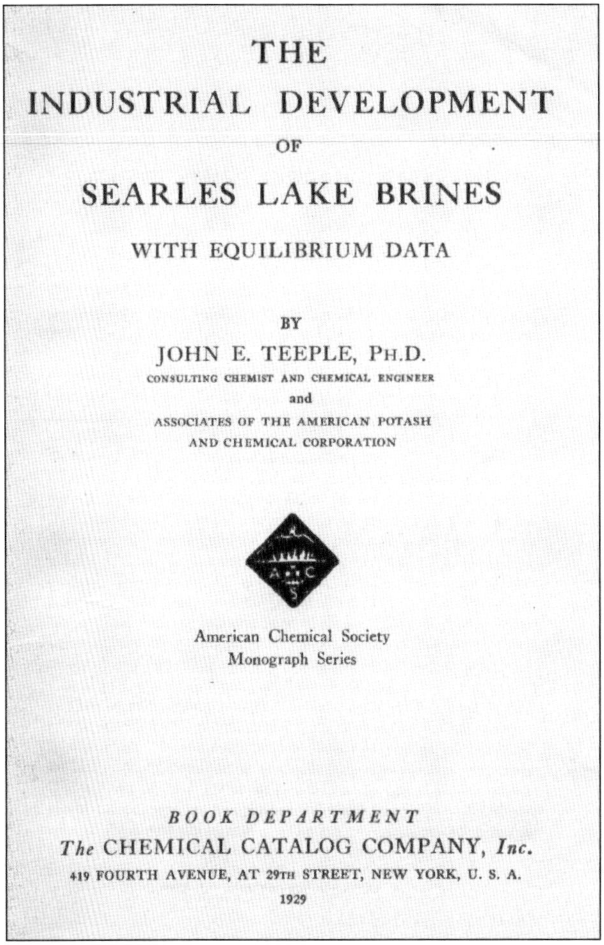

THE
INDUSTRIAL DEVELOPMENT
OF
SEARLES LAKE BRINES
WITH EQUILIBRIUM DATA

BY
JOHN E. TEEPLE, PH.D.
CONSULTING CHEMIST AND CHEMICAL ENGINEER
and
ASSOCIATES OF THE AMERICAN POTASH
AND CHEMICAL CORPORATION

American Chemical Society
Monograph Series

BOOK DEPARTMENT
The CHEMICAL CATALOG COMPANY, *Inc.*
419 FOURTH AVENUE, AT 29TH STREET, NEW YORK, U. S. A.
1929

For his work at Searles Lake, Dr. John Teeple was awarded the Perkins Medal by the American Chemical Society on January 14, 1927. In 1929, he published the solubility data on Searles Lake in the *ACS Monograph*, "The Industrial Development of Searles Lake Brines with Equilibrium Data." This was the first *ACS Monograph*; there have been many since.

While American Trona Corporation was entering the potash market during World War I, another company on Searles Lake was doing the same. This was the Borosolvay Corporation, a joint venture of the Solvay Process Company of Syracuse, New York, and the Pacific Coast Borax Company. This photograph shows the Borosolvay Plant late in its construction. The plant and associated housing areas cost $1.75 million.

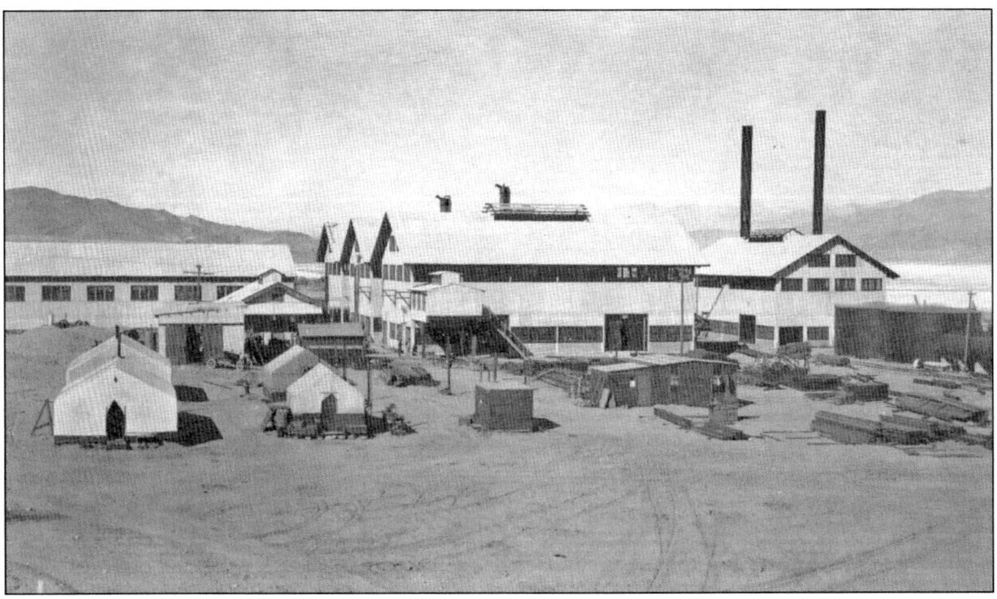

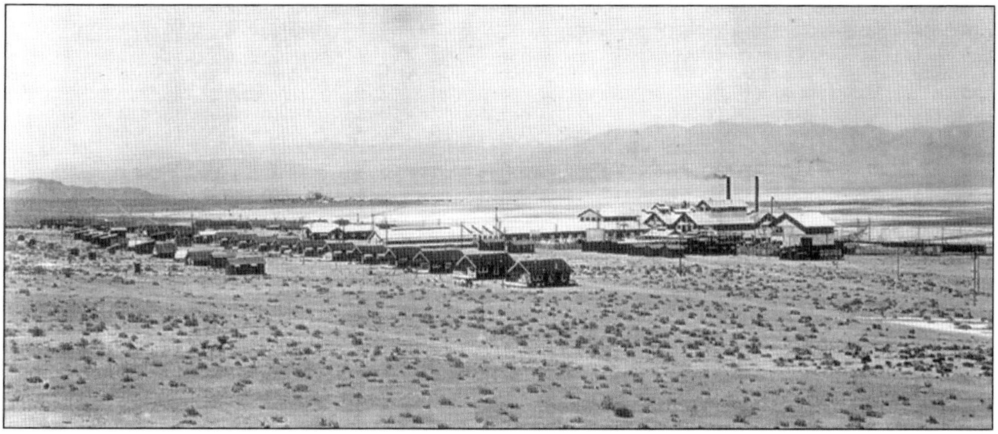

Pictured here is the Borosolvay Plant operating. Borosolvay used a process very similar to that in the Trona plant, except that they were prohibited from producing borax by the partnership agreement. When the price for potash dropped by 90 percent following the end of World War I, the Borosolvay Plant became unprofitable and was closed permanently on February 1, 1921.

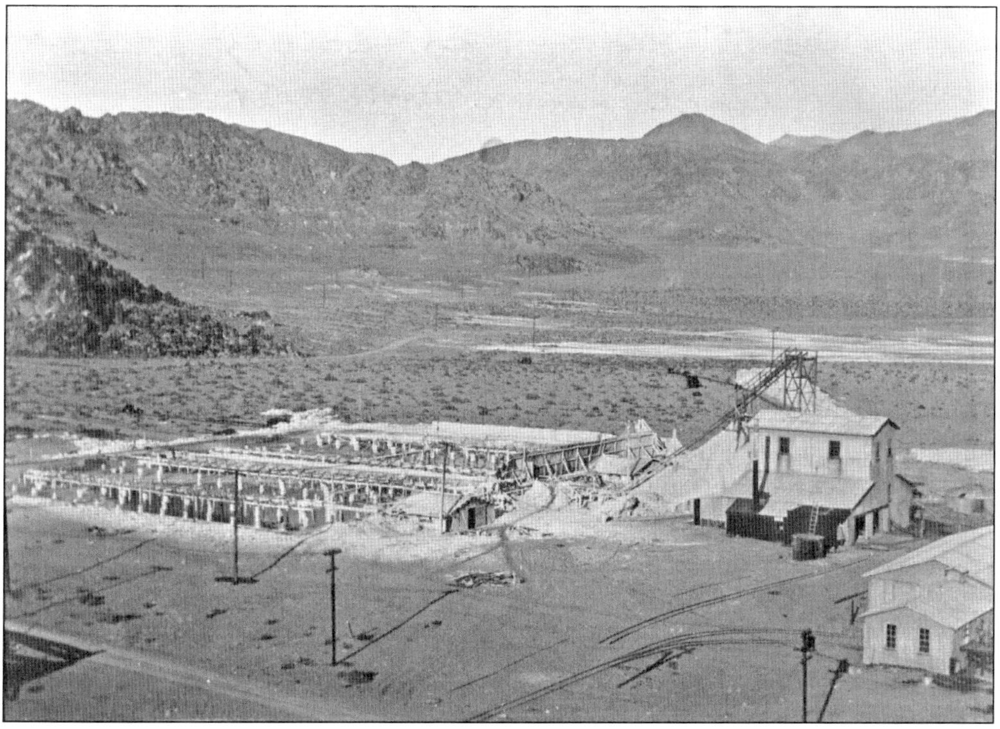

When Francis M. "Borax" Smith went bankrupt on May 6, 1913, he lost control of the Pacific Coast Borax Company he had founded many years earlier. By 1918, he tried to reenter the borax market by acquiring federal leases on Searles Lake. However, his early attempt to recover borax from the brine resulted in failure. This first attempt is pictured here in 1918 He called this the West End Chemical Company.

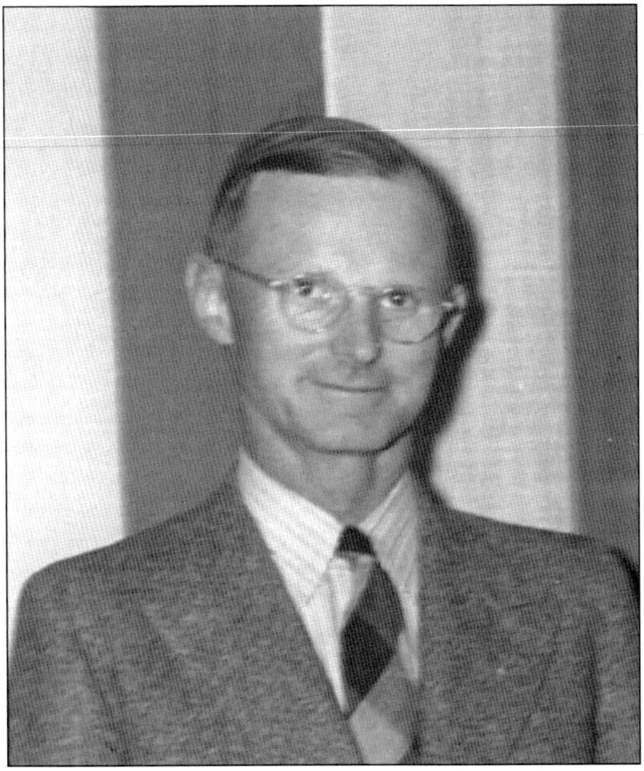

Borax Smith hired a young chemist, Henry Hellmers, to help him with process development at the Anniversary Mine, his Nevada borax property. By 1925, Hellmers had turned his attention to Searles Lake, and by 1926 Hellmers had a plant operating at Searles Lake producing borax. The plant was expanded in 1927 to also produce soda ash.

Gradually, the plant of the West End Chemical Company grew and prospered, even developing a small community to support its operation. The process invented by Henry Hellmers 90 years ago is still profitable today. This aerial photograph shows the plant in the late 1930s.

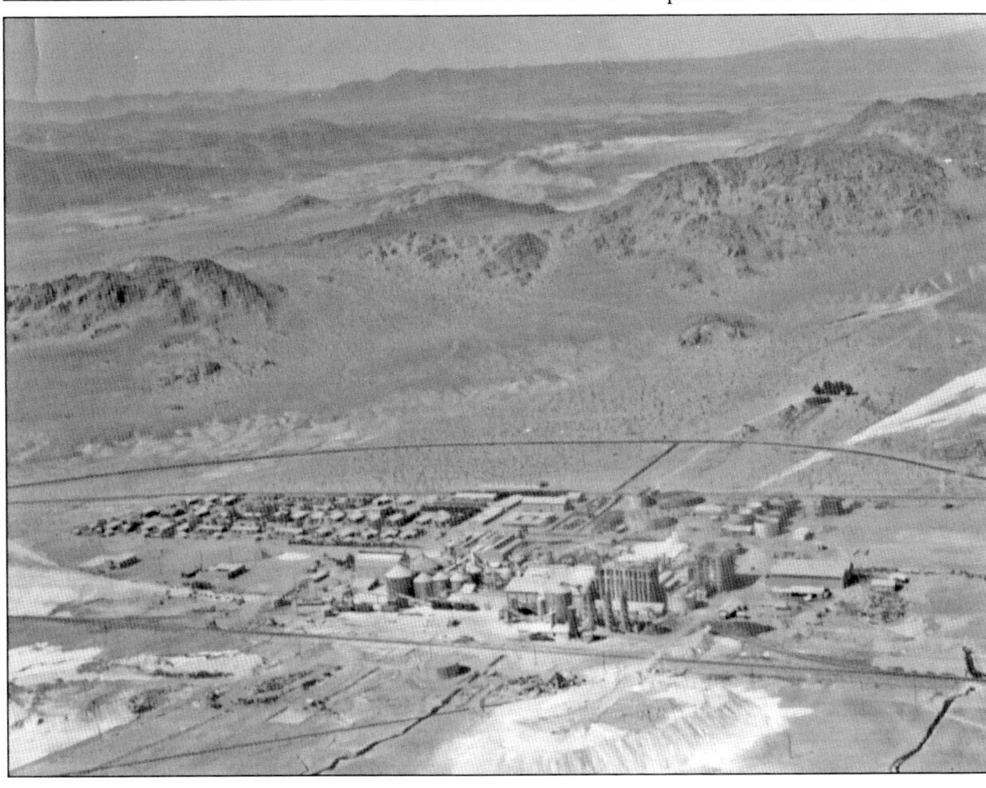

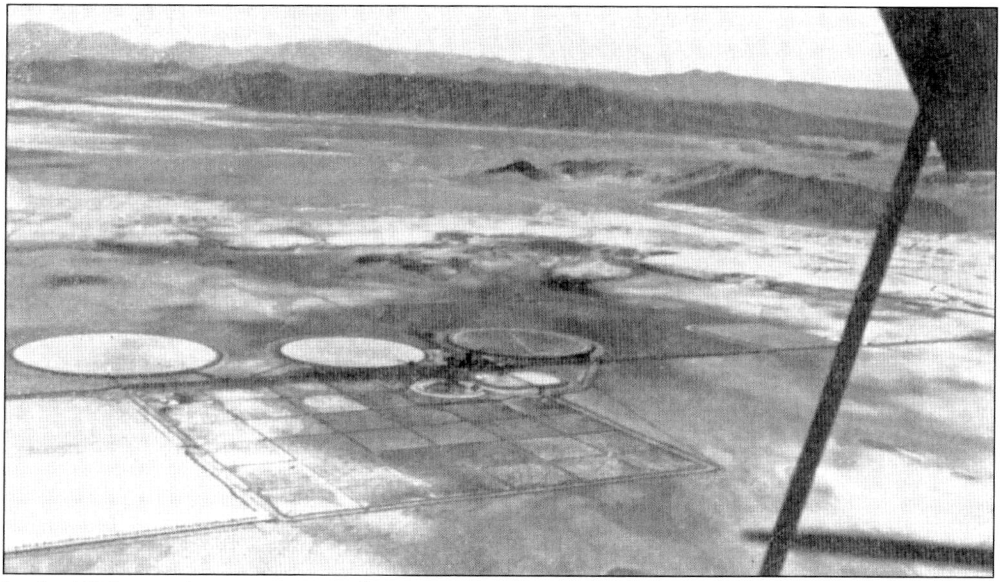

In the 1920s, another enterprising chemist, George B. Burnham of Berkeley, California, attempted to recover products from Searles Lake. His idea was to separate chemicals from the brine using nature's way. This method used solar evaporation to concentrate potash and borax and natural variations in brine temperature that occur in ponds and vats exposed to ambient conditions to adjust solubility. This aerial photograph captures Burnham's solar ponds and brine vats.

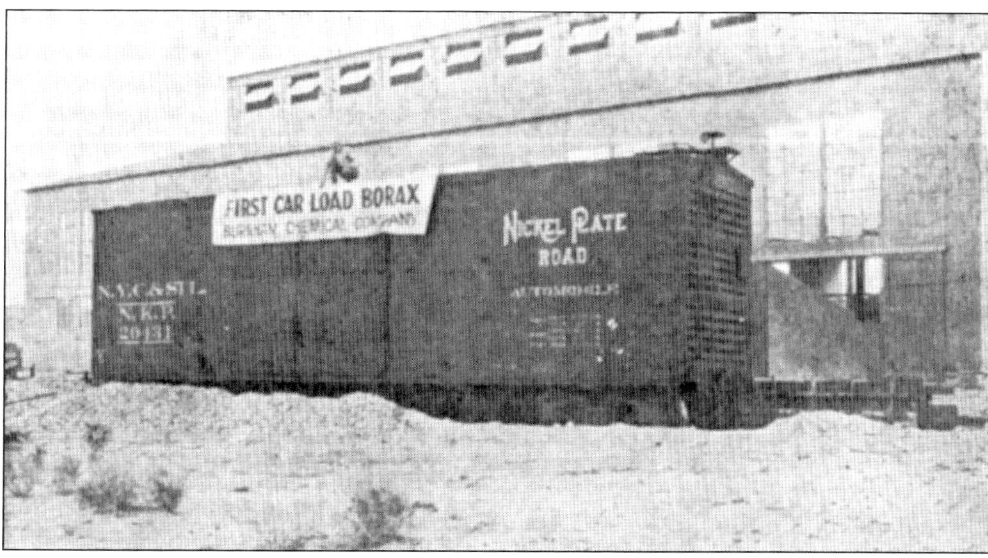

To protect his processes, Burnham obtained over 30 patents. But, weather is unpredictable, and chemical production needs some level of control to be successful. While he was able to produce over 3,000 tons of borax, he was never able to produce at a rate that would pay his costs. He also tried to start his business in 1929, just before the Great Depression sank the entire US economy and Burnham with it.

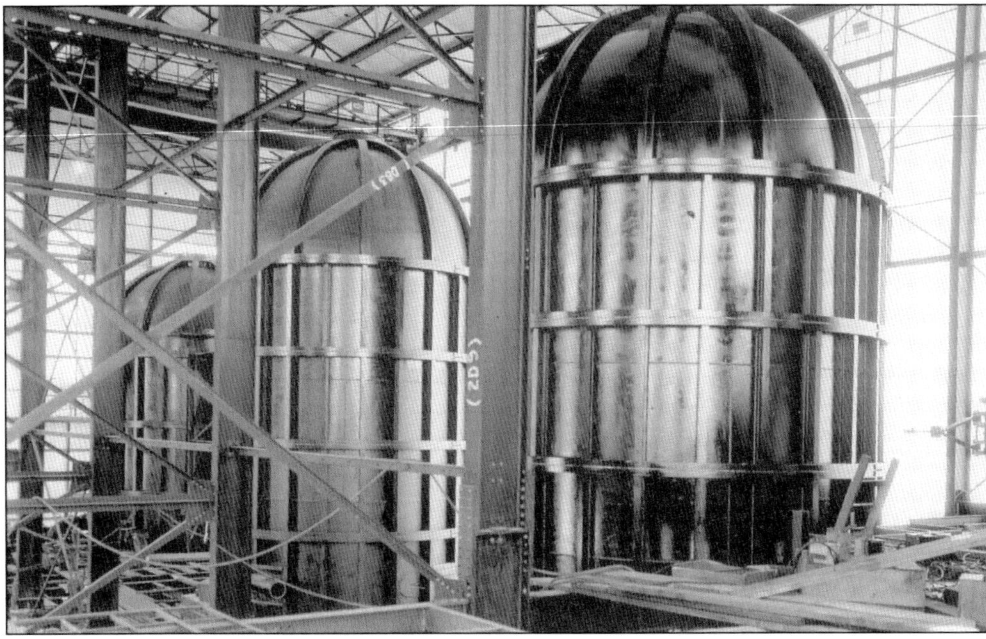

In 1929, American Potash and Chemical Corporation (AP&CC), the successor to American Trona Corporation, announced a major expansion of its plant. Although the country entered the Great Depression shortly after the expansion was announced, plant construction merely slowed but never stopped completely. The expansion included a new brine evaporator, 50 percent larger than the first two built in 1917 and 1918. This photograph shows the No. 3 evaporator during its construction in 1931.

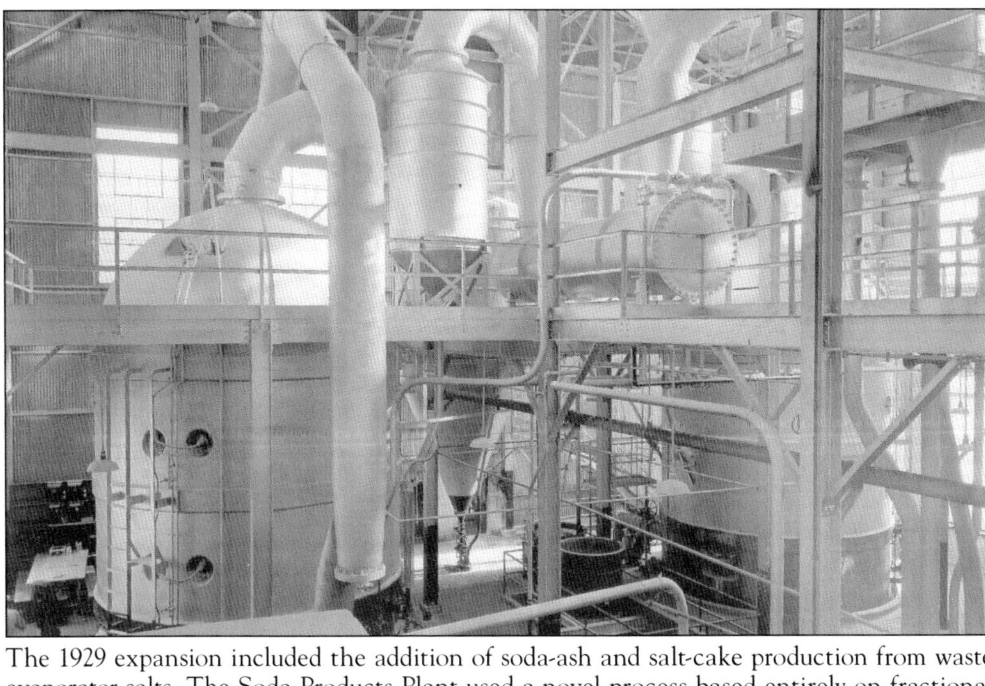

The 1929 expansion included the addition of soda-ash and salt-cake production from waste evaporator salts. The Soda Products Plant used a novel process based entirely on fractional crystallization through temperature manipulation. Pictured here is the soda-ash evaporator.

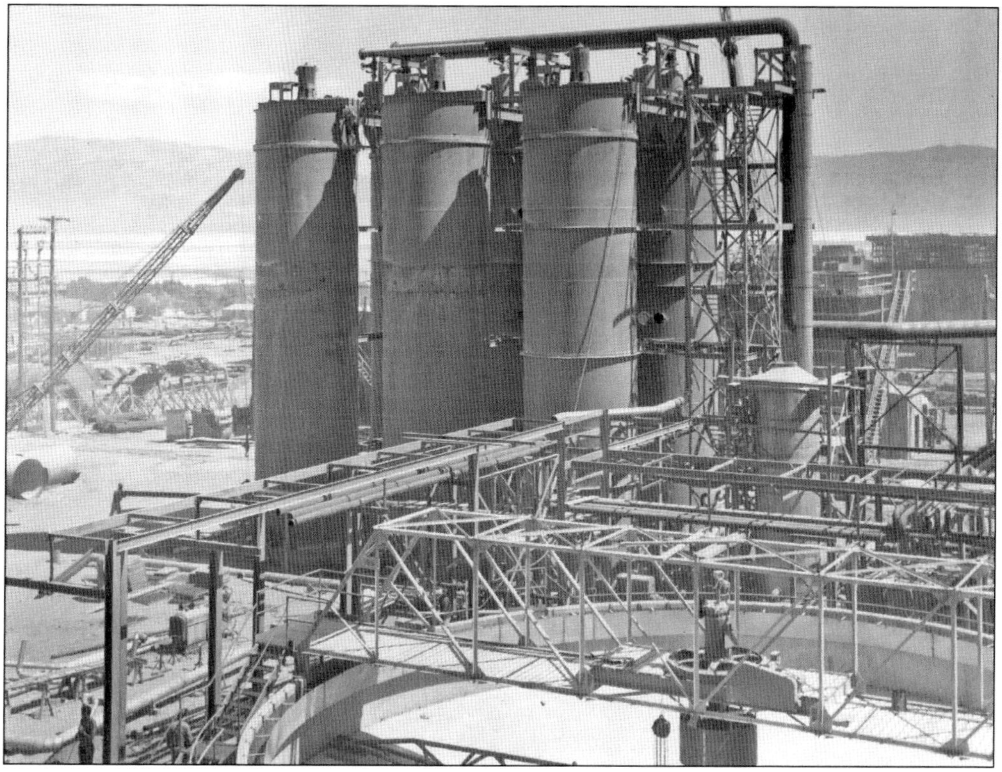

By 1948, AP&CC was expanding again, this time using the process patented by Henry Hellmers for the West End Chemical Company. Pictured here are the carbonation towers for the Trona Carbonation Plant after they were erected but before the piping and access platforms were installed.

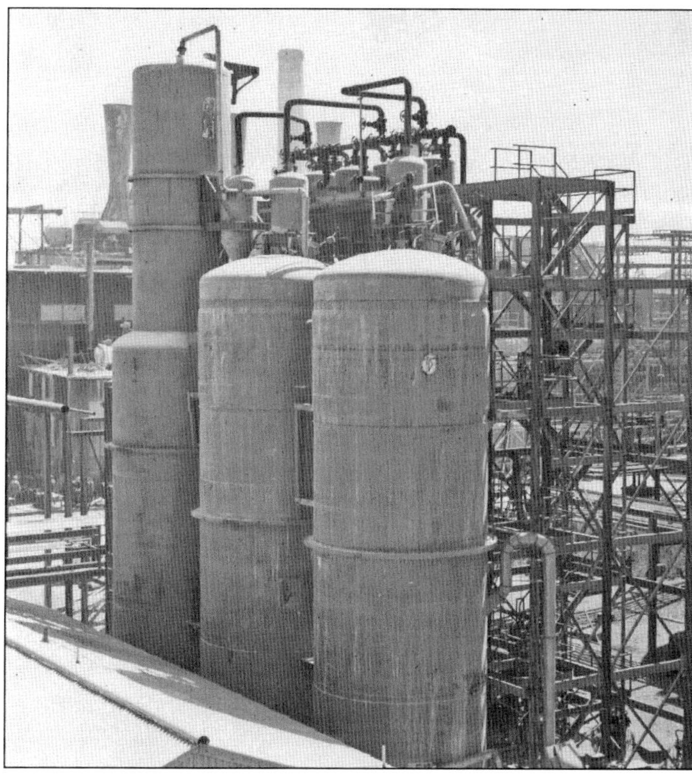

The 1948 carbonation plant expansion included new borax crystallizers, pictured here during construction. The crystallization was done using three stages of vacuum cooling.

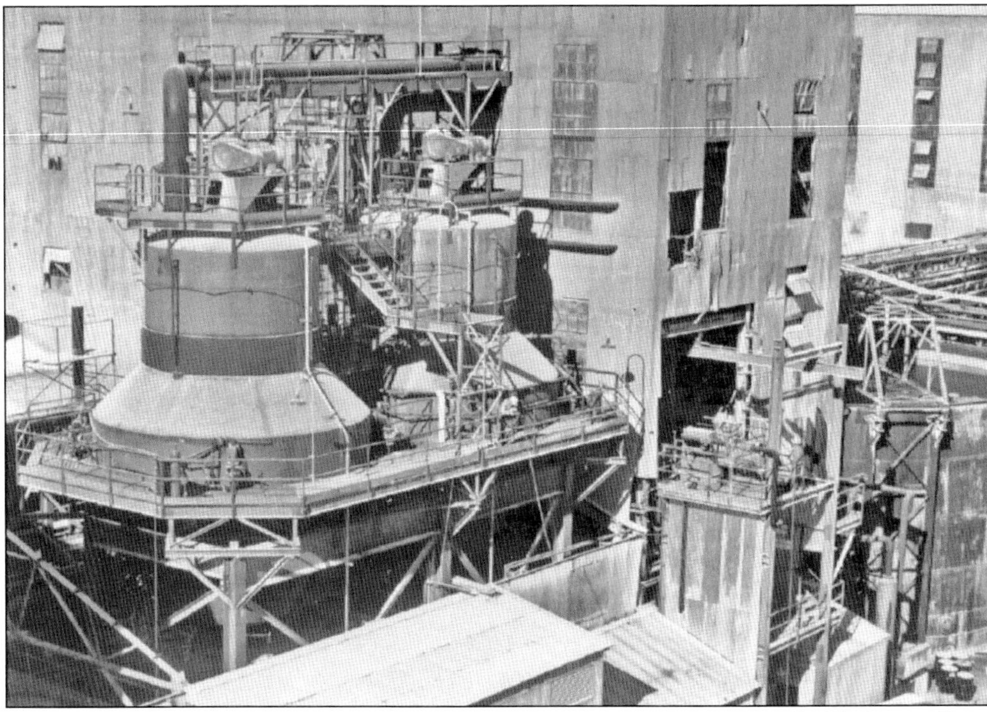

In 1959, AP&CC installed new potash crystallizers, the first large-scale use of baffled crystallizers that can grow crystals to a larger, more desirable size.

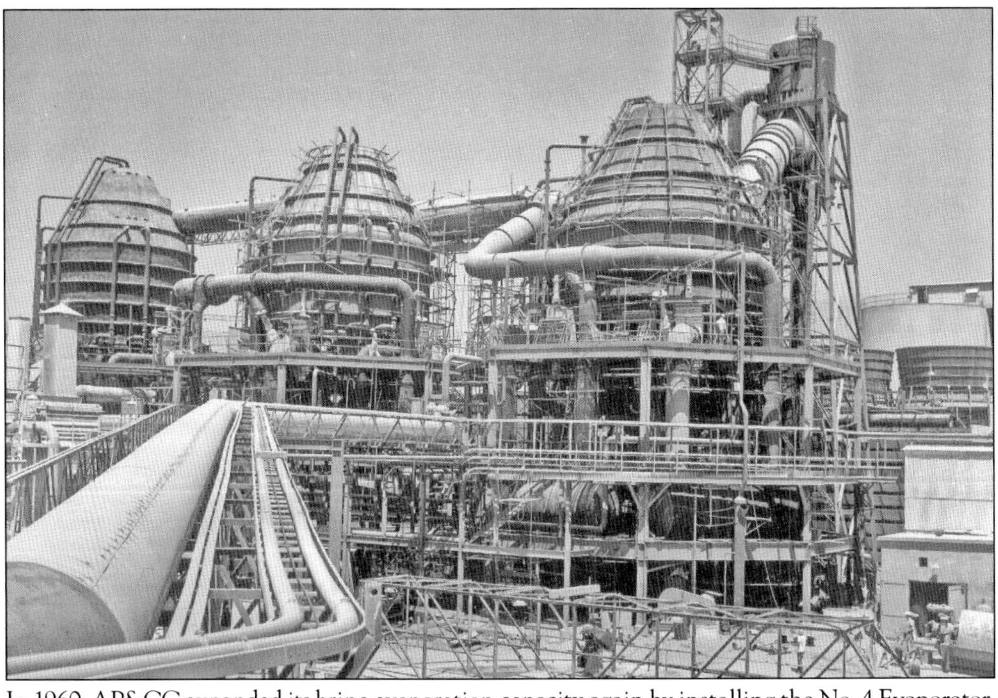

In 1960, AP&CC expanded its brine evaporation capacity again by installing the No. 4 Evaporator. When installed, this was the largest triple-effect steam evaporator in the world, with evaporator pans 34 feet in diameter.

In 1962, AP&CC expanded boric-acid and potassium-sulfate capacity using a new and novel solvent-extraction process. At the time, this was the world's largest use of solvent extraction to produce industrial chemicals. For this achievement, the team of engineers at AP&CC was given the prestigious Kirkpatrick Award for Chemical Engineering Achievement on December 3, 1963.

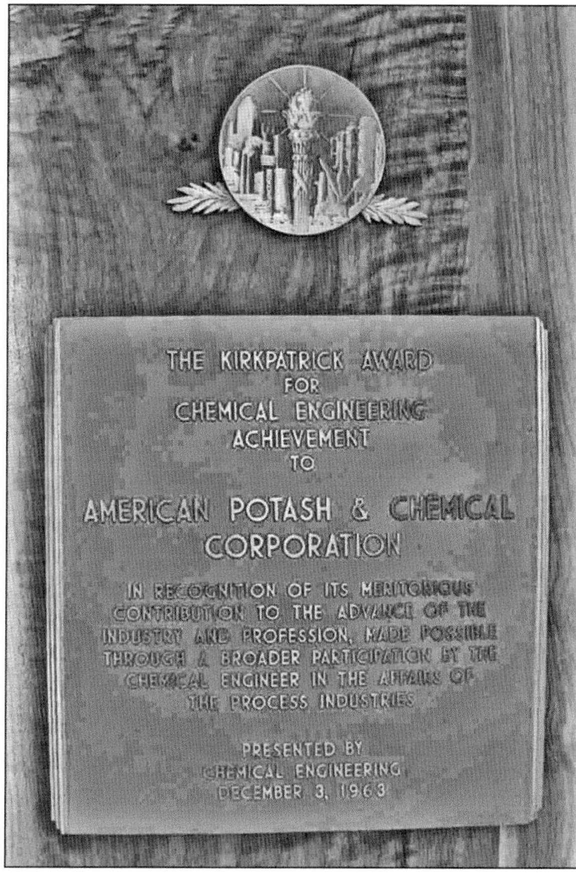

In addition to solvent extraction, the new boric-acid plant included an evaporator, pictured here, to crystallize the extracted boric acid and potassium sulfate.

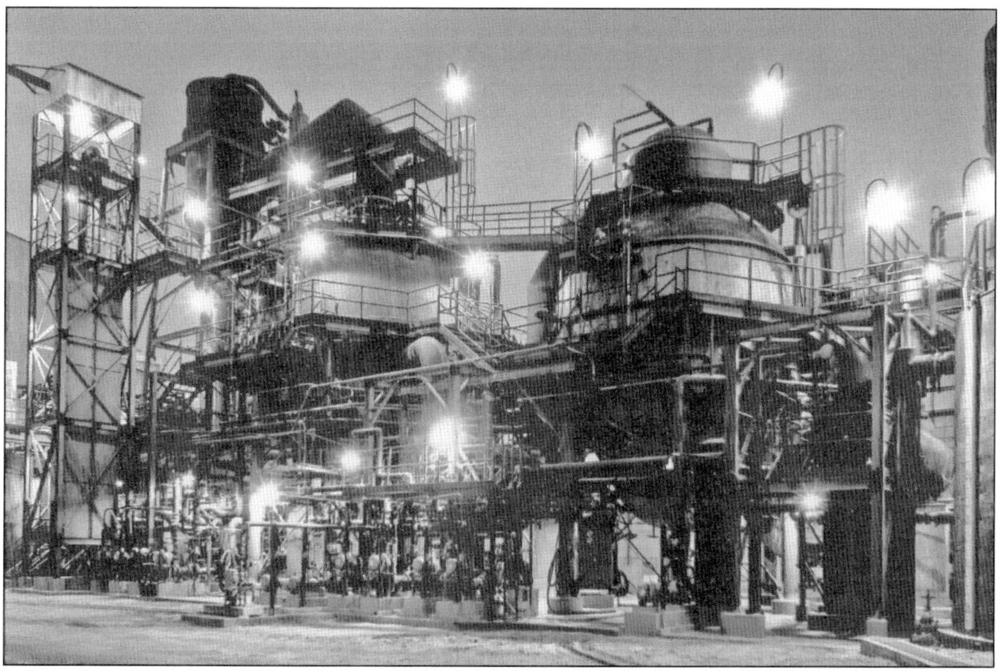

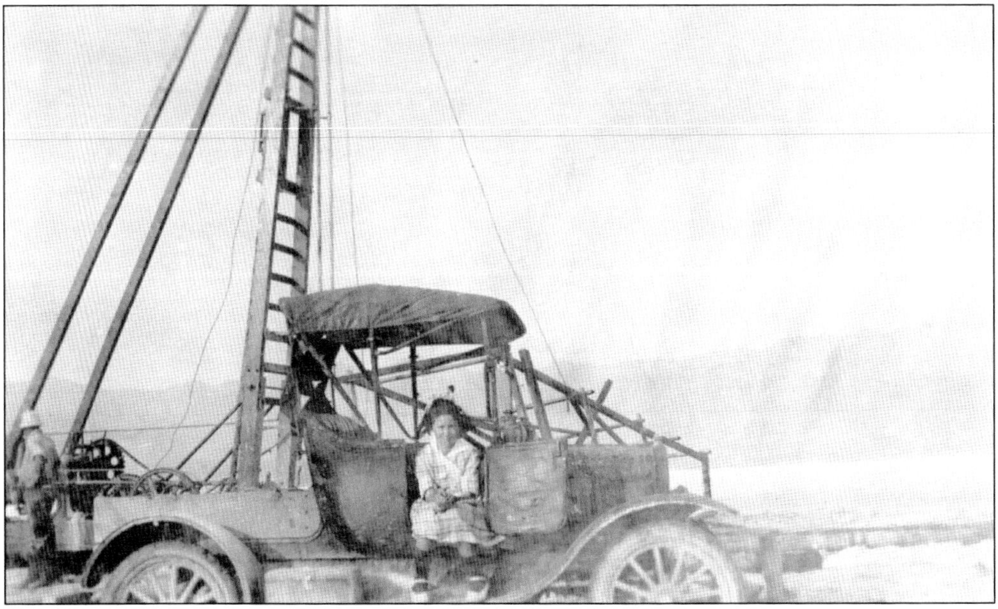

To operate processes based upon brine, wells must be drilled into the salt deposit to pump brine out of the porous salt. Pictured here is the 1915 Ford truck drill rig used by American Trona Corporation.

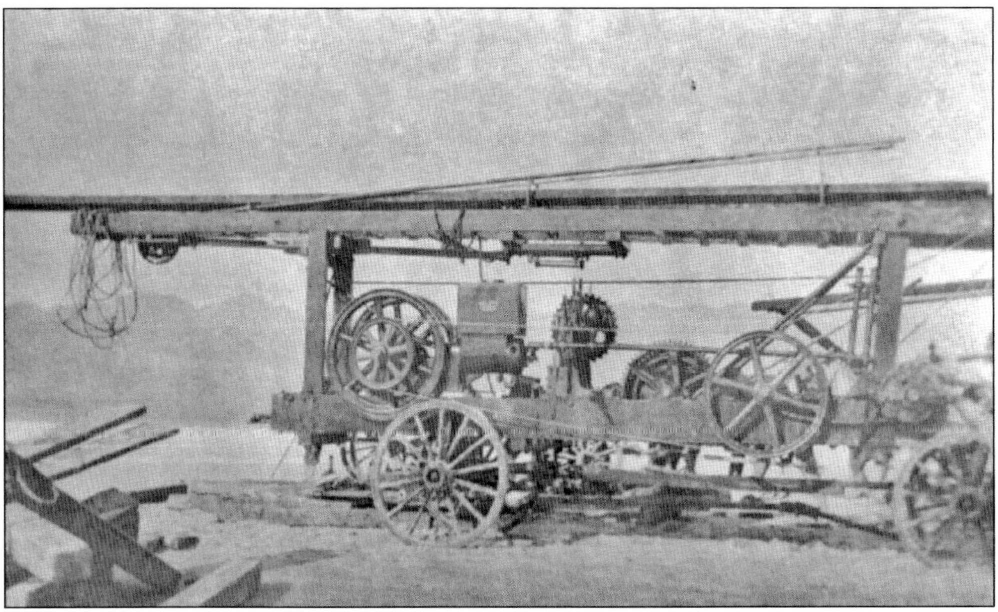

This is a slightly more modern drill rig, although it was still pulled from one location to another by horses. It was a cable-tool drill rig that repeatedly lifted and dropped a heavy weight down a hole to pulverize the rock (or salt) and thereby gradually deepen a vertical hole. Later, rotary drill rigs were used that cut their way through the salt in Searles Lake.

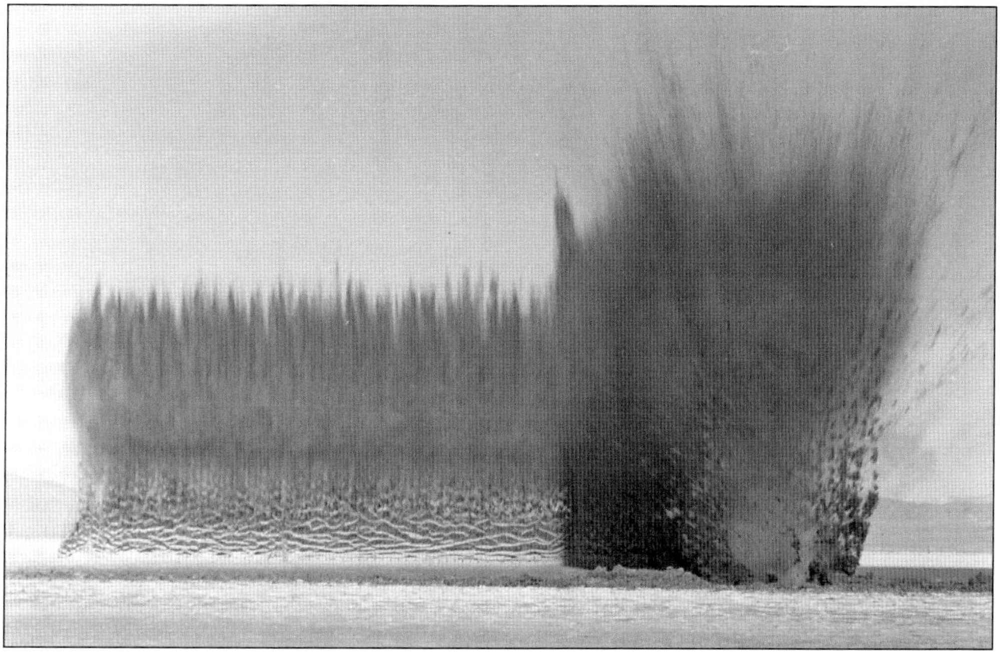

In 1943, AP&CC leased 10,000 acres at the south end of Searles Lake that contained large volumes of potash-rich brine needed to support potash production during World War II. In this area, the brine lay beneath soft mud up to 20 feet thick. To explore these leases and later pump brine from wells, access had to be developed. One early way to develop access was to use high explosives to form a trench across the surface of the mud. Pictured here is one of the blasts that created the trenches.

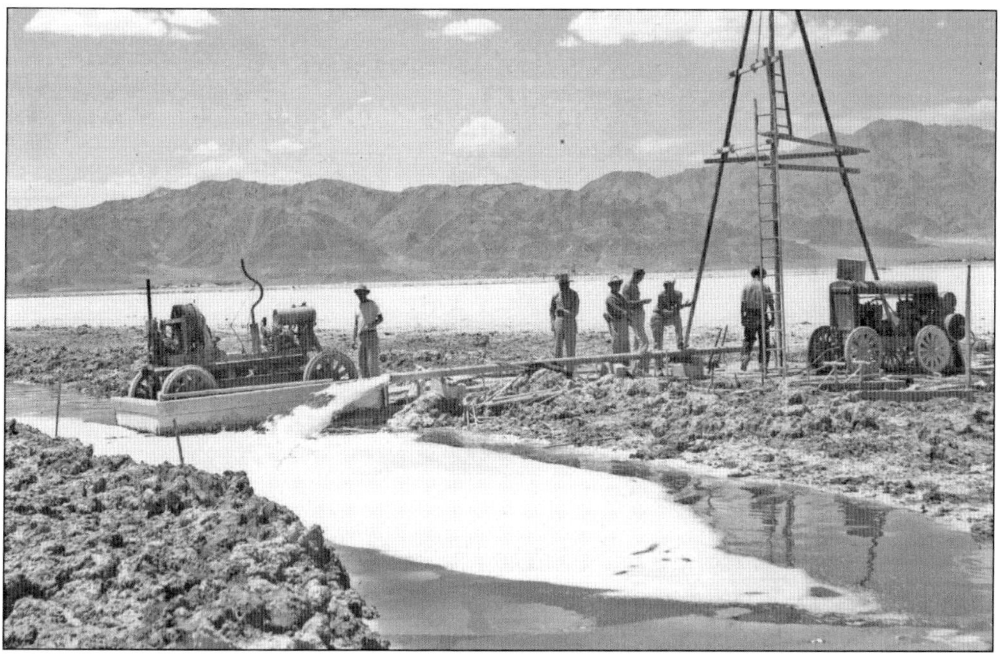

Once a trench had been blasted, it was filled with brine to create a canal, making it possible to float a barge to the drill site. After taking the drill rig off the barge, drilling could begin.

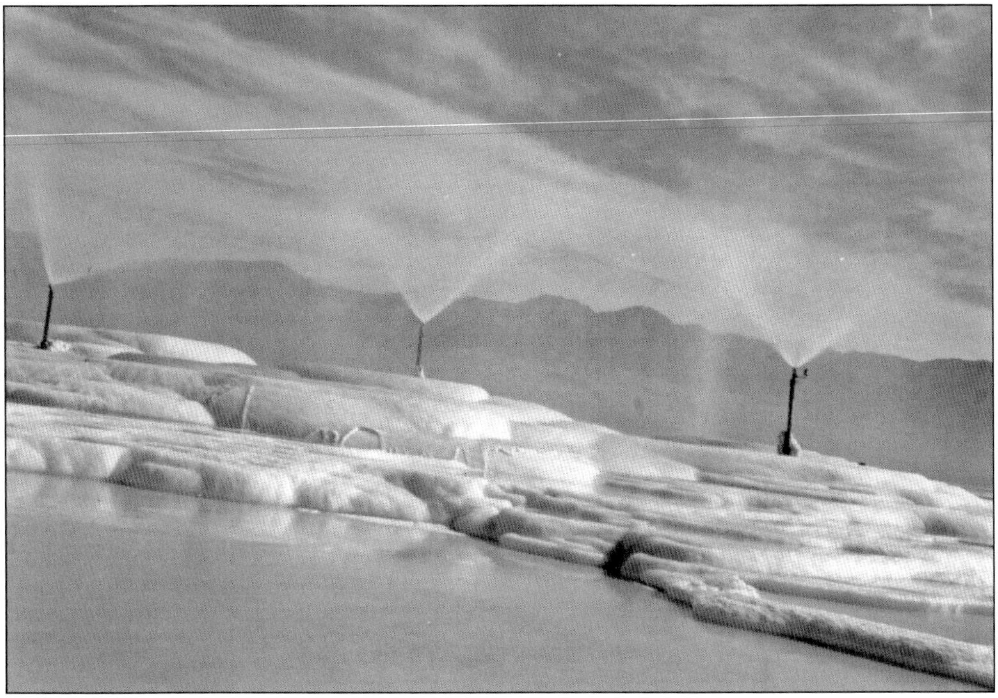

In the 1950s, AP&CC took advantage of cold winter nights. Whenever the air temperature was below 40 degrees Fahrenheit, brine was sprayed into the air through tall pipes. The cold air cooled the brine enough to cause sodium sulfate decahydrate, also known as Glauber's salt, to crystallize. Over the winter, a deep pile would form.

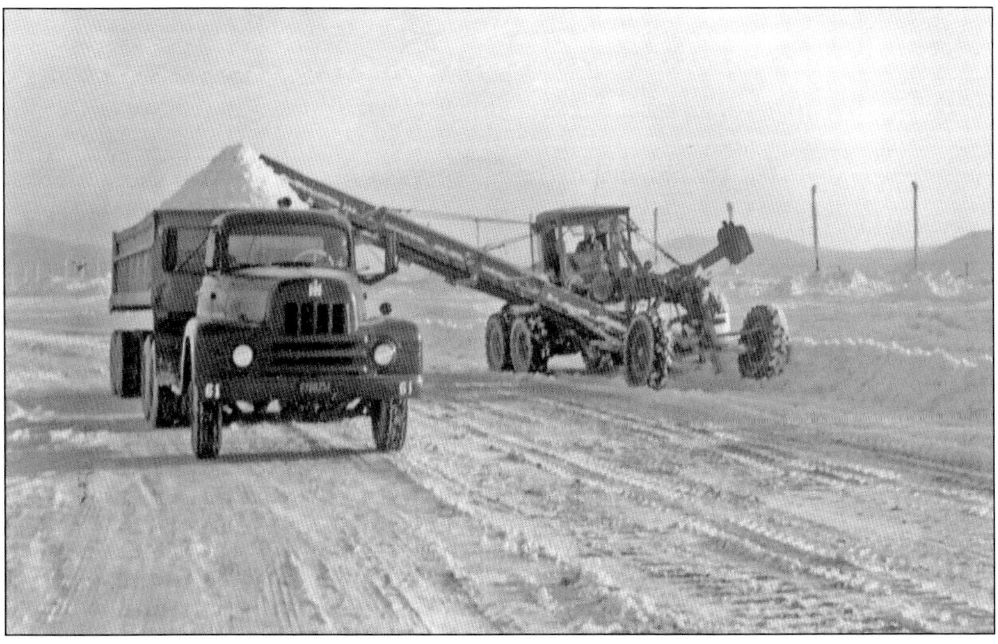

Glauber's salt was then used to produce sodium sulfate. The first step to produce sodium sulfate was to scrape the Glauber's salt into long piles. A loader-conveyor was then used to put Glauber's salt into trucks to be hauled into the Trona plant, where final processing occurred.

Five

Transportation

Some people see Searles Valley as the end of the world, as it lies over 100 miles from any population center, and there is mostly just harsh desert between those places and Trona. When the 49ers escaped from Death Valley in January 1850, they walked through Searles Valley. No one other than native peoples traveled through the area for the next eight years. Beginning in 1858, hardy prospectors returned to look for gold and silver. Some of these miners had the luxury of horses, but most traveled by foot with a burro carrying their gear. Nevertheless, prospectors had enough success to create many mines throughout the deserts west of Death Valley.

From the 1860s until 1914, crude roads passed through Searles Valley to the mines, making it increasingly possible to travel by horse, carriage, and even stagecoach, allowing goods and the output of the mines to be moved in freight wagons. During this period, John Searles built large freight wagons that he hooked in tandem and pulled with teams of 16 to 22 mules and horses, often using teams of 20, thereby creating the first 20-mule teams in California's borax industry. By the early 1900s, automobiles began using the mine roads to travel across the desert. All early roads were gravel, rock, or sand, making for a rough ride. Flash floods and snow could make the roads impassable.

Travel improved substantially on November 5, 1908, when Southern Pacific Railroad completed the Owenyo Branch to Searles Station, 30 miles west of Trona. Then, in 1914, American Trona Corporation completed construction of the standard-gauge Trona Railroad to connect Trona to Searles Station. This made it possible to travel from Los Angeles to Trona on smooth steel rails in just 12 hours. The standard-gauge railroad also allowed products from Searles Lake to be shipped to markets at competitive costs.

As mining on Searles Lake improved, so did travel to Trona. Scheduled bus service between Los Angeles and Trona began, and in the mid-1970s, Trona even had scheduled airline service.

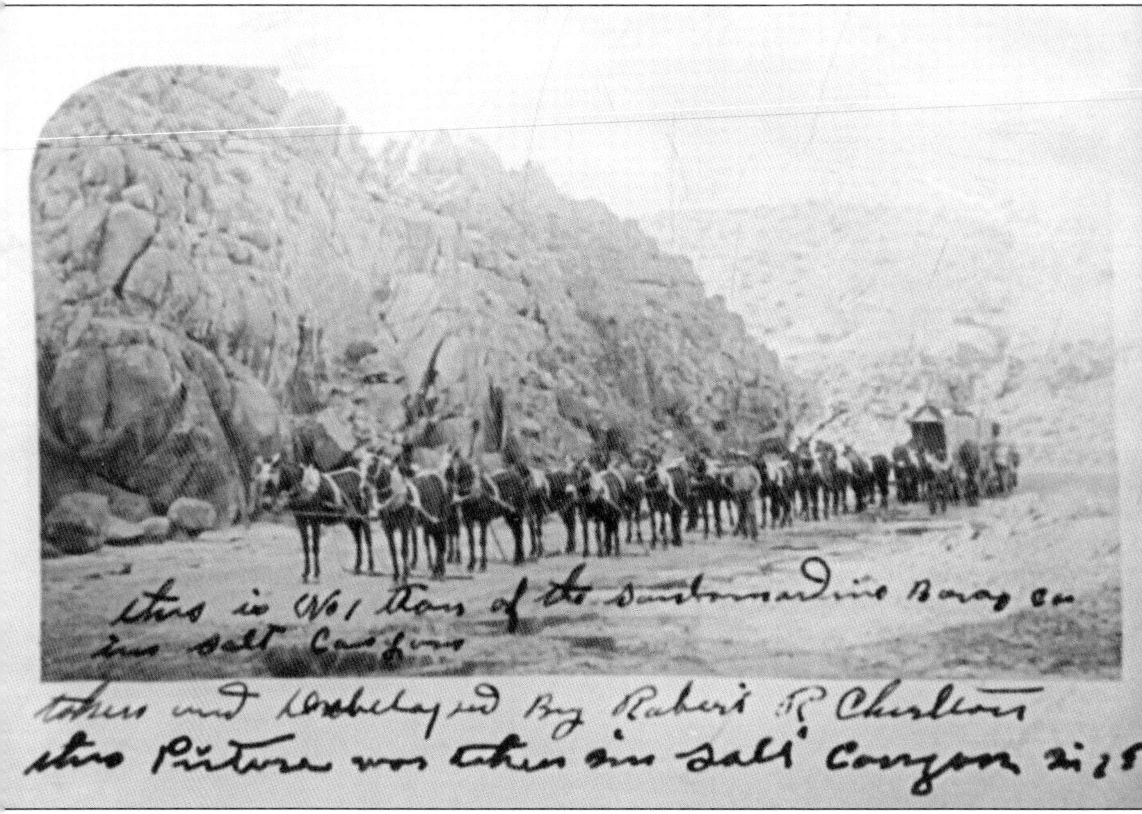

The San Bernardino Borax Mining Company, with John Searles as its superintendent, first shipped borax from Searles Lake in 1874, hauling it 175 miles to San Pedro. On August 6, 1876, the railroad reached Mojave, shortening the haul to just 80 miles. Searles constructed roads to his mill with three overnight stations about 20 miles apart, all with water. The four large wagons he built could each haul seven and a half tons of freight. The trips to Mojave used two of these wagons in tandem, and after he changed to fuel oil for his boiler, Searles added an oil-tank wagon between them. Depending on load and road conditions, he used between 16 and 22 mules or horses to pull his wagon train. Of course, Searles often used 20 animals, mostly mules, making his the first 20-mule teams hauling borax across the California deserts, nearly nine years before the highly promoted 20-mule teams out of Death Valley. (SD)

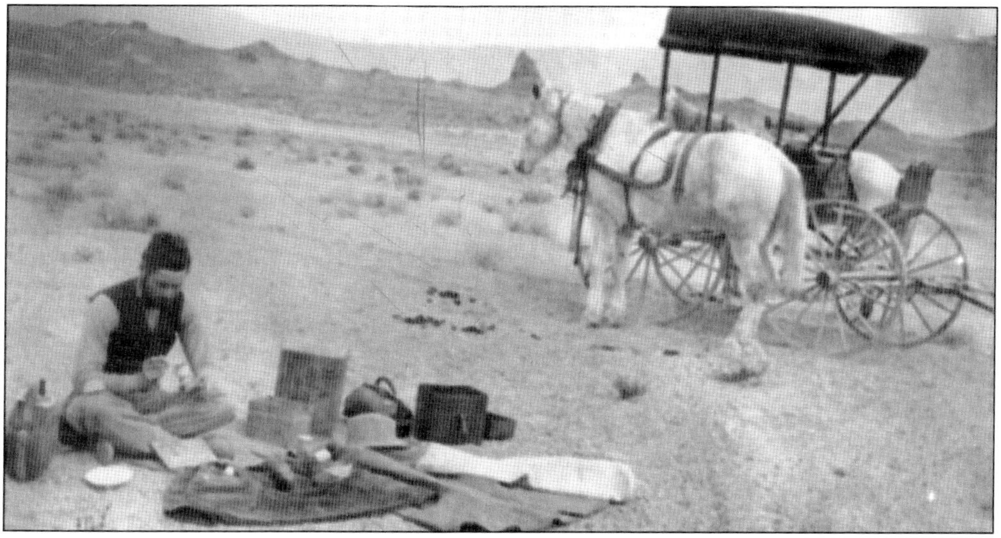

In the summer of 1890, Dennis Searles III visited his father, John, at his mill at Searles Lake. He traveled there with Robert R. Charlton, manager of Searles's Mojave office. Charlton, an avid photographer, took many photographs of the Searles operation. In this photograph he captures Dennis's trip to Searles Lake in a surrey drawn by two horses. They are having lunch near tufa pinnacles along their route. (SD)

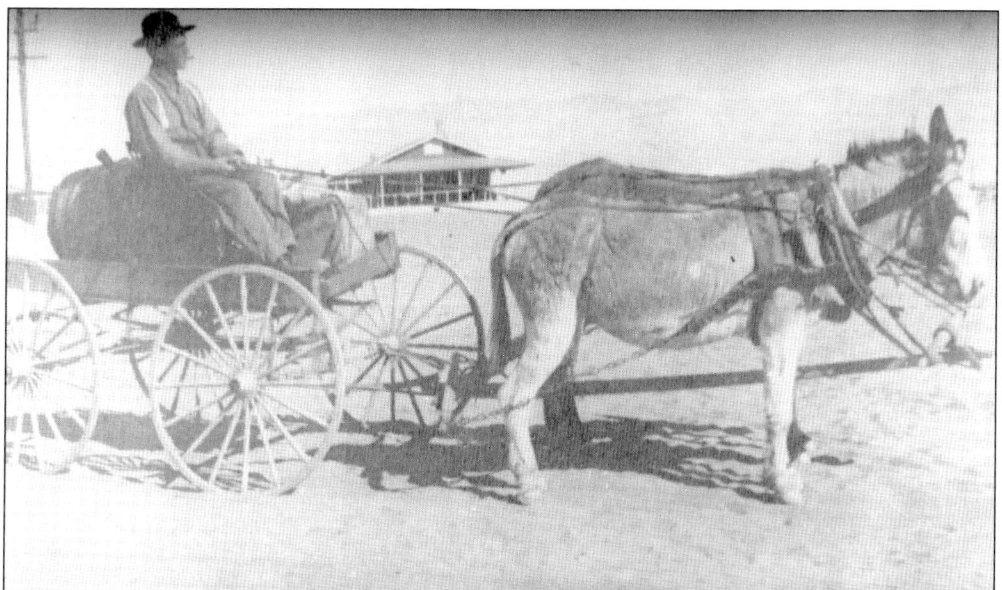

Some of the more successful gold miners in the Slate Range were able to travel to their mines by burro-drawn wagon. Shown here is Benny Truman with the burros he called his "Mockingbirds" on their way to the Copper Queen Mine.

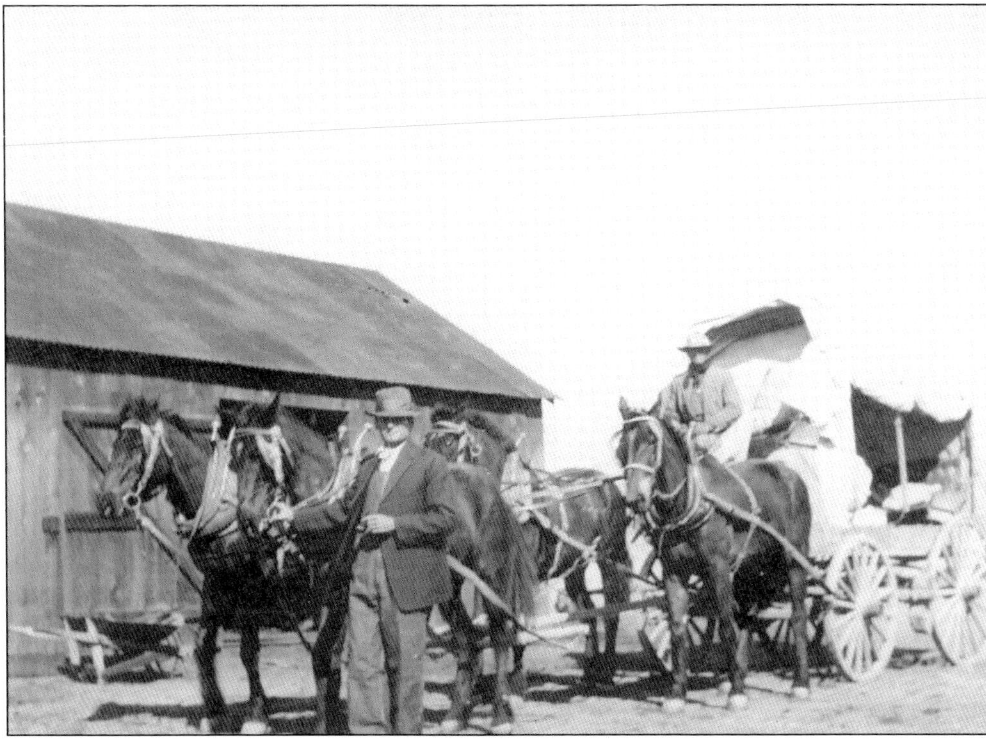

In 1906, the stagecoach between Johannesburg and the gold-mining boomtown of Skidoo in the Panamint Mountains west of Death Valley passed through Searles Valley. The first change of horses was at The Tanks, six miles north of Trona. (Courtesy of J. Bart Parker)

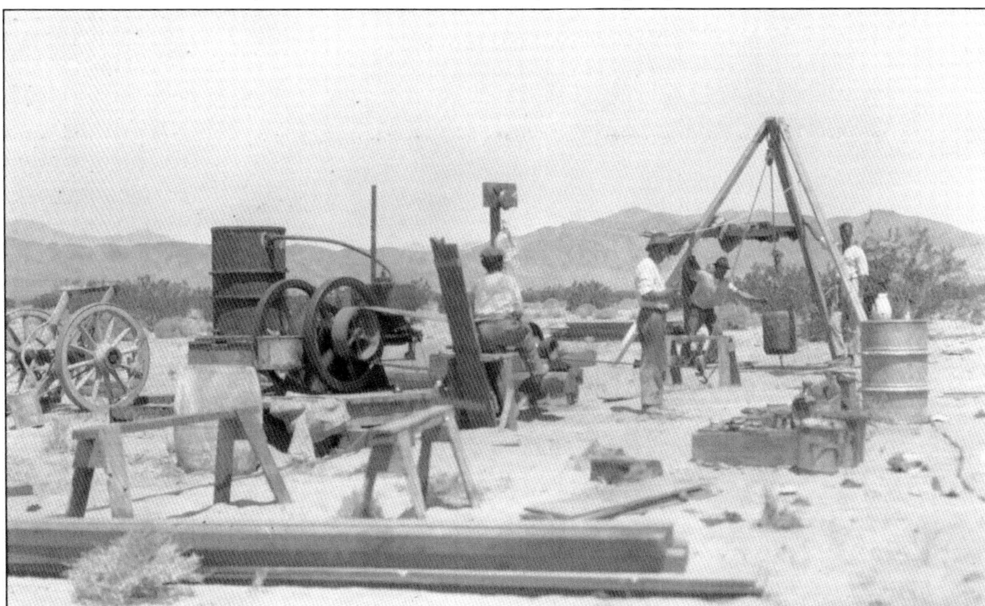

The Tanks included a well from which drinking water could be drawn. Water was drawn up using a gasoline motor with two large flywheels, a clutch operated by the man sitting down, and a cable to a bucket that could be lowered into the well empty and then raised once it was filled.

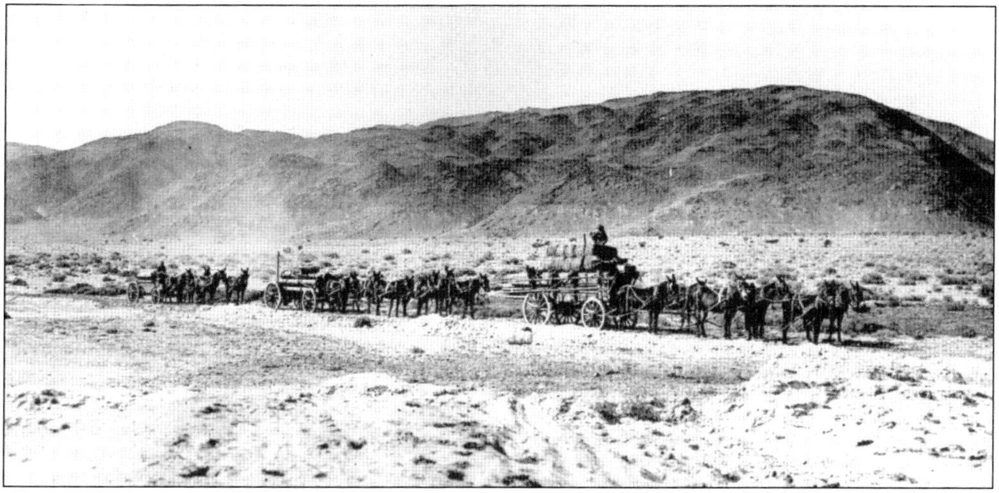

On October 8, 1908, the Southern Pacific Railroad Company completed its Owenyo Branch to Searles Station, just 30 miles from where California Trona Company was modifying the old Searles mill to produce soda ash. Wagons drawn by mule teams transported much of the construction materials from Searles Station to Trona.

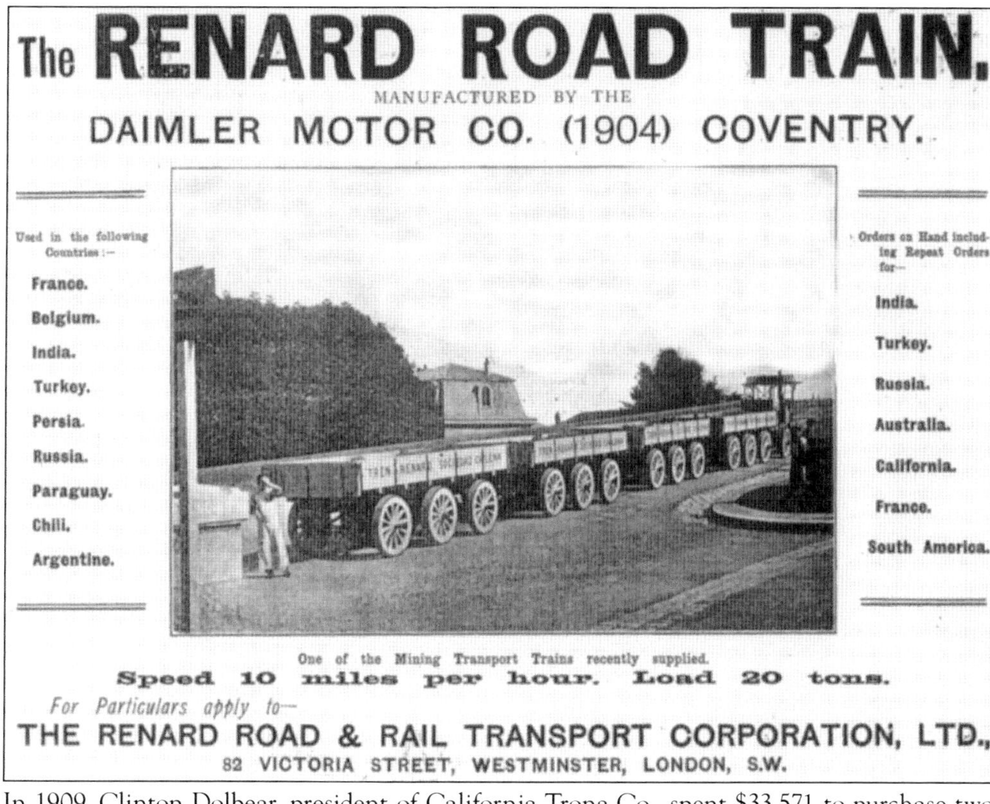

In 1909, Clinton Dolbear, president of California Trona Co., spent $33,571 to purchase two Renard road trains to transport materials to modify the idle Searles borax mill he had purchased and haul supplies for its operation. The Renard trains also transported mined trona from reefs on the eastern edge of Searles Lake to Dolbear's mill, and Dolbear hoped to also transport soda-ash product to the railroad at Searles Station, although he never produced any to haul.

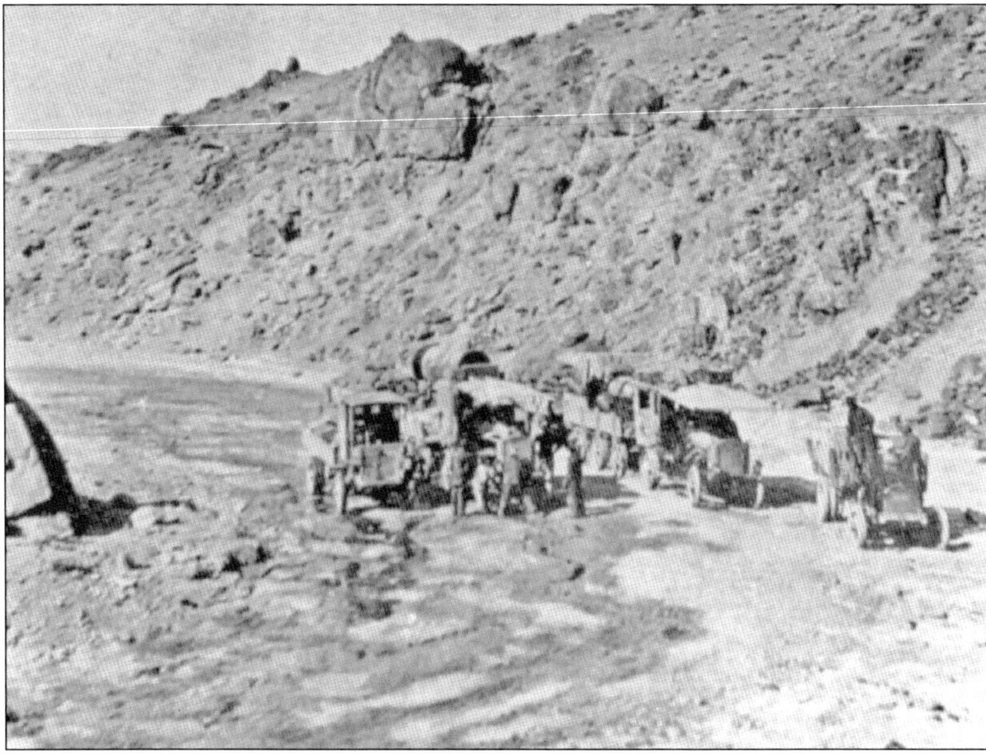

The California Trona Company transported material from Searles Station to Trona by truck and with the Renard road trains. Both are shown here traveling on the rocky wash bottom where the road passed through the west end of Salt Wells Canyon, now known as Poison Canyon. Oscar Johnson was the first driver of the Renard road train.

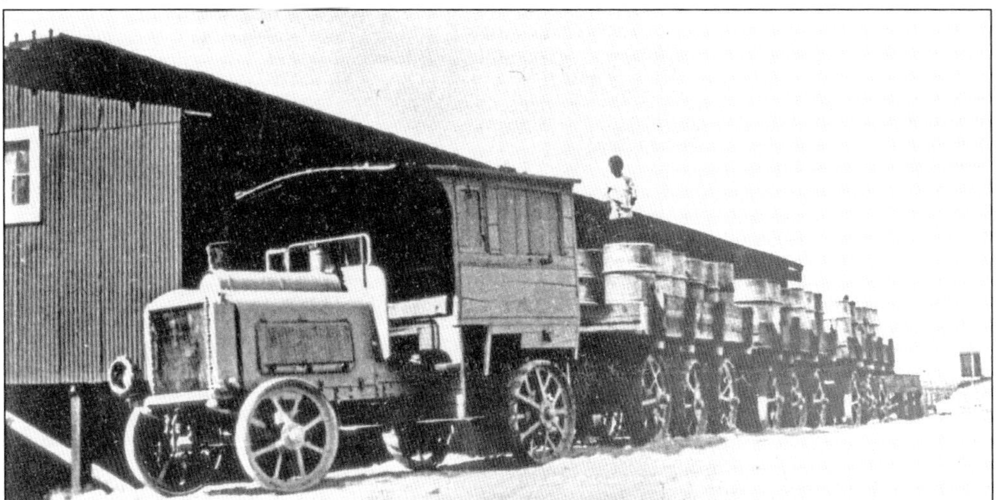

Renard road trains were designed for travel over rough mining roads around the world. They were unique in that they had six wheels on each trailer, with the center axle driven by the motor in the tractor. Driving the trailer wheels required a long driveshaft stretching from the tractor to the last trailer, with universal joints connecting the driveshaft between each unit in the train. With each unit receiving power, the trains could traverse very rough terrain.

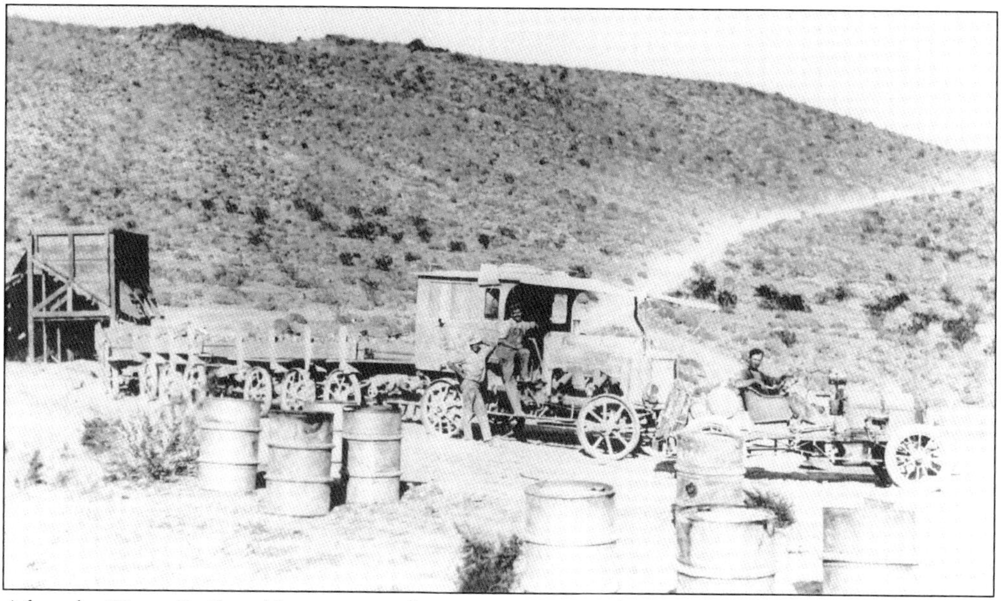

After the Trona Railroad began providing transportation between Trona and Searles Station, the Renard trains were sold to mining companies. Pictured here is antimony ore trucked from Wildrose Canyon being loaded onto a Renard road train at Slate Range Crossing for transport to the railroad in Trona.

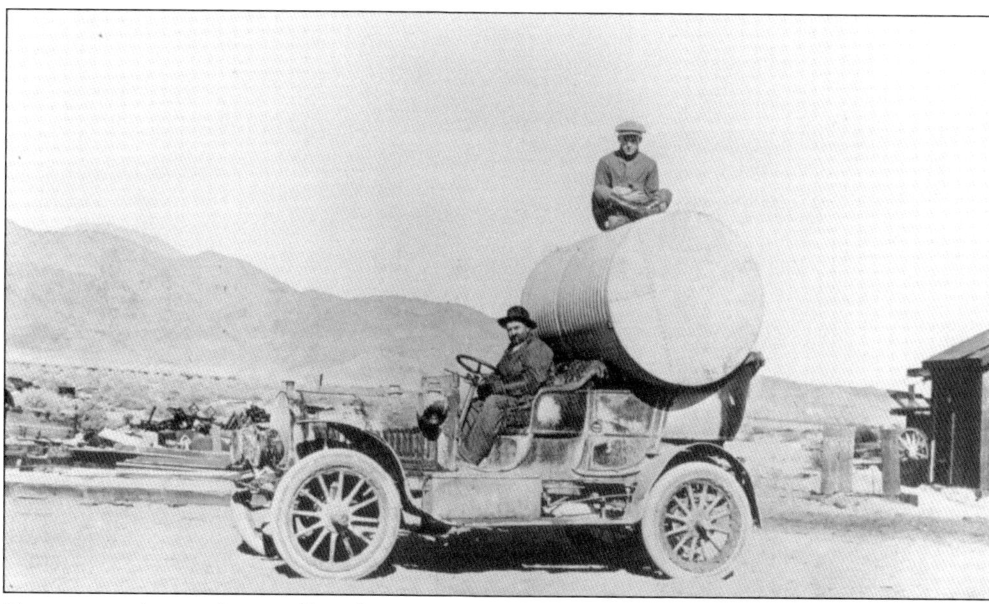

Transporting large volumes of liquids presented special problems to the California Trona Company. One innovative solution used in November 1913 was to stack a large tank onto the back of a sedan car. The tank in this photograph would hold 400 to 500 gallons. With water in the tank, it would weigh over one and a half tons, a huge load on the rear axle. However, the tank was empty and merely being moved to a permanent location.

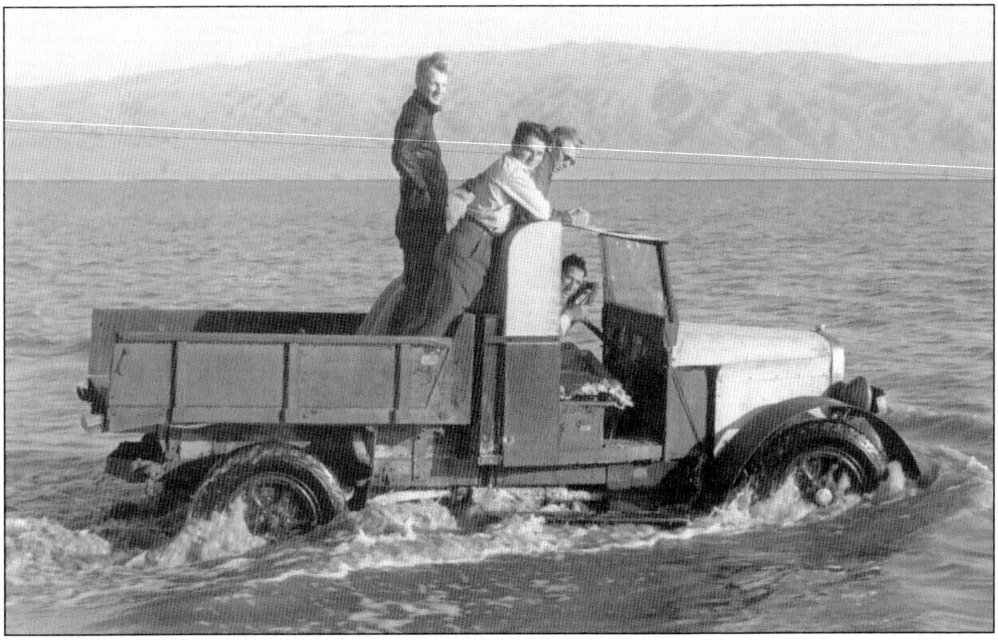

The salt surface of Searles Lake is very hard, making it possible to safely drive anywhere across it, even when flooded. However, the surface is surrounded by a strip of mud over a mile wide, and when the mud is saturated with water, it is very soft. There is one account of a bulldozer sinking completely out of sight into the mire.

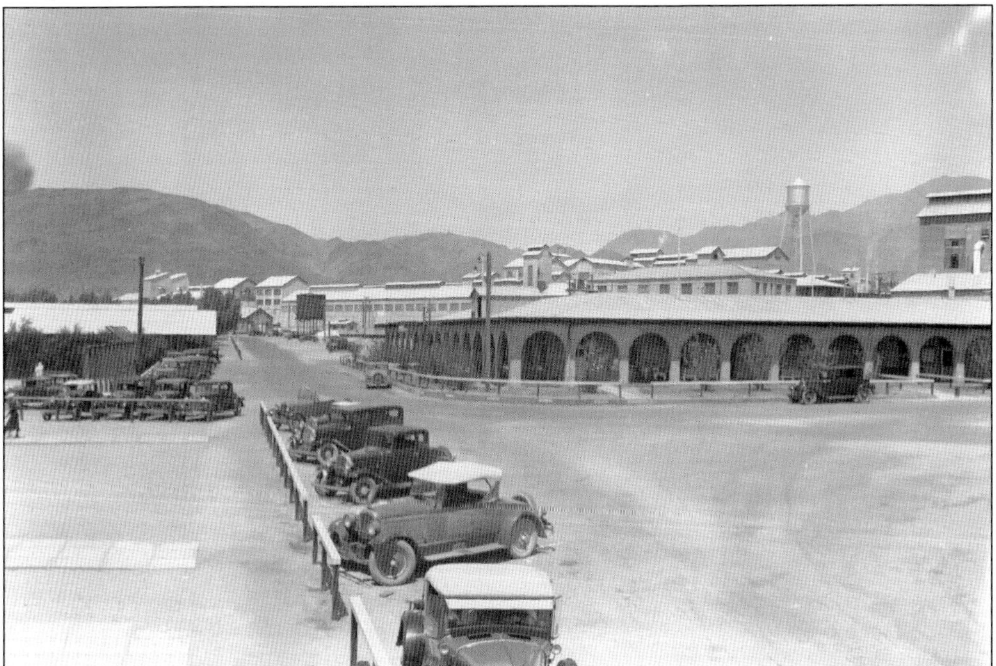

The road into Trona was not paved until the mid-1930s. Nevertheless, there were a substantial number of automobiles in Trona, all driven there across rough desert roads. This photograph shows several cars parked near Austin Hall.

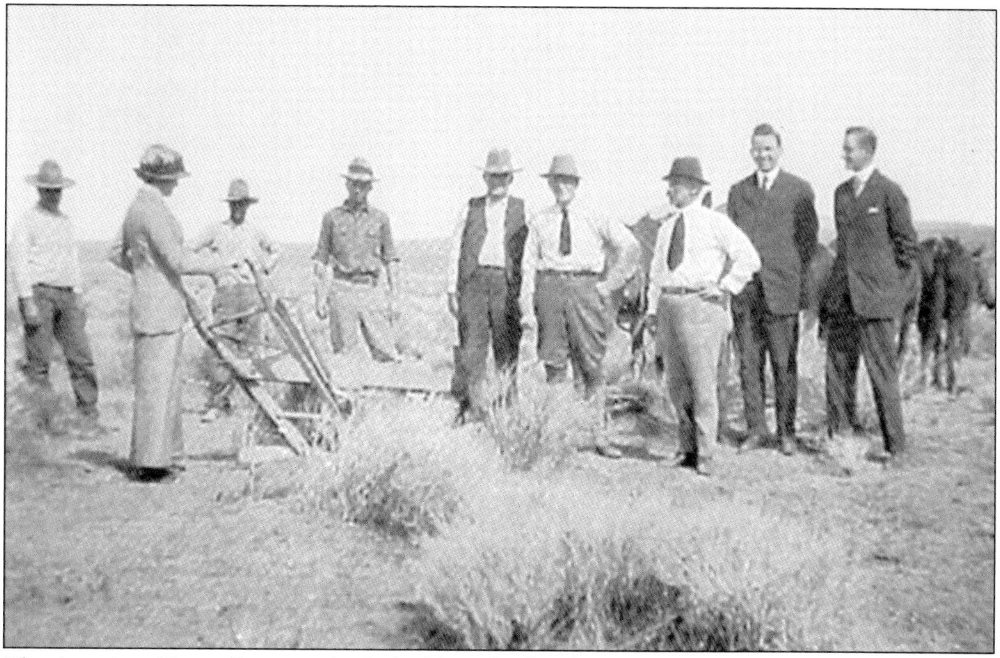

The American Trona Company built the Trona Railroad in 1913–1914 for a total cost of $600,000. The ground-breaking ceremony, held at Searles Station near the Southern Pacific Railroad, was attended by dignitaries including Raymond Ashton, the man in the dark shirt fourth from left, who led the design survey party for the railroad route.

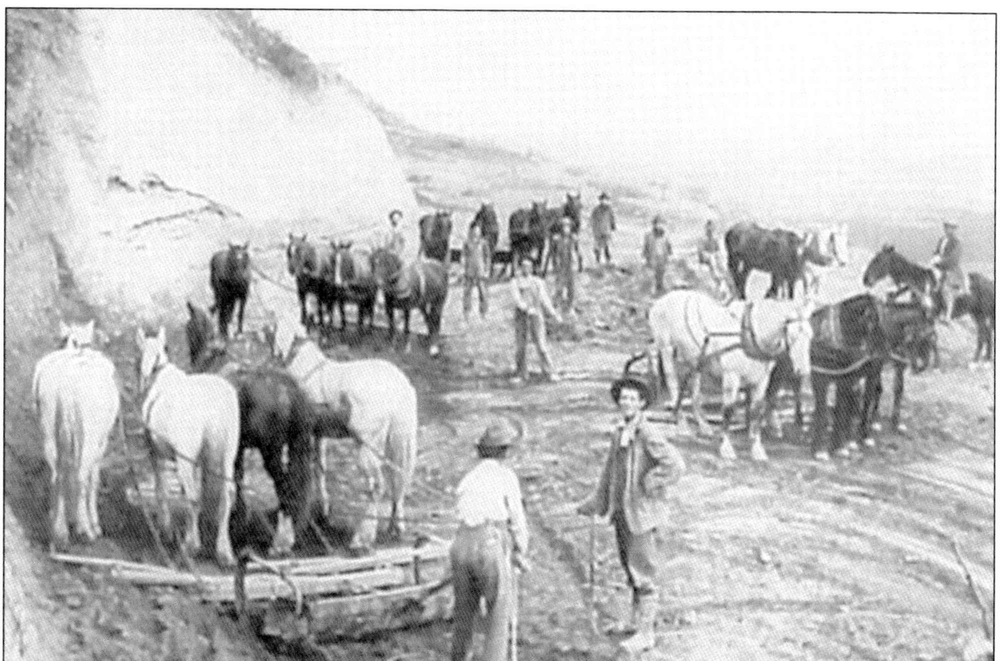

Although the Trona Railroad initiated modern transportation into Searles Valley, the actual construction was largely done using teams of horses to excavate the cuts and smooth the roadbed before laying tracks.

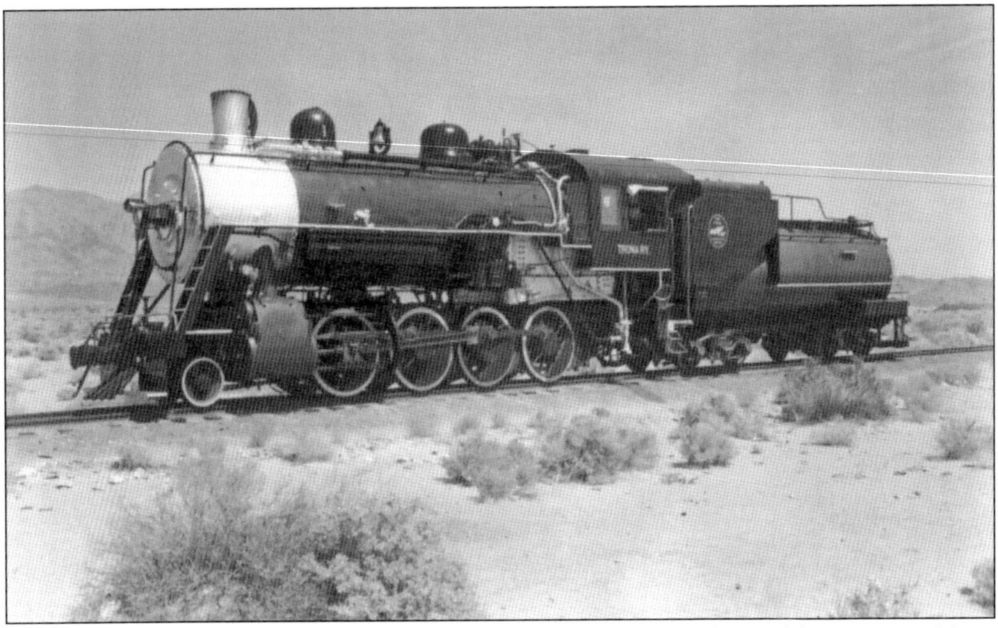

The Trona Railroad Company began operating in 1914 with two identical locomotives, No. 1 (pictured here) and No. 2. Each was a Baldwin model 2-8-0 weighing 208,000 pounds, with oil-fired boilers that produced steam at 200 pounds pressure to power them. In 1937, the larger Alco steam locomotive 2701 joined the two earlier units. All were in regular service until 1949.

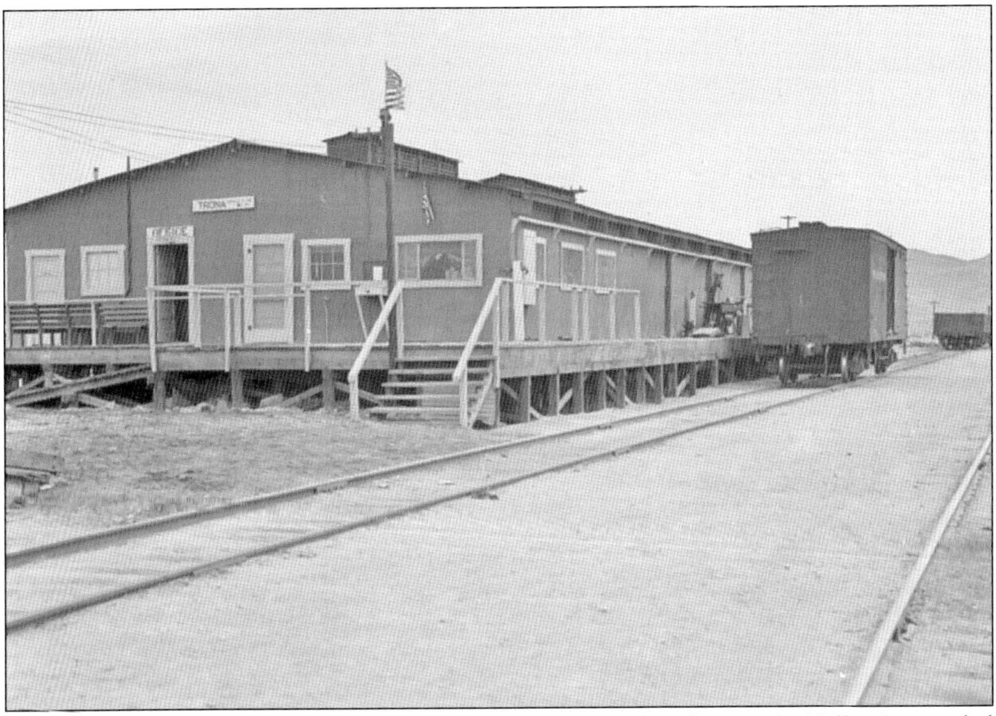

The Trona Railroad Station was the terminus of the Trona Railroad in Searles Valley. It provided a limited warehouse as well as a waiting area for passenger service. The high platform helped passengers board the train and workers remove freight from boxcars.

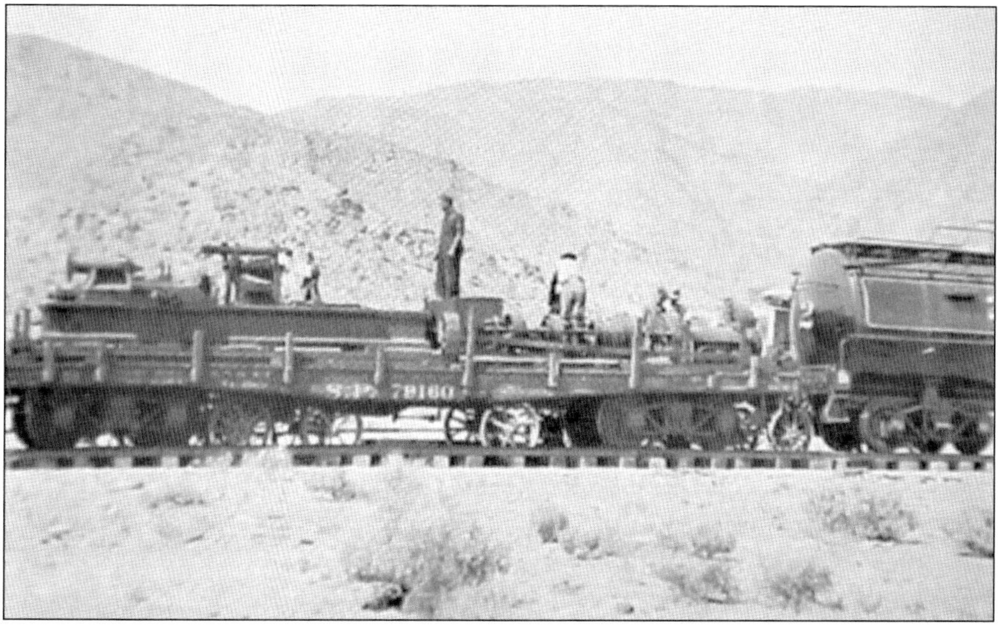

The Trona Railroad played a key role in the construction of the Searles Lake potash mines during World War I by transporting all materials used to construct the Trona plant of American Trona Corporation, the railroad's owner, and the competing Borosolvay Corporation Plant. Trona Railroad carried construction materials for Borosolvay because it was a common carrier, and the law required it to. Materials are pictured here being unloaded at Borosolvay Siding.

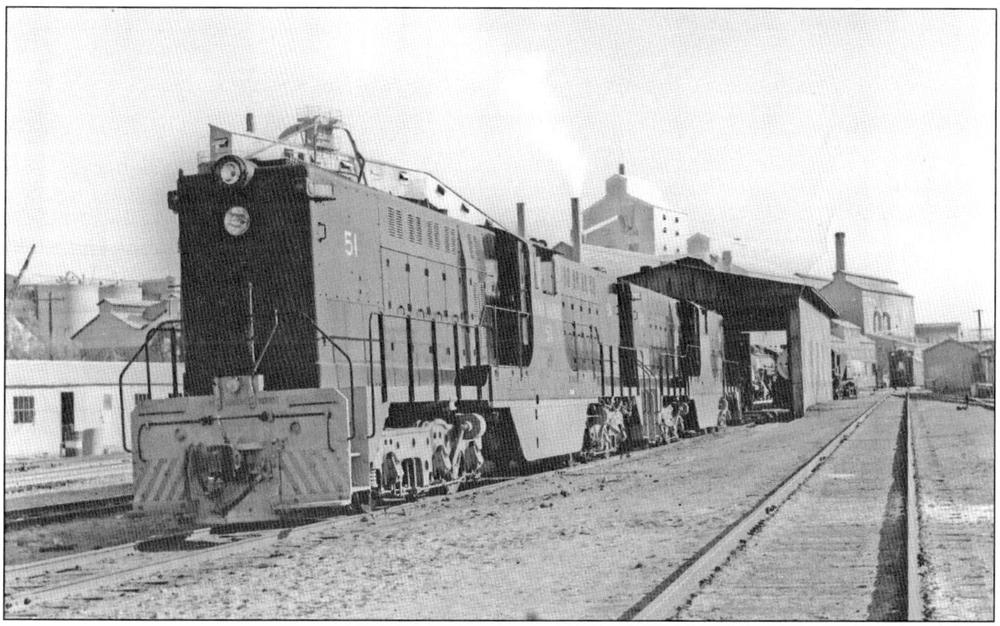

Pictured here are locomotives 51 and 50 at the Trona plant of American Potash and Chemical Company. These 2,000-horsepower locomotives were purchased new from the Baldwin Locomotive Works in April 1949. They were joined over the next 37 years by three smaller Baldwin AS 616 locomotives that had 1,600 horsepower each. All were retired from service in March 1993, by which time each had logged over one million miles.

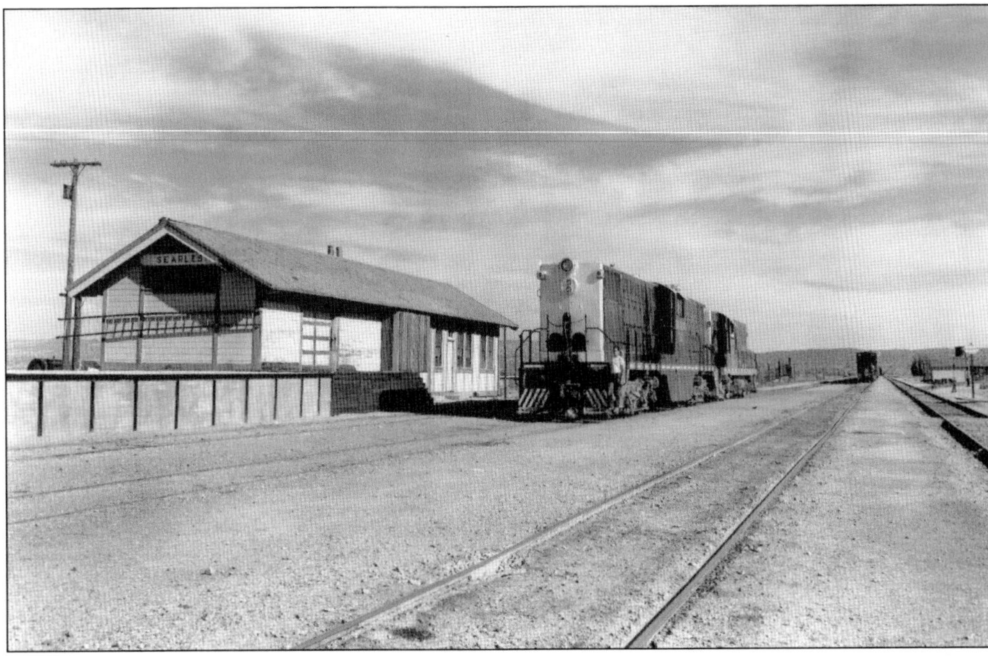

Searles Station was the transfer point for freight and passengers between the Trona Railroad and the Southern Pacific Railroad. In addition to a freight platform, there was a small waiting room for passengers. While loaded freight cars could be switched from one railroad to another, passengers could only ride in passenger cars operated by each railroad company.

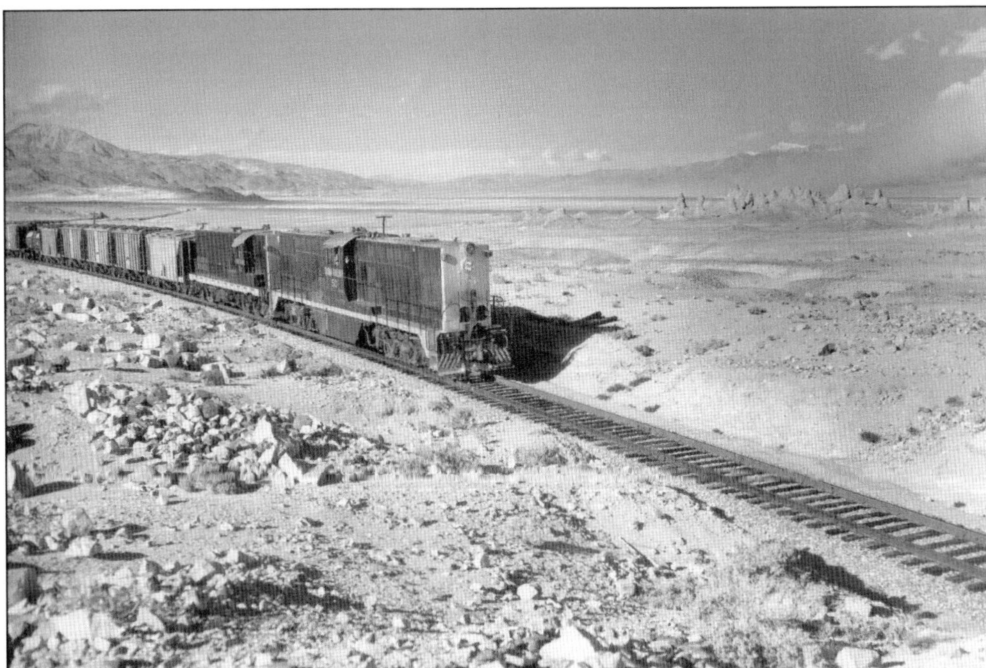

The route of the Trona Railroad passes the Trona Pinnacles National Natural Landmark on its way to Searles Station. This 1956 photograph shows locomotives 50 and 52, the Pinnacles, and Searles Lake in the distance.

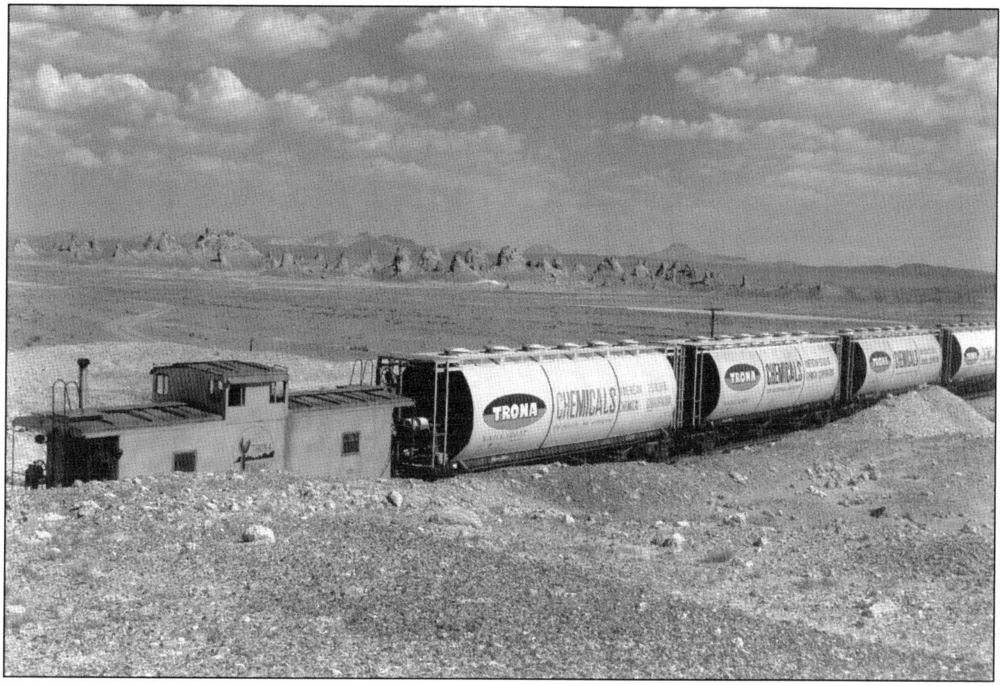

Four large hopper cars of AP&CC, each able to carry 100 tons of product, approach the Trona Pinnacles. The caboose in the photograph is now owned by the Searles Valley Historical Society.

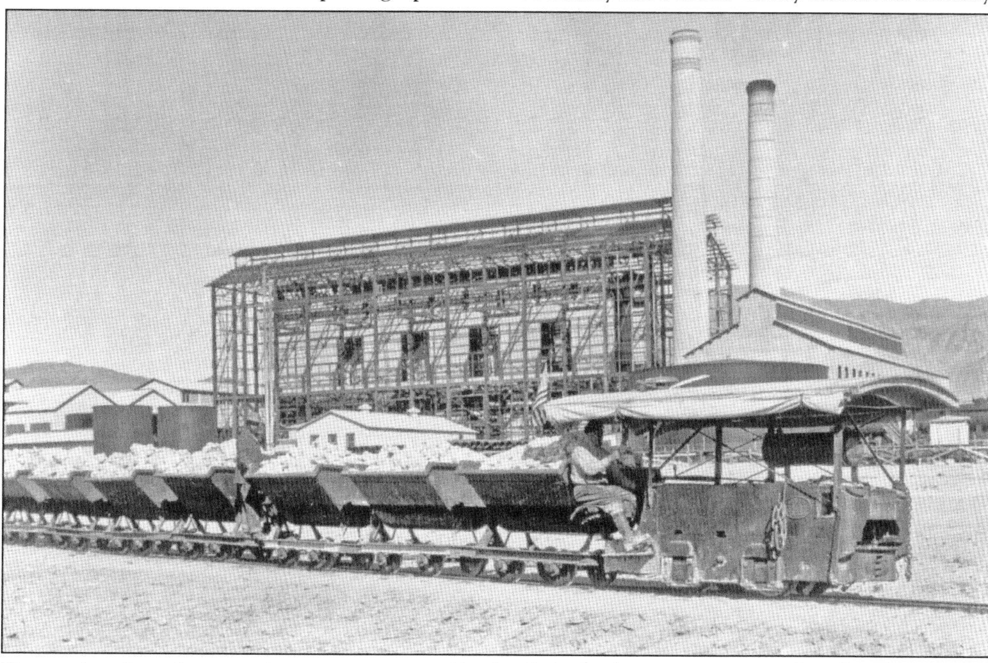

Two early mineral-extraction companies on Searles Lake had narrow-gauge railroads. The narrow-gauge Mexican Central of American Trona Corporation could have been used in underground mining with its small gasoline engine and side-dump cars. It moved dirt from excavations for the new plant and crude trona from the east side of Searles Lake, and provided access to brine wells on Searles Lake. This photograph was taken during the construction of the Trona plant.

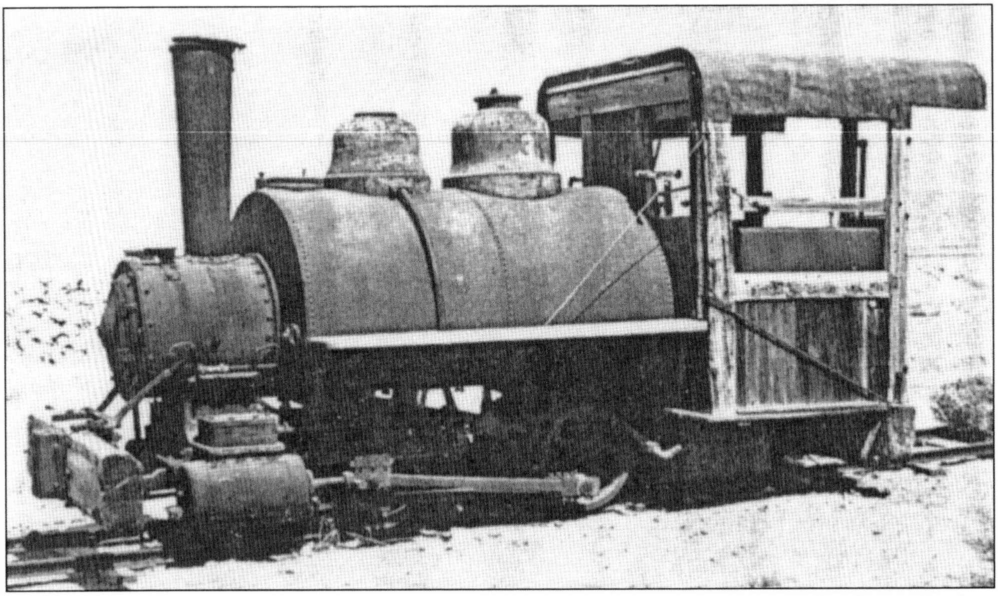

The Westend narrow-gauge railroad used a small Baldwin steam locomotive that burned oil. It provided access to the Westend brine wells on Searles Lake.

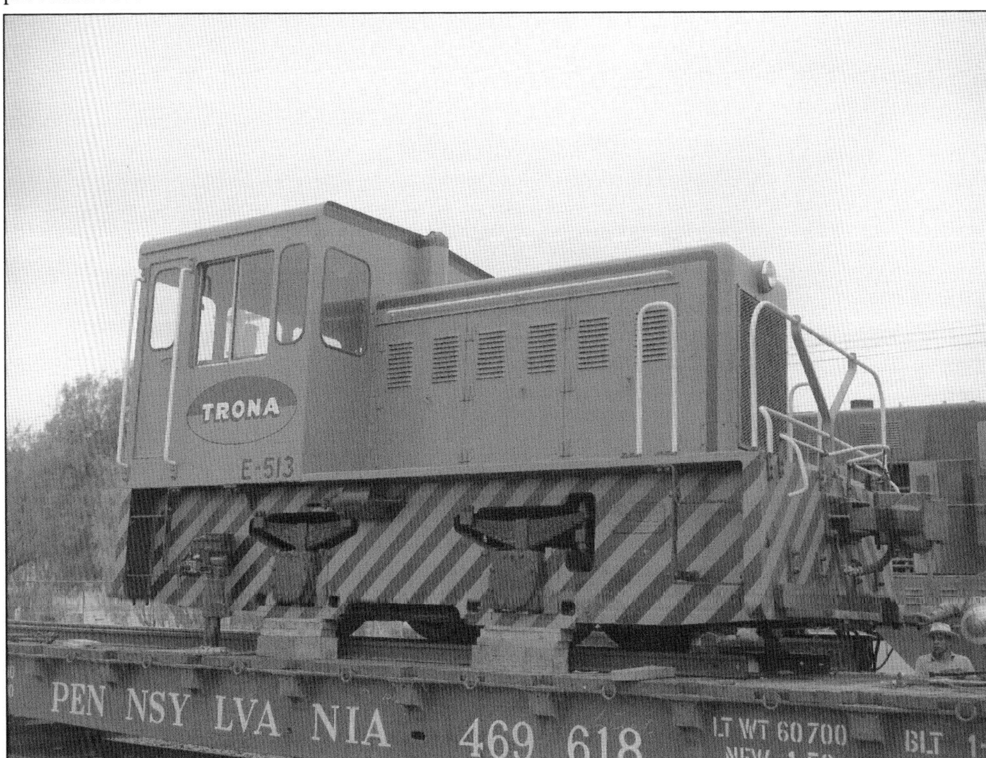

In 1950, the Trona Railroad purchased a small switch engine to move short strings of railcars inside the Trona plant. It was delivered new on a Pennsylvania Railroad flatcar from the Baldwin Locomotive Works. The 80,000-pound locomotive used diesel-electric power. It was used until 1971, when it was acquired by a museum.

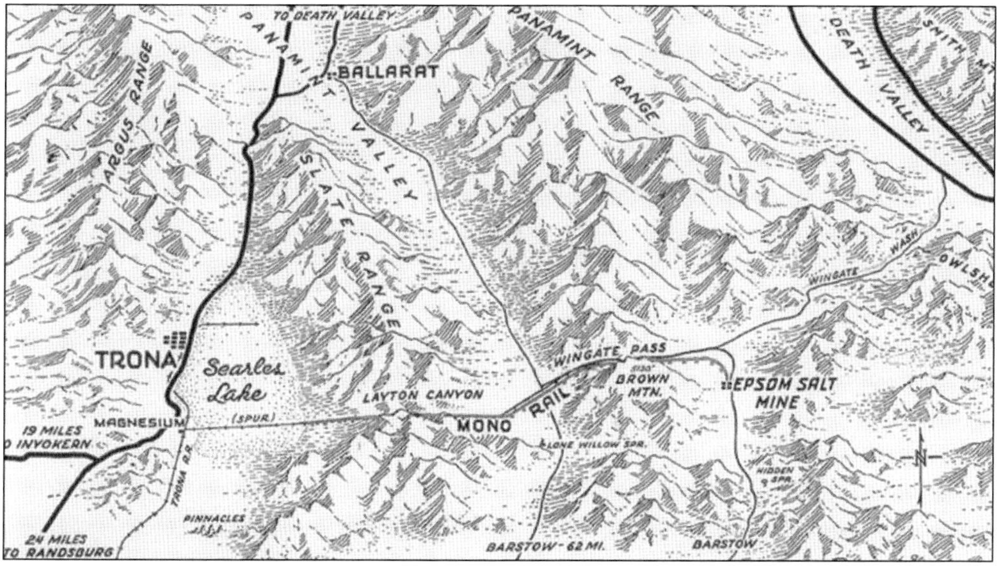

In 1917, an Epsom-salt deposit was discovered at the southern end of the Panamint Mountains. In 1919, claims were acquired by Los Angeles florist Thomas Wright. Wright began construction of a monorail at Magnesium Siding on the Trona Railroad, six miles south of Trona, in 1922. It ran eastward across Searles Lake, over the Slate Range via Layton Canyon, across Panamint Valley, over Wingate Pass, and south to the mine. Construction took two years and cost about $200,000.

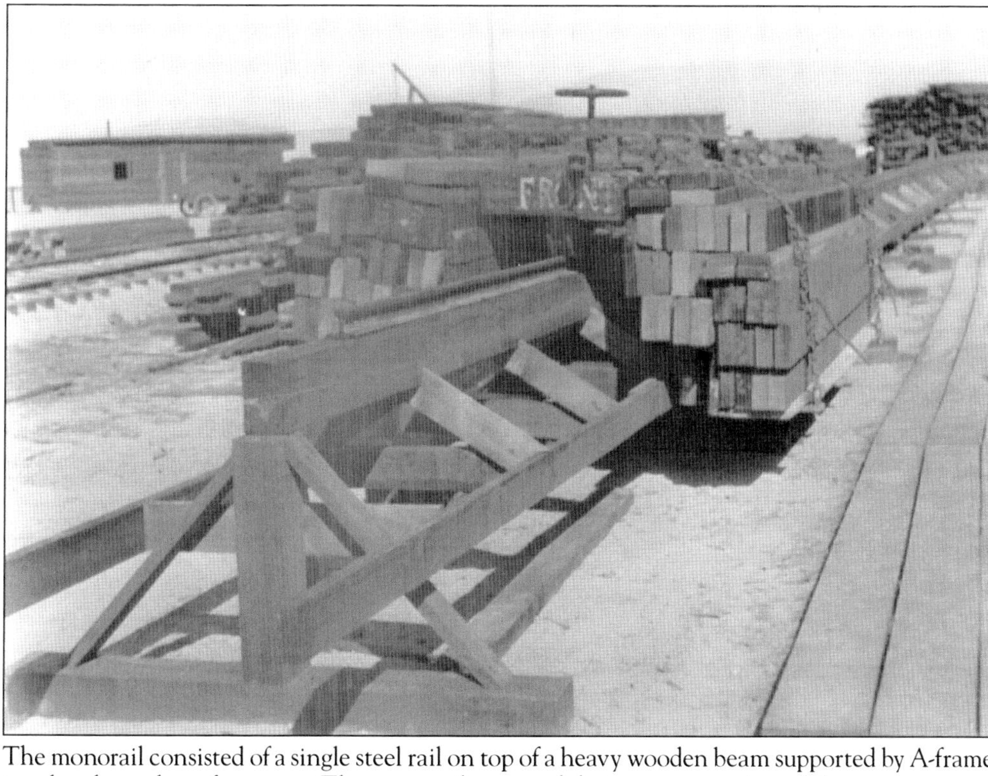

The monorail consisted of a single steel rail on top of a heavy wooden beam supported by A-frame trestles about three feet apart. The monorail was used during construction of the route to carry the rail and timber as the route extended eastward from Magnesium Siding.

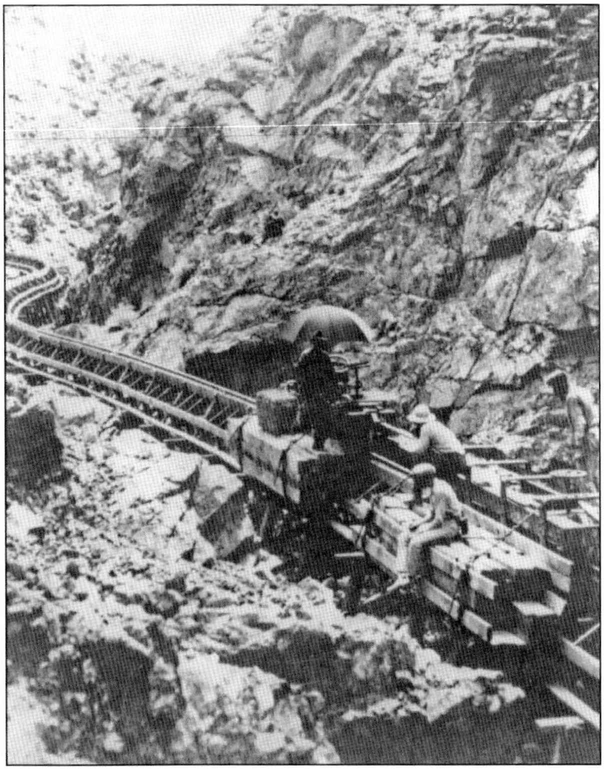

The route through Layton Canyon was particularly treacherous because the canyon was steep, an eight-percent grade, and curves were frequent and sharp. Wingate Pass was even steeper, with grades up to 12 percent. Total loads were limited to just six tons. Some passengers described harrowing descents down the steep canyons, as braking was not always adequate. The canyon washes were also subject to flash floods that washed out trestles.

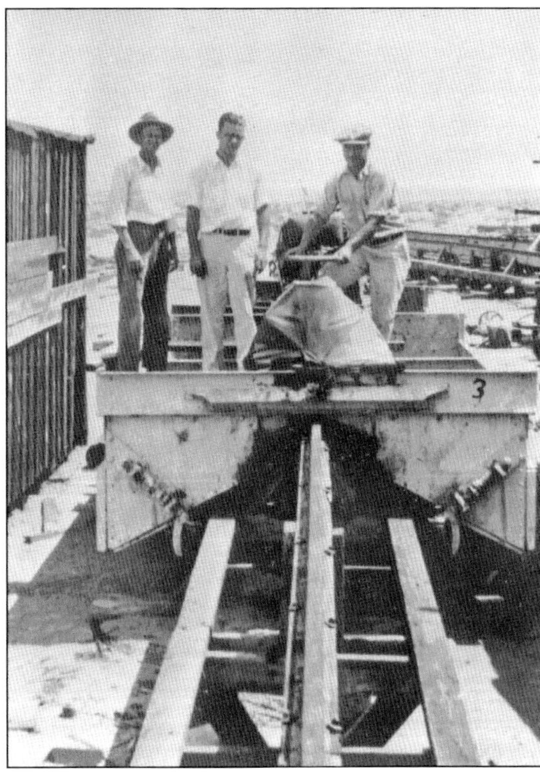

The monorail locomotives and cars ran on just two wheels. Stable operation required the load be balanced with equal loads on each side, much like pack saddles on a mule's back. Simple in concept, the line never worked properly. After several attempts to increase efficiency, the operation ceased in 1927. In the late 1930s, the rail and beam were salvaged, leaving only A-frames, most of which have since disappeared.

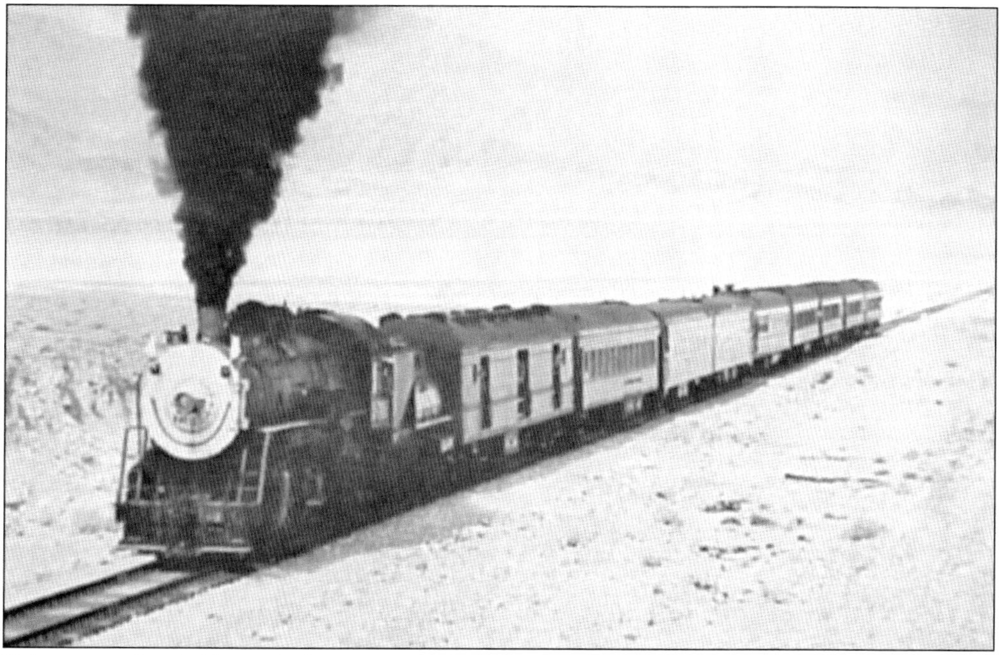

When completed, Trona Railroad provided the most comfortable travel to Trona. Travel from Los Angeles to Mojave was on the Southern Pacific Railroad. In Mojave, the traveler transferred to the Owenyo Branch of Southern Pacific, which took them to Searles Station. At Searles they transferred again, this time to the Trona Railroad, which took them into Trona. The entire trip was completed in just 12 hours. This service continued until September 1937.

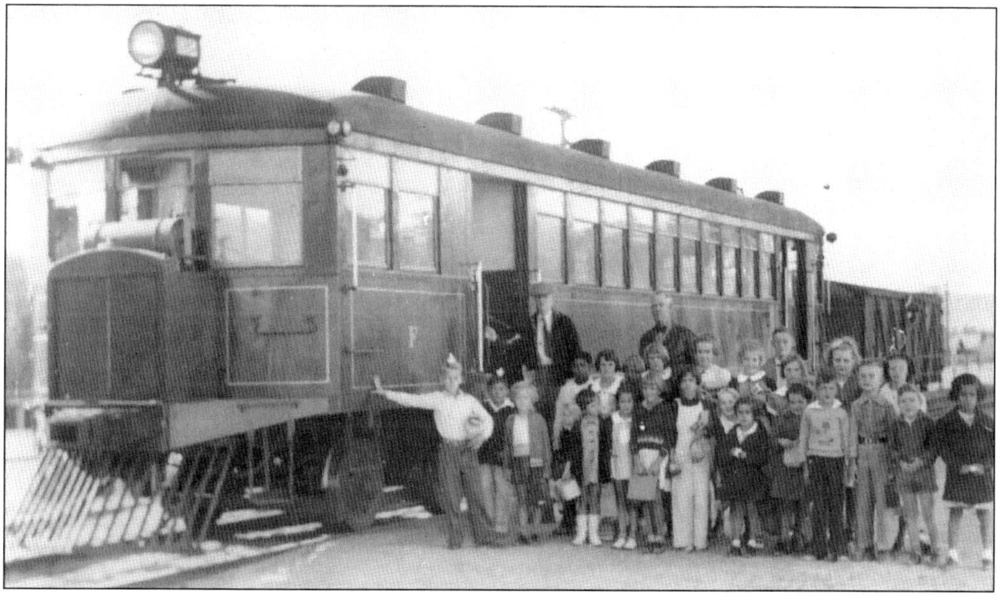

The Trona Railroad also transported children from Westend, Burnham, and Borosolvay to school in Trona. At first, they used regular passenger service with a full train. Then, in 1936, the Trona Railroad purchased a self-propelled passenger car to transport the children. The power was supplied by a 150-horsepower gasoline motor. This service continued until a school bus was purchased in December 1938.

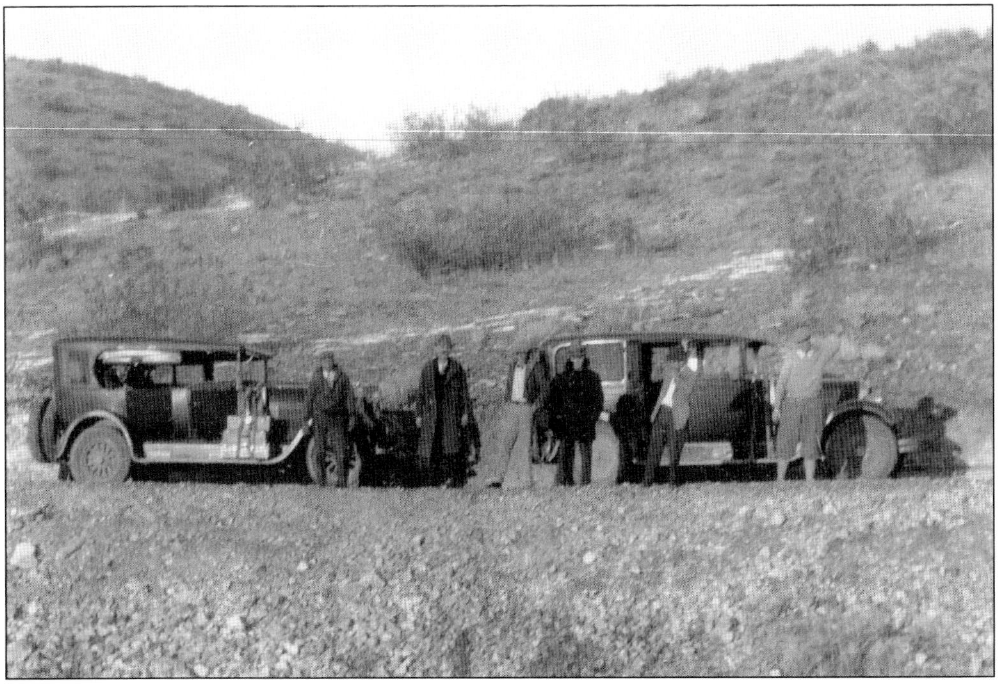

In 1914, James Proper purchased five seven-passenger Studebaker touring cars and started taxi service in Los Angeles. Later, he provided taxi service to mines in the desert east of Mojave. His initial service into Searles Valley carried workers to construct and later operate the Borosolvay plant. Quickly, he realized that transporting workers for American Trona Corporation could be even more profitable. Pictured here are two Studebakers near Randsburg on their way to Trona.

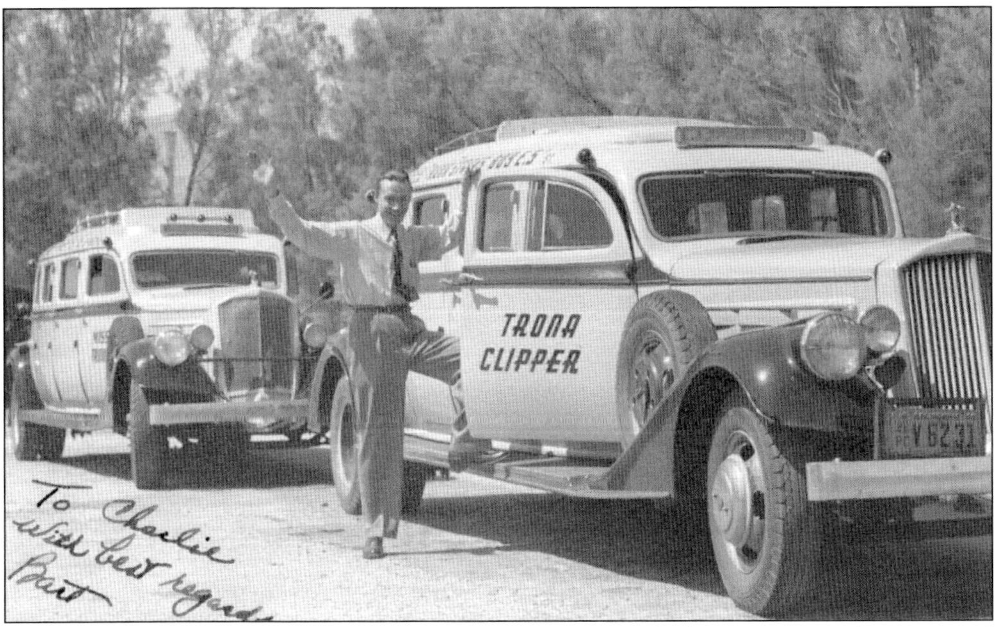

By 1937, James Proper had purchased Pierce Arrow motor cars for his Trona Stage business, and named one *Trona Clipper* and another *Miss Trona*. This service allowed passengers to travel to Trona in luxury in less than four hours, much faster than just a few years earlier by railroad.

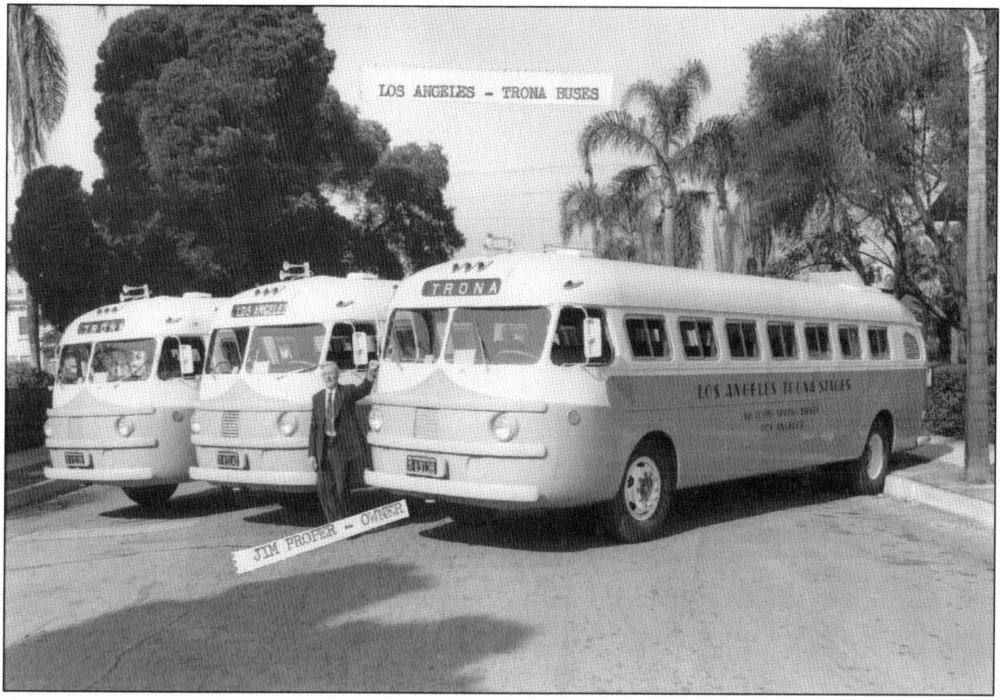

On November 20, 1942, the Los Angeles–Trona Stage Company took delivery of three new buses. The purchase was almost one year after the start of World War II, when buying just about anything for civilian use was nearly impossible. J.L. Robinson, president of the Trona Railroad, helped James Proper with his purchase of the buses because AP&CC needed workers, and it was difficult for men to travel to Trona. Gasoline for private cars was severely rationed, and the Pierce Arrows did not have the capacity to carry the number of men needed.

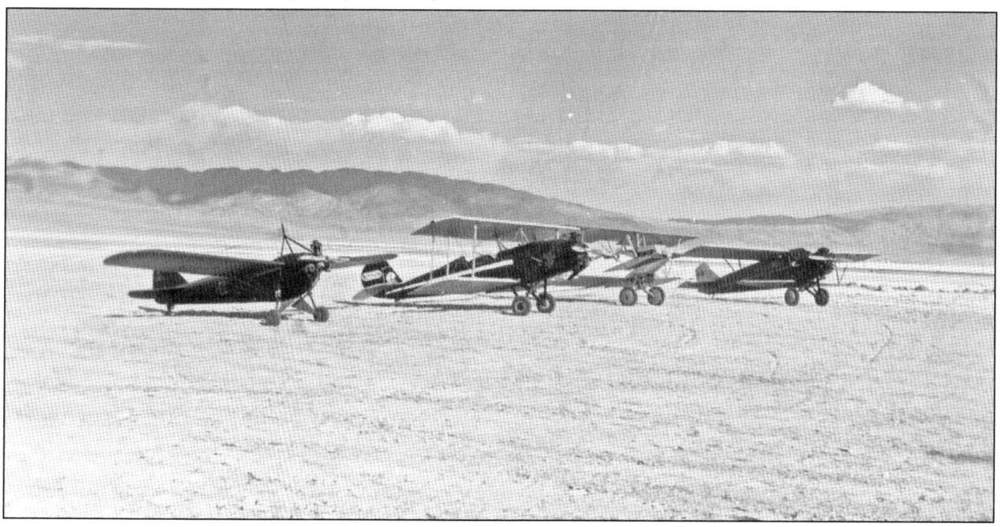

The first airport in Searles Valley was on the edge of Searles Lake, east of Trona's schools. The airport served local private pilots, even providing hangar space for a few of the airplanes. For only a few weekends in 1928, the lakeside airport actually hosted commercial aerial service to Los Angeles. This airport was replaced during World War II when the Army Air Corp constructed auxiliary landing facilities that later became the present Trona Airport.

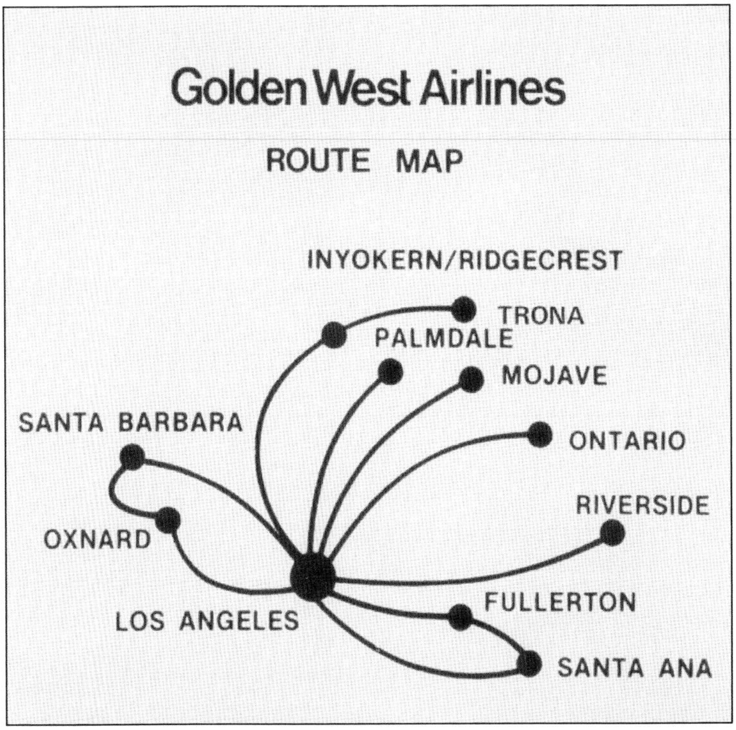

In early November 1975, Golden West Airlines initiated scheduled airline service to the Trona Airport. At the time, Kerr-McGee Chemical Corporation was starting construction of new facilities that would result in a major increase in production capacity. Scheduled airline service to Trona would support those efforts, allowing engineers, company management, and workers to travel from Los Angeles to Trona in just over one hour.

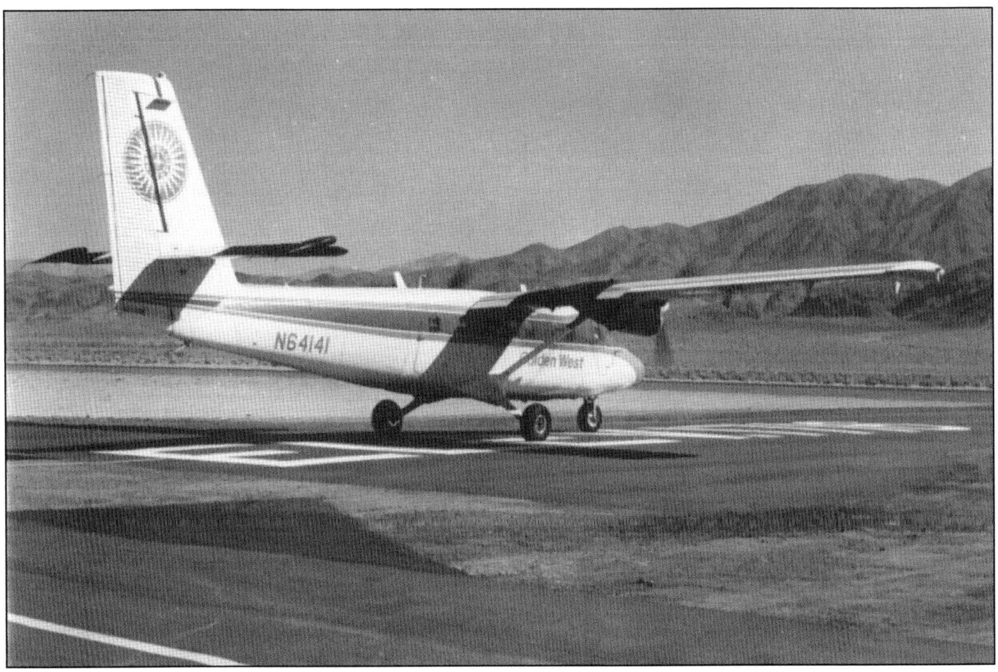

Golden West operated De Havilland DHC-6 Twin Otter aircraft for its service to Trona. The main ground facility provided by Golden West was a passenger waiting room at the Trona Airport. Today, the waiting room is a visiting pilot's lounge. Among the first passengers was Dean McGee, cofounder and chairman of Kerr-McGee Corporation, the owner of the Searles Lake mining operations.

Six

Trona Helps Win Another World War

In World War I, the men and women of Trona produced potash from the brine of dry Searles Lake to help meet the nation's dire need for this critical crop nutrient. Throughout World War II, Trona continued to pour out not only potash but also potassium sulfate, borax, dehydrated borax, boric acid, lithium carbonate, soda ash, sodium sulfate, and bromine, all chemicals for victory. These products increased the food supply, were used to make instrument glass for bombsights and range finders, as well as percussion caps, flares, smokeless powder, shell cases, and synthetic rubber—to list a few of the war materials made from AP&CC products. Because of the critical importance of these products from Trona, and on the recommendation of the War Production Board, the US War Department presented American Potash & Chemical Corporation and its employees with their first Army-Navy E Award on June 23, 1943. Before the end of the war, they would earn three more.

During the award presentation, Robert Patterson, undersecretary of war, praised the people of Trona, saying, "The men and women of Trona are proud of their war work, proud of the 370 of their number who have gone into their country's armed services, proud of the E Award flag that will be raised to fly over their community with their Minuteman flag, proud of the lapel pin which every man and woman in your plant may wear as a symbol of high contribution to American freedom, and proud of the long trainloads of chemicals for victory they are sending forth daily to make materials and food for United Nations forces on every front."

The E Award ceremony at AP&CC was an extraordinary first because it was in the Mojave Desert in a modern community built by the men and women of Trona, surrounded by a desert rich in the romance of early California.

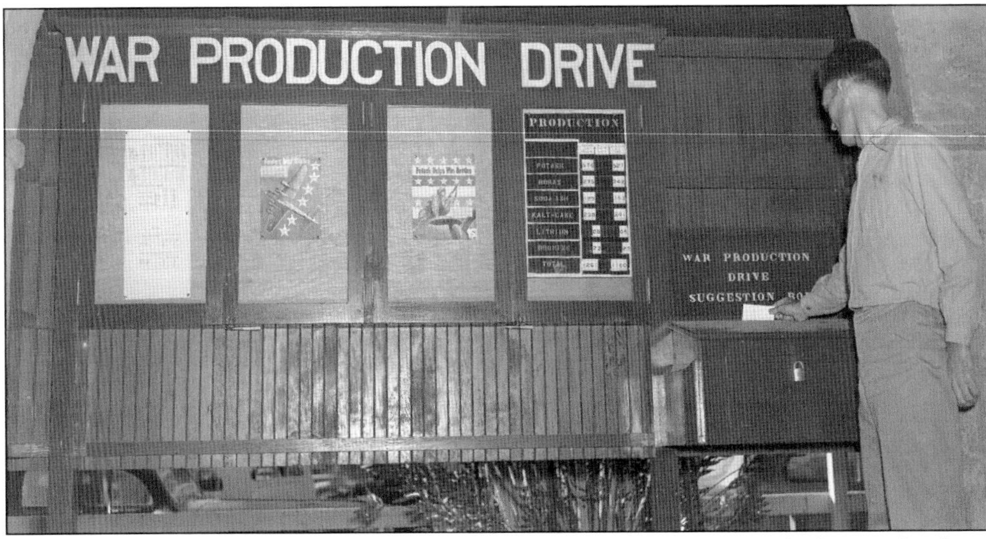

By the middle of World War II, over 10 percent of Searles Valley's residents had entered military service, draining manpower from AP&CC, which could have reduced production. Nevertheless, the people at AP&CC produced nine percent more than the previous year. AP&CC created a display board to show how much product was being made and how it helped win the war, and encouraged suggestions for ways to produce even more.

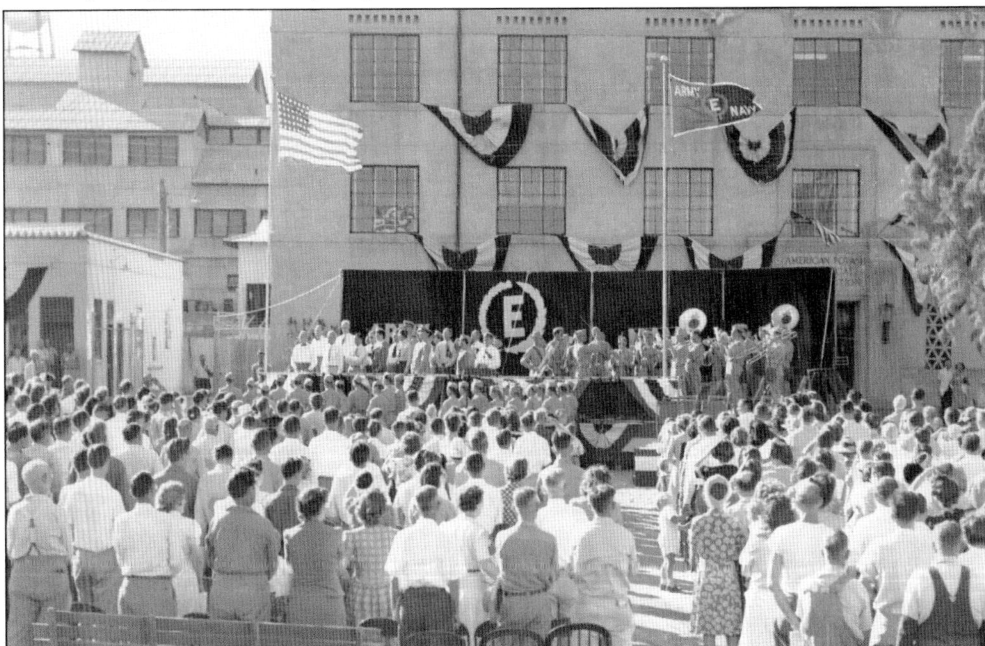

During a ceremony on June 23, 1943, AP&CC and its employees received their first Army-Navy E Award for high production of critical war materials. The ceremony was in front of the Trona administration building. The Muroc Army Air Base Band played, and speeches were given by Robert W. Kenny, California attorney general; Maj. C.W. Clark, assistant district chief, Los Angeles Ordnance Region; and F.C. Baker, president of AP&CC. Before the war was over, AP&CC had won four E Awards.

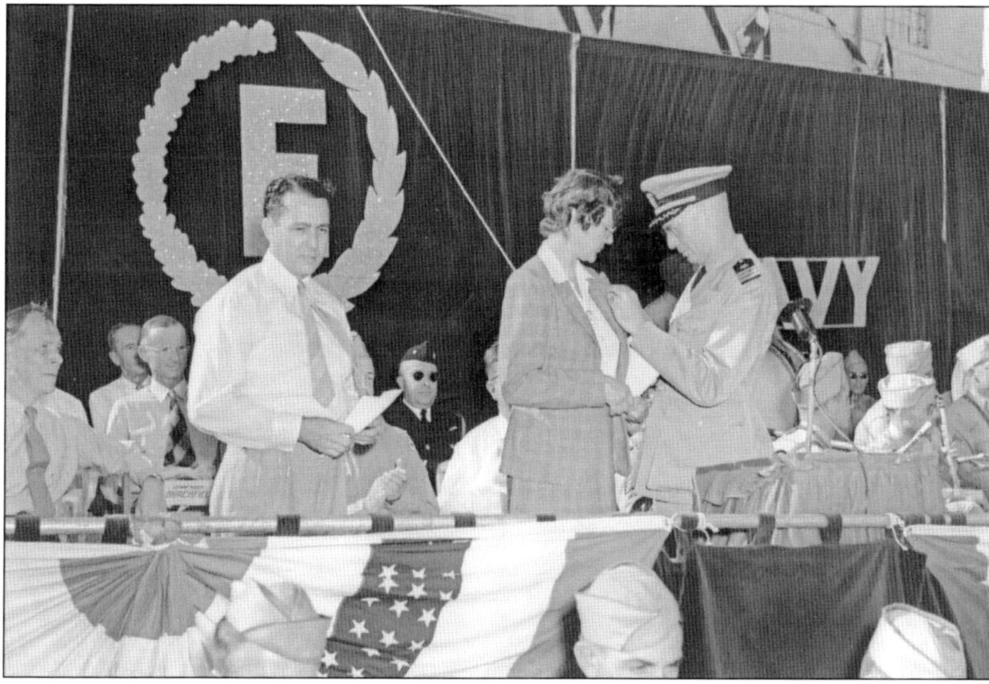

The most important part of the E Award ceremony was the presentation to every AP&CC employee of an E Award pin that they could wear with pride. In this photograph, Johnnie H. Lewis receives her pin from Lt. Comdr. Churchill Carmalt, USNR, as J.J. Eason looks on.

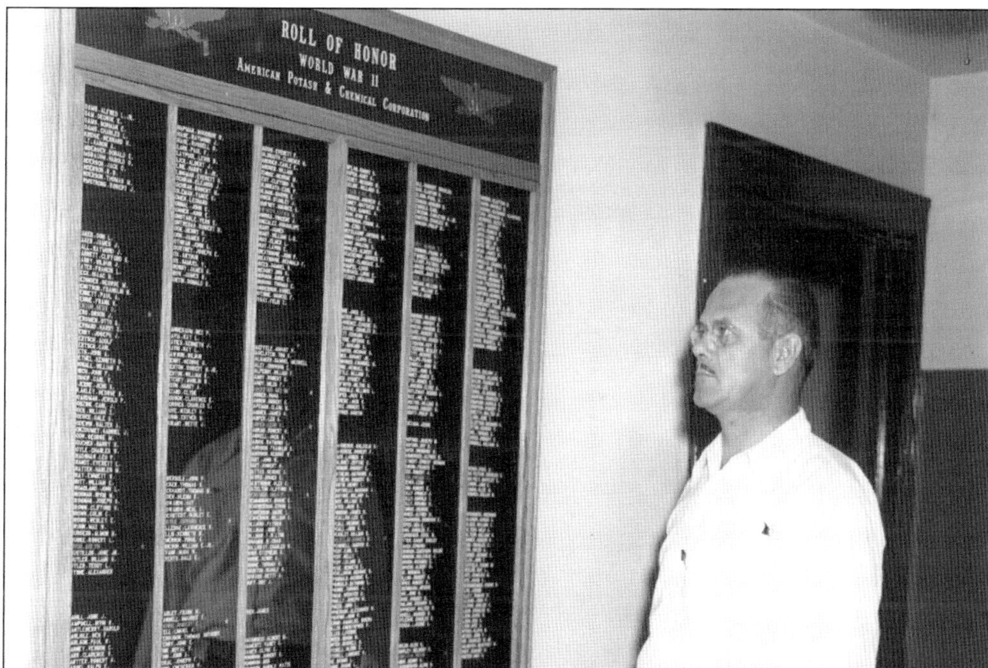

AP&CC encouraged its employees to sign up for the systematic purchase plan to buy war bonds with every paycheck. Part of the plan to boost support was to post an honor roll with the names of every Trona employee who signed up. Here A.H. Meyer checks the board.

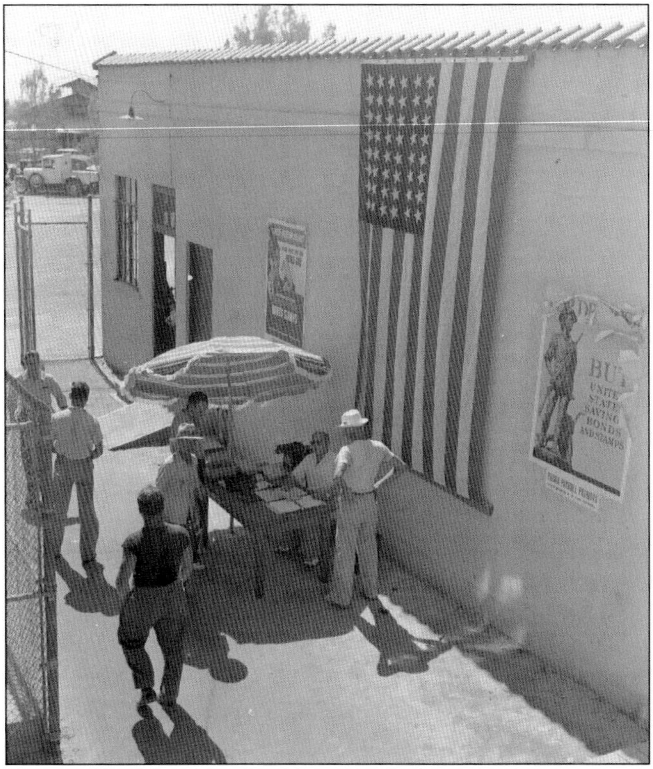

As employees entered or exited the American Potash chemical plant, they passed a booth where they could sign up for systematic purchase of war bonds or purchase bonds in addition to their regular commitment.

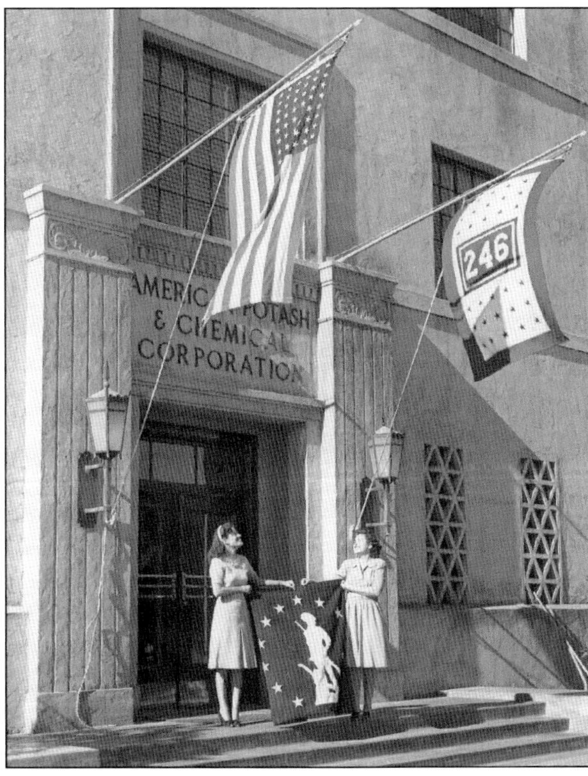

By October 21, 1942, over 90 percent of AP&CC employees had signed up for the systematic purchase plan, to invest at least 10 percent of their earnings in war bonds. For this achievement, they were awarded the Minuteman flag, held here by Sylvia Maes (left) and Eleanor Cochran. The flag reading "246" signifies that 246 employees of AP&CC had already entered military service.

AP&CC and its employees were also awarded a certificate signed by Harry Morgenthau Jr., secretary of the US Treasury. By August 26, 1943, the actual percentage to sign up for at least 10 percent of earnings was 96.1 percent, with all 11 departments above 94 percent.

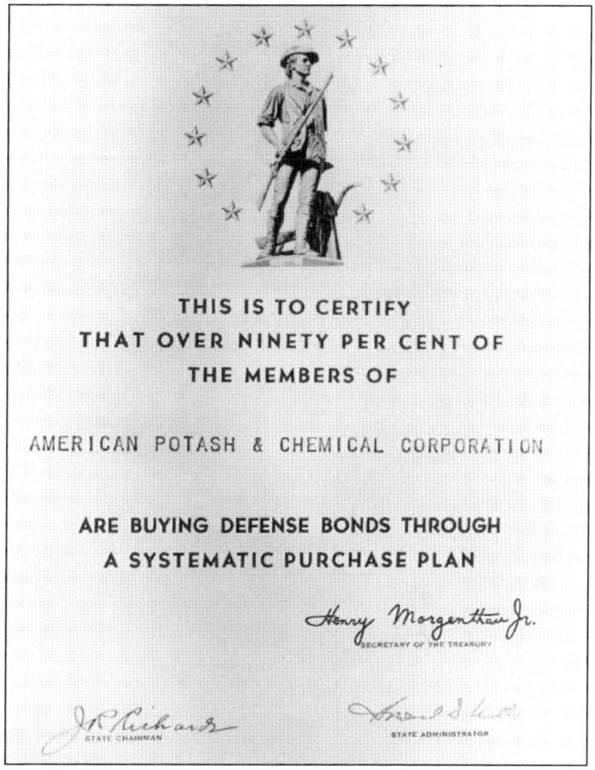
THIS IS TO CERTIFY
THAT OVER NINETY PER CENT OF
THE MEMBERS OF
AMERICAN POTASH & CHEMICAL CORPORATION
ARE BUYING DEFENSE BONDS THROUGH
A SYSTEMATIC PURCHASE PLAN
Henry Morgenthau Jr.
SECRETARY OF THE TREASURY
STATE CHAIRMAN
STATE ADMINISTRATOR

Everyone in Trona, not just AP&CC, worked hard to protect American freedoms and way of life against hostile foreign forces during World War II. The people here formed the Trona Committee for Victory to encourage everyone to do all they could to support the fighting forces.

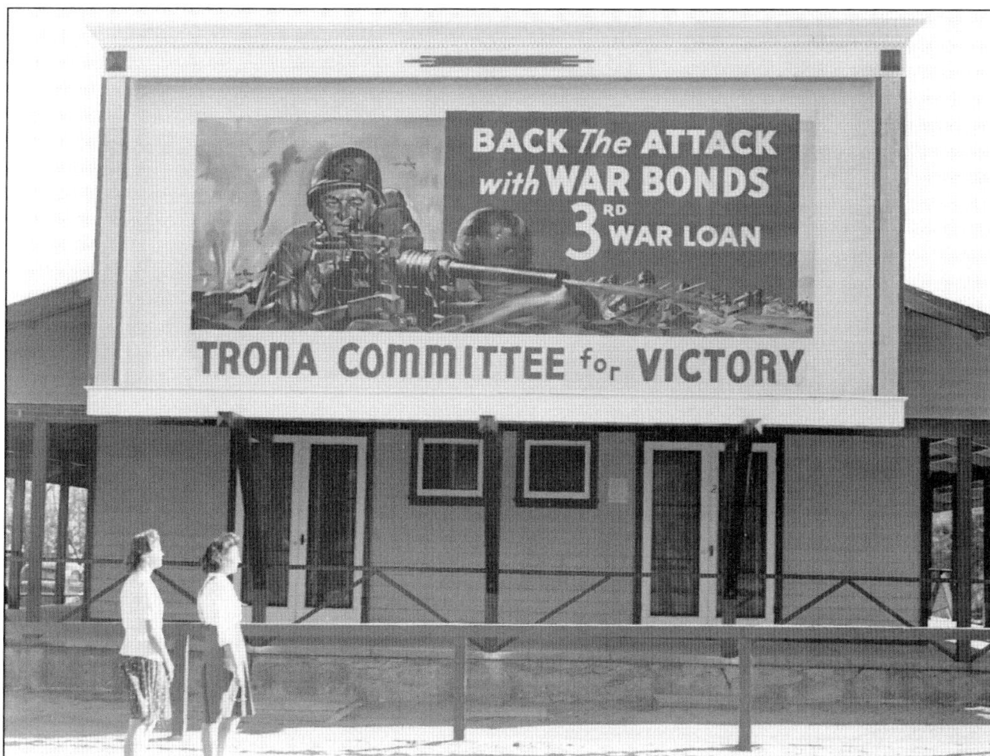

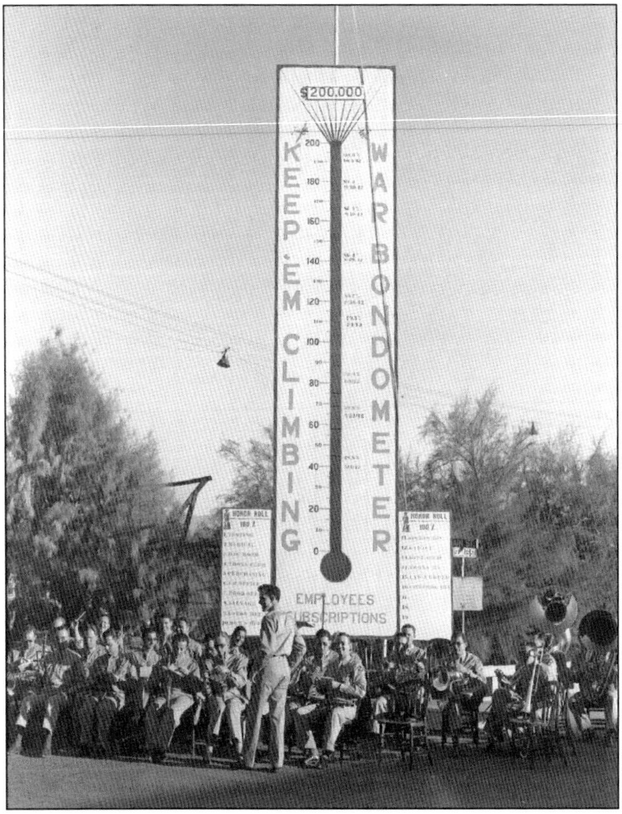

Everyone watched the Bondometer rise, showing Trona's progress toward reaching its goal for war bond purchases. When they reached their goal of $200,000, a brass band from the Army helped them celebrate.

At the Trona schools, patriotism ran high when the 1942–1943 school year began. In October 1942, fired with enthusiasm, Trona High School students salvaged as much scrap metal as could be found in the towns, desert, and mountains surrounding Trona. The boys' and girls' physical education classes worked two hours daily collecting scrap metal in trucks loaned by AP&CC.

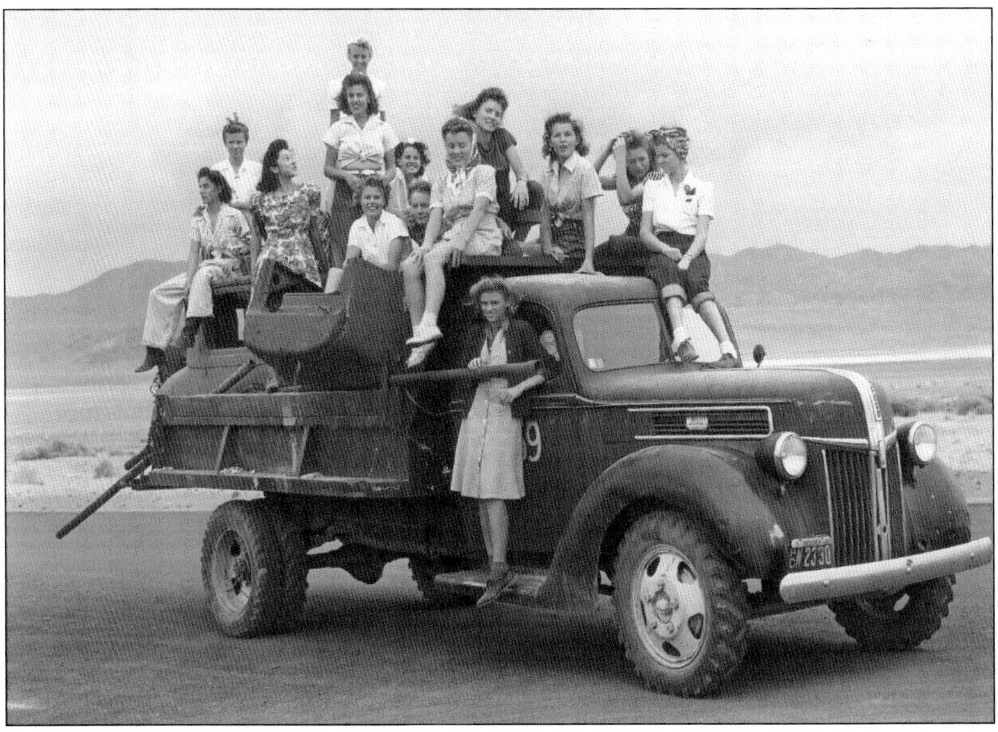

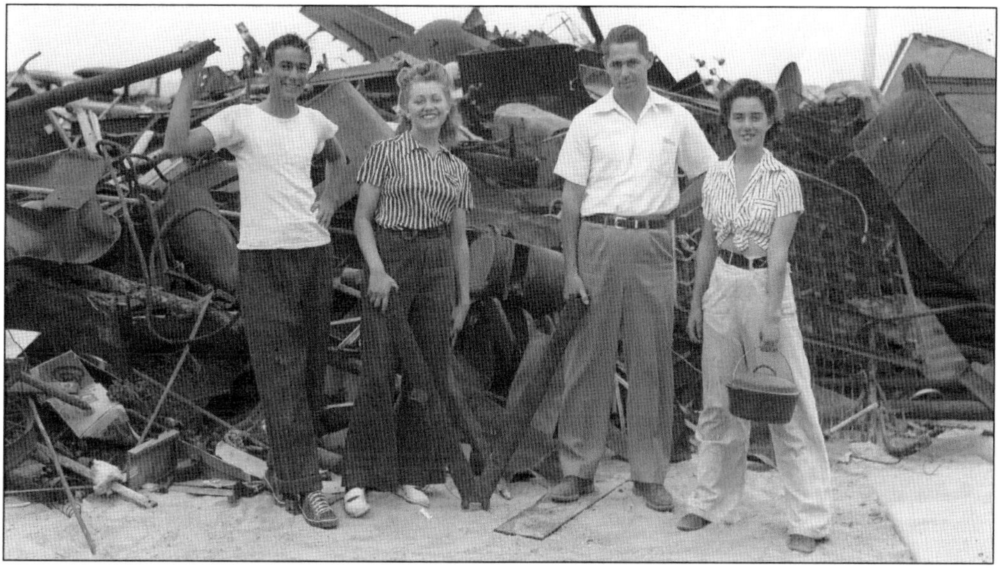

Within 10 days of starting, 20 tons of scrap metal were piled around the flagpole in front of the school. Pictured here are, from left to right, Bill Ryan, Virginia Rorick, Clair Franklin, and Marydith Tyler. Samuel B. Levin, chairman of the Searles Valley Defense Council, arranged for its transfer to a designated government center within a month.

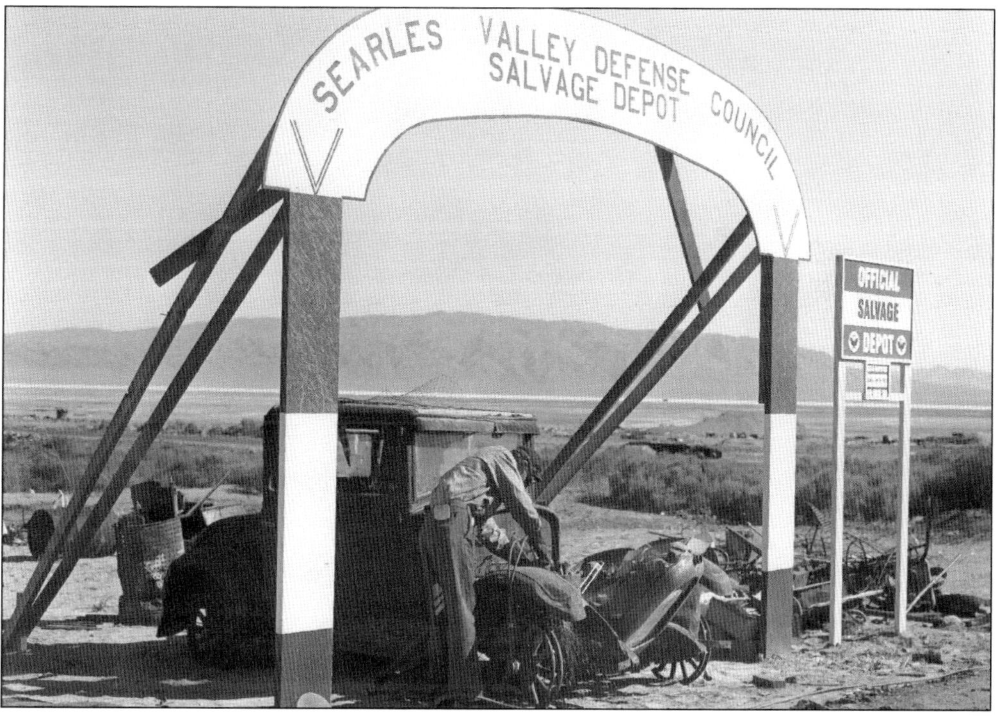

For 1942, the Searles Valley goal was 100 pounds of scrap for every person living here. The school students certainly did their part. AP&CC also donated many thousands of pounds, and West End Chemical Company donated 25 tons. The total for the whole valley was over one million pounds of scrap material, about three times the goal. In addition to the school, there were also salvage depots at Argus and Westend.

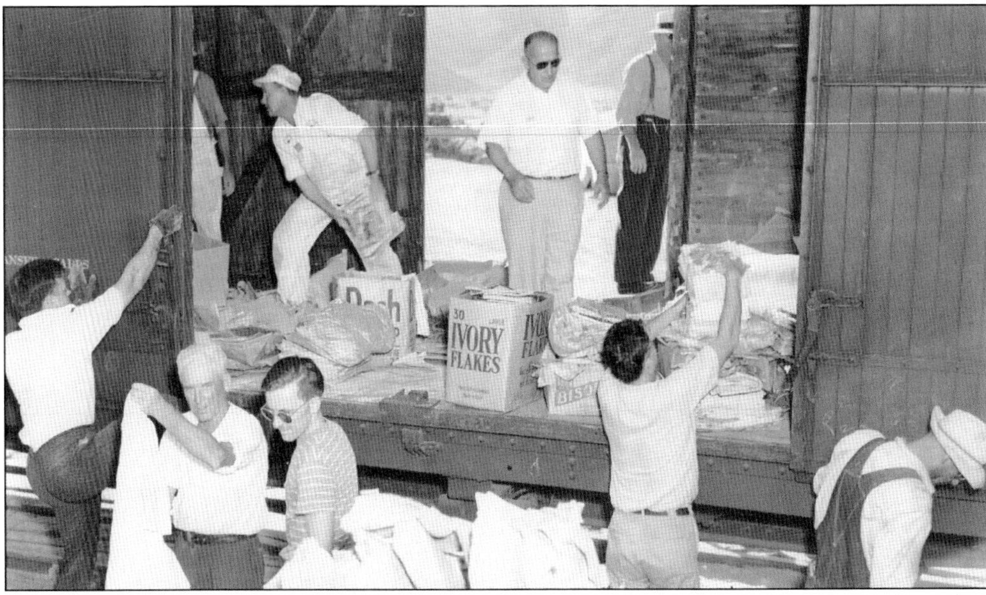

As with many other communities, individuals in Trona donated many different items from their homes. These included unused clothes and bedding, waste paper and boxes, empty cans and bottles, old appliances, and even containers of lard. They brought these to the railroad station to be loaded into a boxcar for shipment to where they were needed for the war effort.

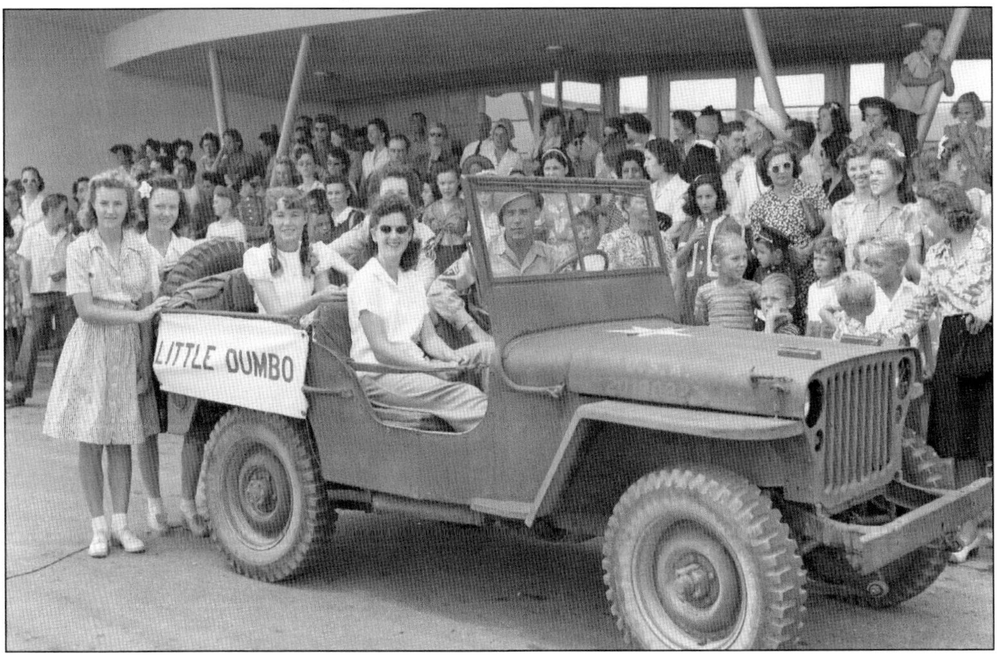

On April 1, 1943, students at the Trona schools kicked off their Jeep Drive, under the inspired direction of Clair E. Franklin and Samuel B. Levin. The original slogan was "Buy a Jeep." Quickly, this changed to "Buy Jeeps" as Trona students purchased war bonds and stamps equivalent to three Jeeps. By the end of the drive on April 30, six and a half Jeeps had been purchased with the $7,789 in war bonds sold. Names for the first three Jeeps, selected by contest, were *Trona Tornado*, *Trona Blitz Buggy*, and *Little Dumbo*.

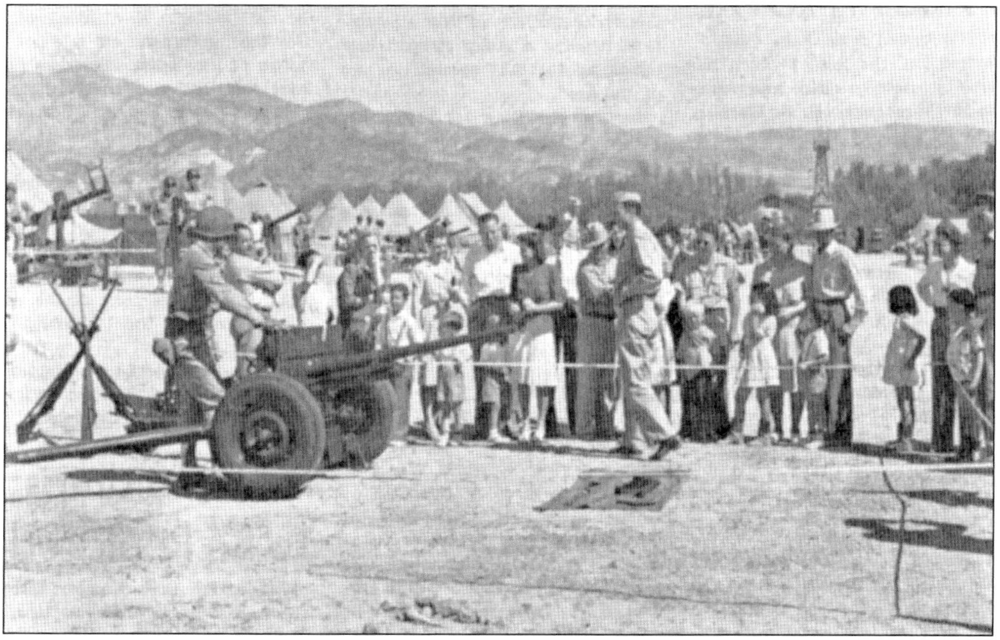

On April 3, 1943, a battalion of Army engineers under the command of Lt. Col. Boyd Yaden passed through Trona on their way to the AP&CC Valley Wells Recreation Area. They had come to construct an auxiliary flying field and camped at Valley Wells until it was finished in mid-August. That World War II auxiliary flying field is today's Trona Airport.

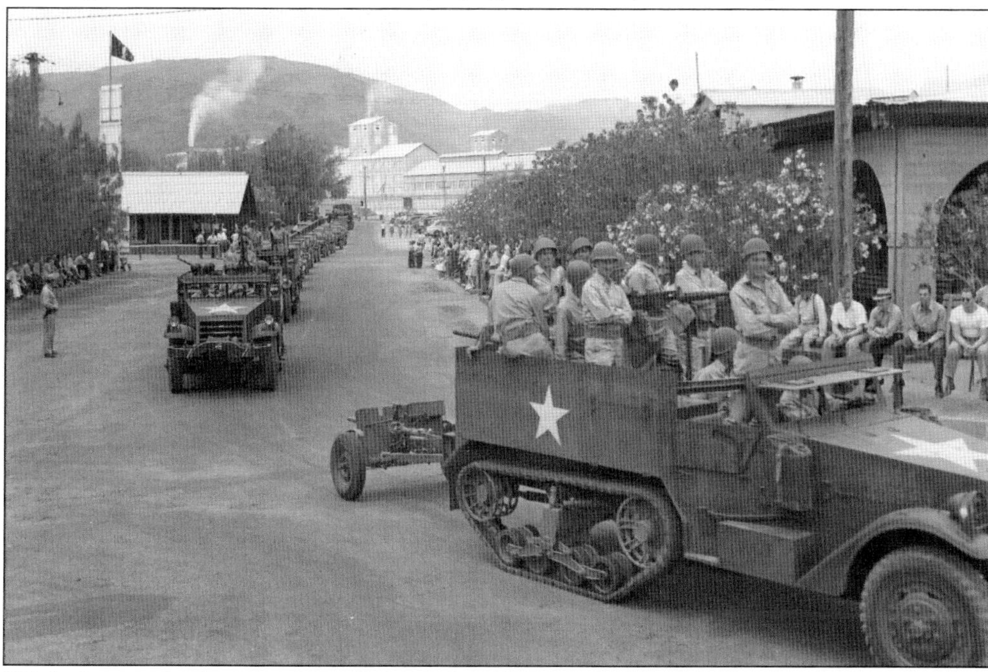

While the people of Trona were only doing their duty, the Army thought Trona's achievements for victory were special and deserved recognition. On May 2, 1943, the Army engineers bivouacked at Valley Wells staged a parade, which included many local people. Jeeps, halftrack trucks, other weaponry, and troops paraded down Main Street in front of the AP&CC plant and Austin Hall.

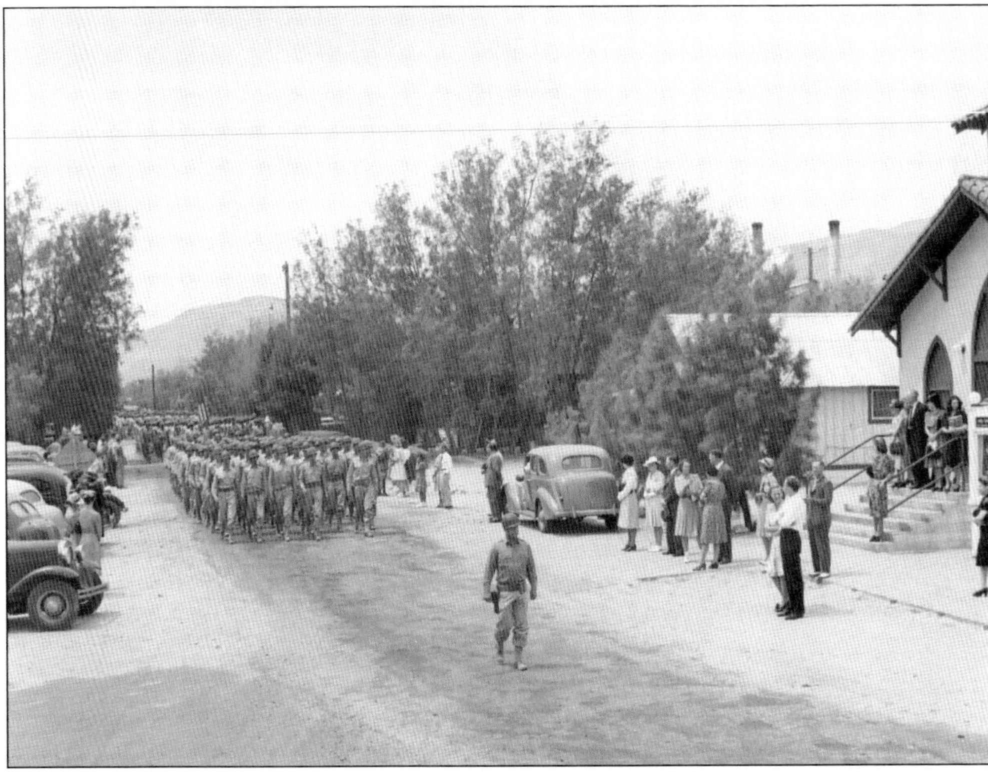

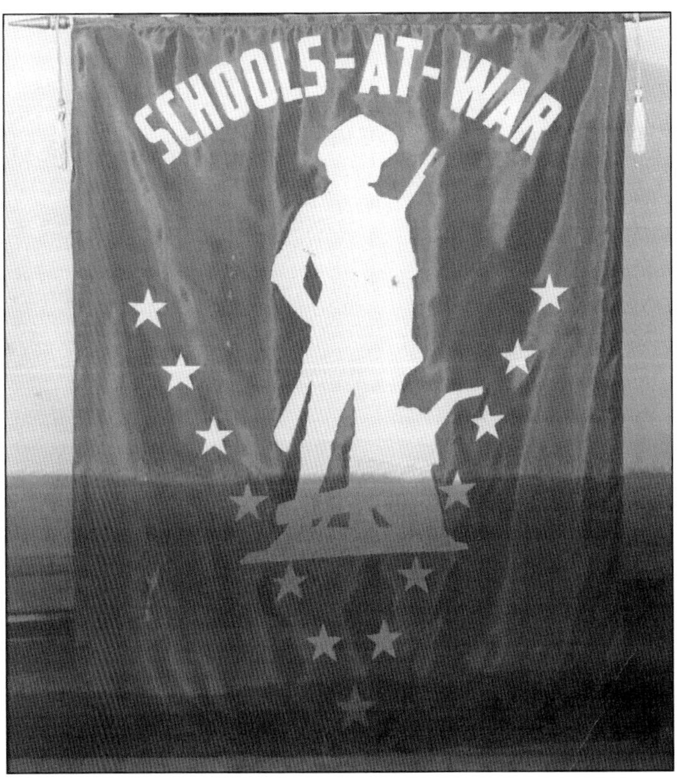

The parade continued down Magnolia Street, with the equipment and troops marching past many local homes and the Trona Community Church. The parade also included the 28-member band, officers, and enlisted men from Muroc Air Base. The California State Guard also sent units for the parade.

The parade ended at the Trona School. There, Trona's students were awarded the Minuteman flag by Samuel B. Levin, head of Trona's bond-selling committee, and officers from the Army. This was to honor the Trona students for exceeding their goal for war-bond sales during their Buy a Jeep war-bond drive in April 1943.

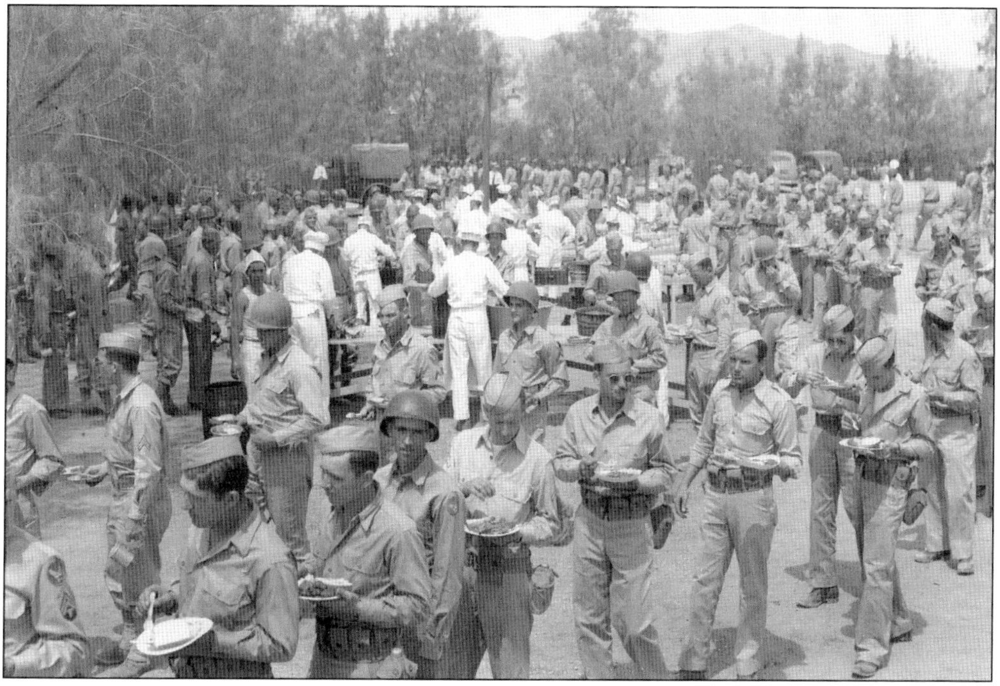

After the parade, the party moved to Valley Wells, where the Army was bivouacked. There, a hearty lunch for 2,000 people was served by the Army. For everyone who was spending at least 10 percent of their income to buy war bonds, the lunch was free. Everyone else could buy their lunch by purchasing a war bond at the event.

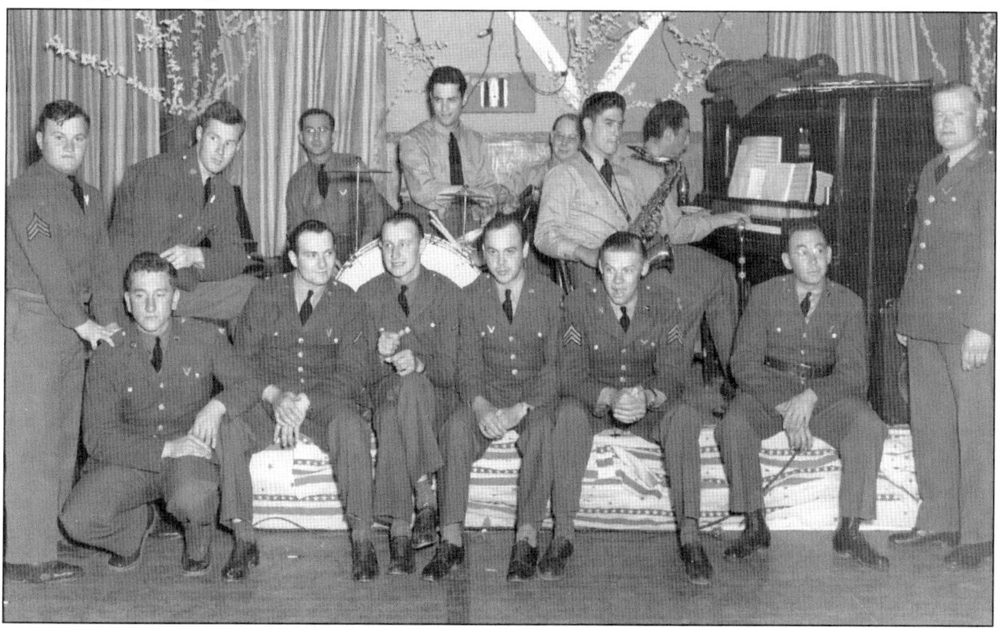

On May 2, 1942, the Red Cross in Trona hosted a victory ball in the Trona Club (recreation center). The featured entertainment was the Victorville Army Camp Orchestra. There were other entertainers, including several from Hollywood. Proceeds from the event, attended by 500 to 600 people, were used to furnish a dayroom at the Victorville Army Camp.

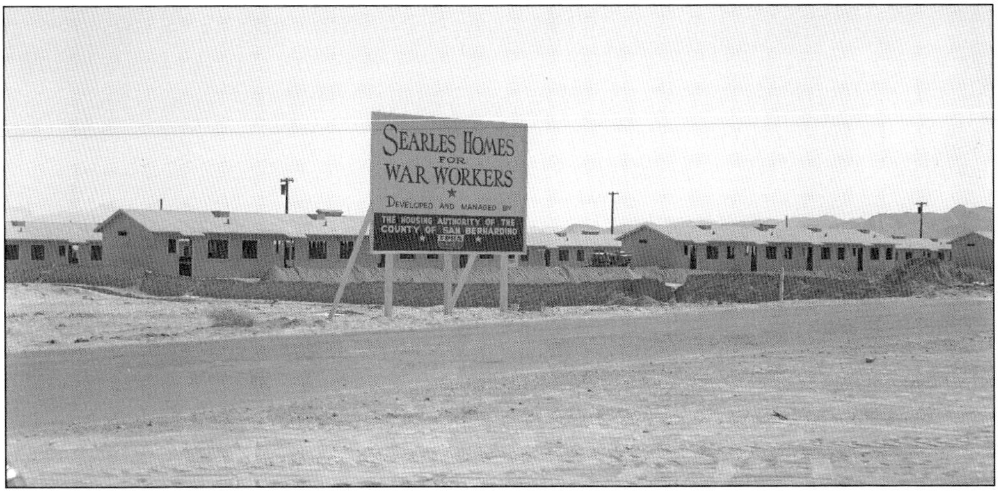

In 1944, using financing from the Federal Public Housing Authority, the County of San Bernardino Housing Authority developed and then managed the Searles Homes for War Workers. Locally, this collection of apartments became known as the Pana Project. The site was cleared in the 1980s.

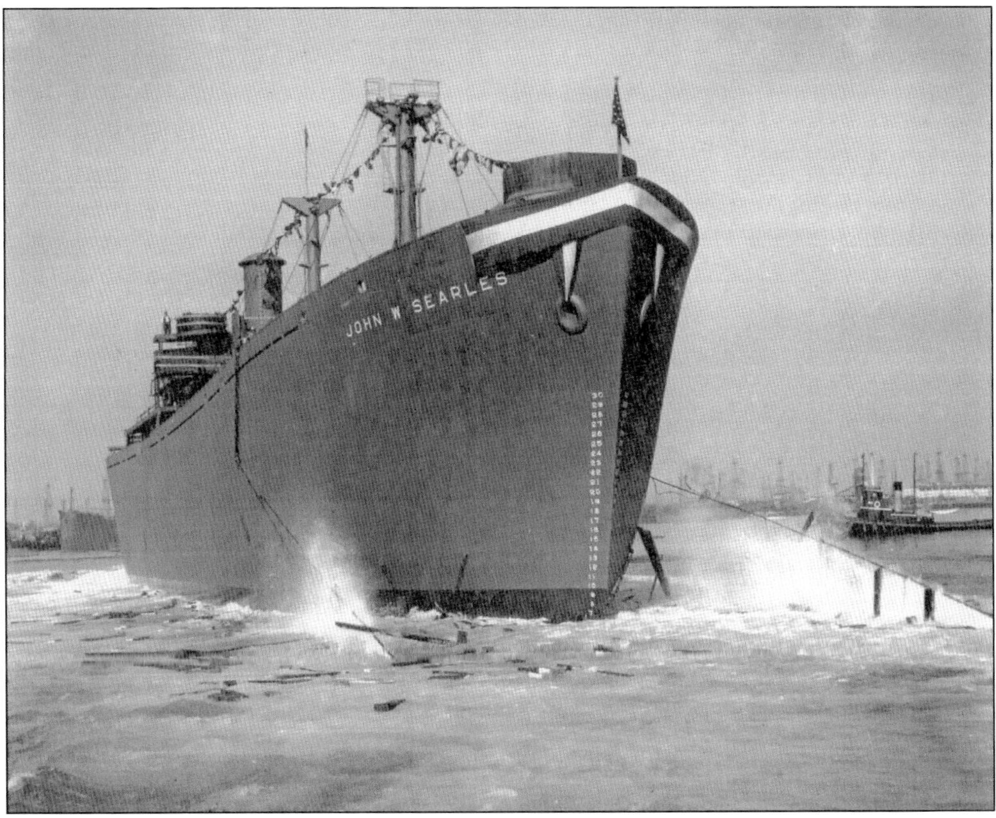

Trona's proudest moment must have been on December 2, 1943, when the US Merchant Marine launched a 10,500-ton Liberty ship, hull No. 2,540, from the California Shipbuilding Corporation yard on Terminal Island, California. This ship proudly displayed the name *John W. Searles* on its bow, honoring the memory of the founder of mining at Searles Lake. It took only 26 days to assemble the entire ship.

Seven

Living in Searles Valley

When Americans arrived around 1860, they were miners seeking gold or silver, and none built permanent communities. The first permanent settlement was at the Searles borax mill with John Searles's substantial home. When Searles sold his business in 1895, the town shrank to just a caretaker and stayed that way until California Trona Company began modifying the Searles mill to produce soda ash.

When California Trona went bankrupt, the court appointed Stafford Austin receiver. To provide services for American Trona Corporation, Austin constructed the iconic Austin Hall in 1913. Over the next eight years, many single-family houses were built for staff, and several large bunk houses were built for the workers, who were mostly single men. This was in the town of Trona. Meanwhile, a similar town, Borosolvay, was rising near the plant of Trona's competitor.

After this early burst of development, town expansion faltered and then ceased as the fortunes of American Trona faded and Borosolvay failed. By 1929, the fortunes of American Trona's successor, American Potash and Chemical Corporation, had reversed, and AP&CC started construction to double its plant's capacity. This spurred another burst of growth, with Trona nearly doubling in size to match the company's growth.

The rapid growth that started in 1929 slowed after 1938, but continued for another 22 years until about 1950. The golden years of Trona were from 1929 until 1955, when Trona was the largest town within 100 miles and offered business and cultural services unavailable elsewhere in the vicinity.

Still, change continued. By 1955, Ridgecrest, just 22 miles west, was undergoing sustained growth, fostered by the Navy at China Lake. Ridgecrest was already larger than Trona and attracting many large businesses. As Ridgecrest businesses grew, they offered more services than Trona's smaller businesses could provide. Gradually, one by one, Trona's businesses closed. Today, only a small business community remains.

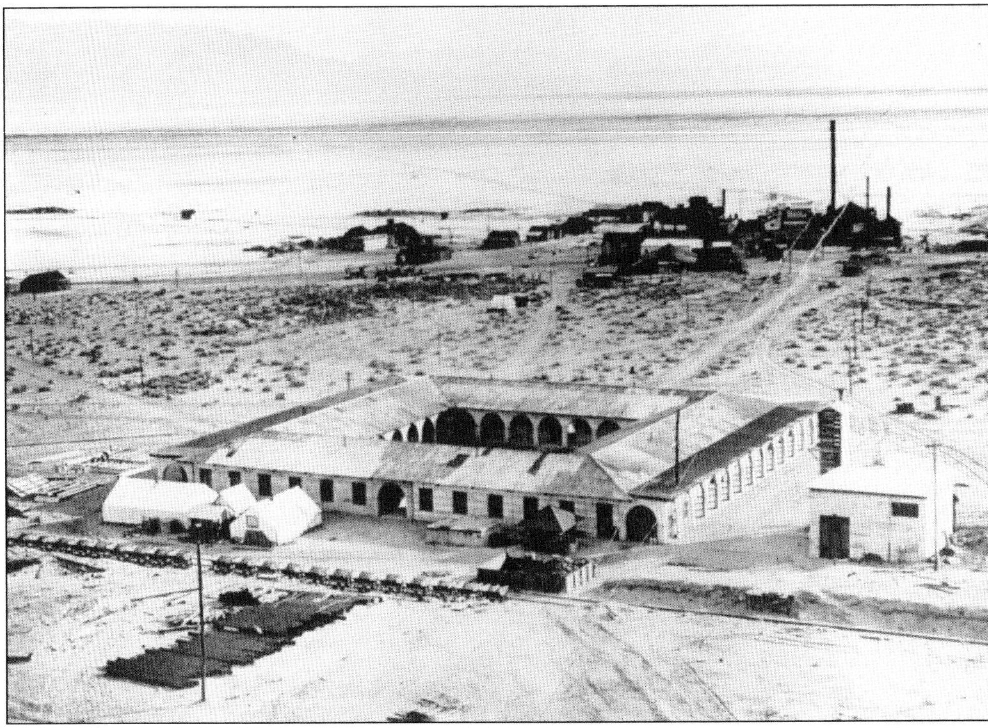

In 1913, Stafford W. Austin, court-appointed receiver for the bankrupt California Trona Company, constructed Austin Hall to house managers and workers who were building the Hornsey plant. It also contained a mess hall for the workers. This 1914 photograph shows Austin Hall with the Hornsey plant, which had failed by this time, in the distance.

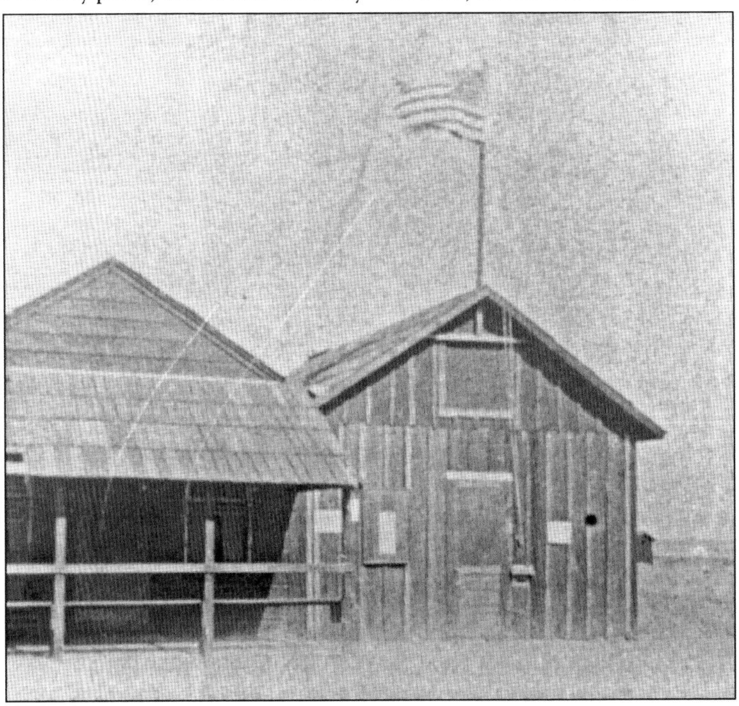

The first post office opened on March 27, 1914, making Trona a legal entity and giving the town its official name. It was in a simple wooden building with a US flag over the door and a covered slot for outgoing letters. Over the weekend of March 28–30, 2014, Trona celebrated its centennial with a history symposium, parade, music festival and concerts, a street fair, and many reunions.

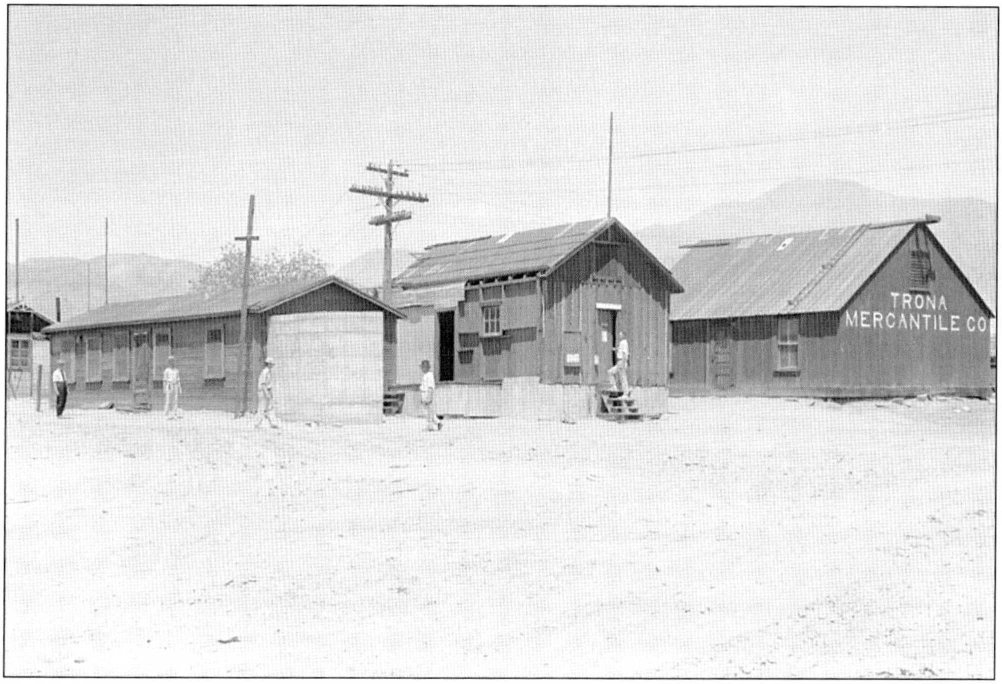

By 1914, the Trona Mercantile Company had been established to supply the growing community. The Trona Mercantile Company not only served the needs of American Trona Corporation, but also brought supplies much closer to the gold miners in the Argus, Slate, and Panamint Mountains.

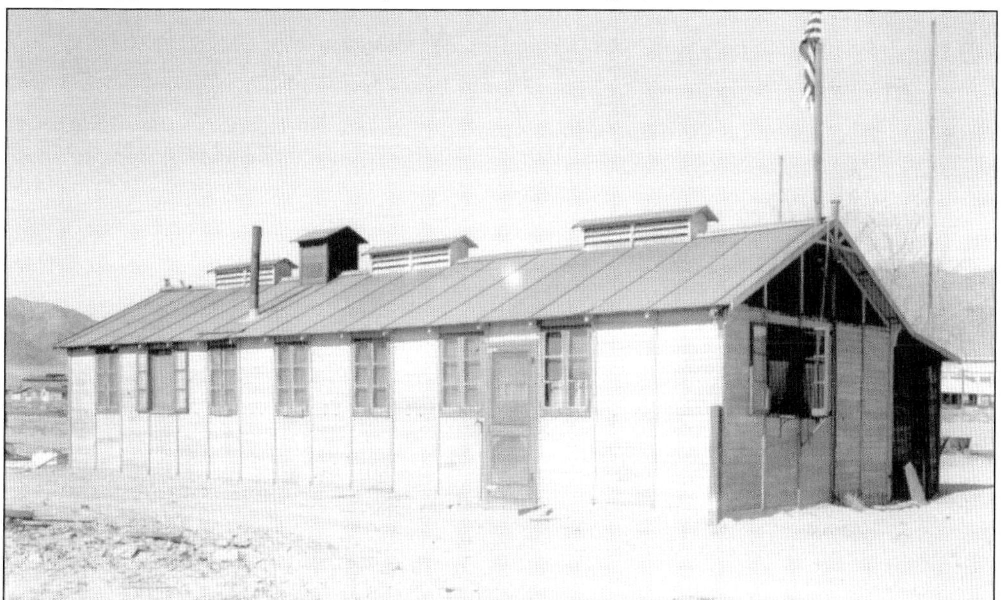

The Trona School District was established on October 16, 1916. American Trona Corporation provided a small building with a single room and just one teacher. At this time, most of the workers in Trona were men who had only come to construct the American Trona plant. The work was only temporary, and the isolation and inhospitable climate and poor housing were unacceptable to most of their wives. This structure was replaced by a new building in 1918.

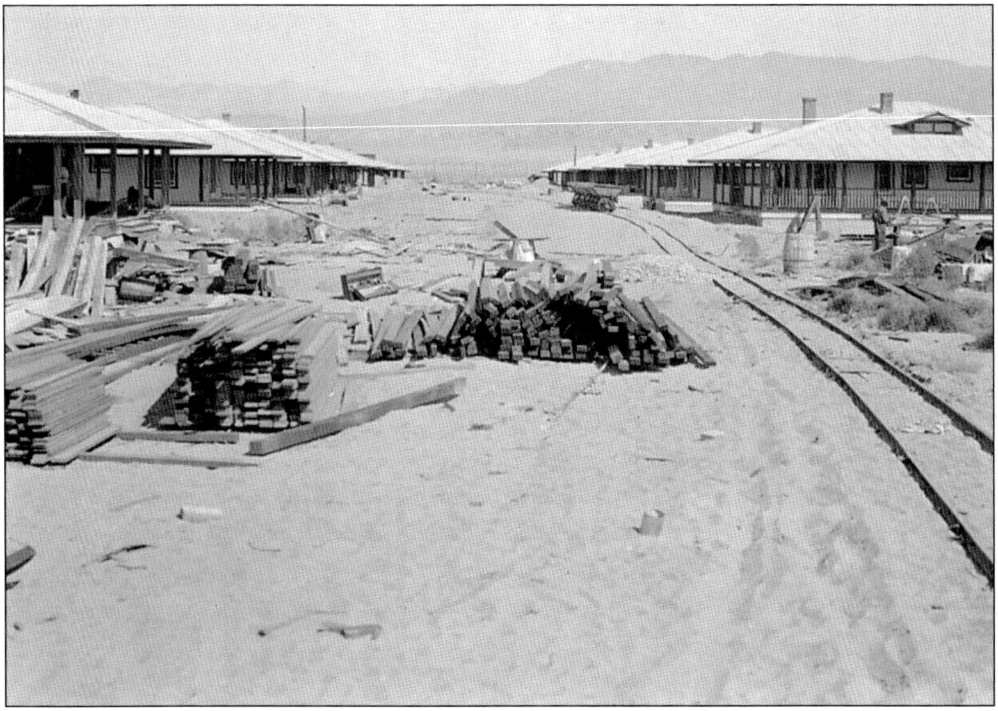

In 1916, American Trona Corporation constructed about 20 luxury houses on Magnolia Street for its executives, and in 1920, the company constructed a similar number of houses on Panamint Street. Air conditioning had not yet been invented, so the houses had wide porches to keep the sun off the walls. On a hot summer evening, people sometimes slept on the porch beneath wet bed sheets. The houses used asbestos sheeting for roofs. Most of the roofs are still in good condition today, and the houses are still occupied. The narrow-gauge Mexican Central Railroad ran down Panamint Street and on across the lake to the east side.

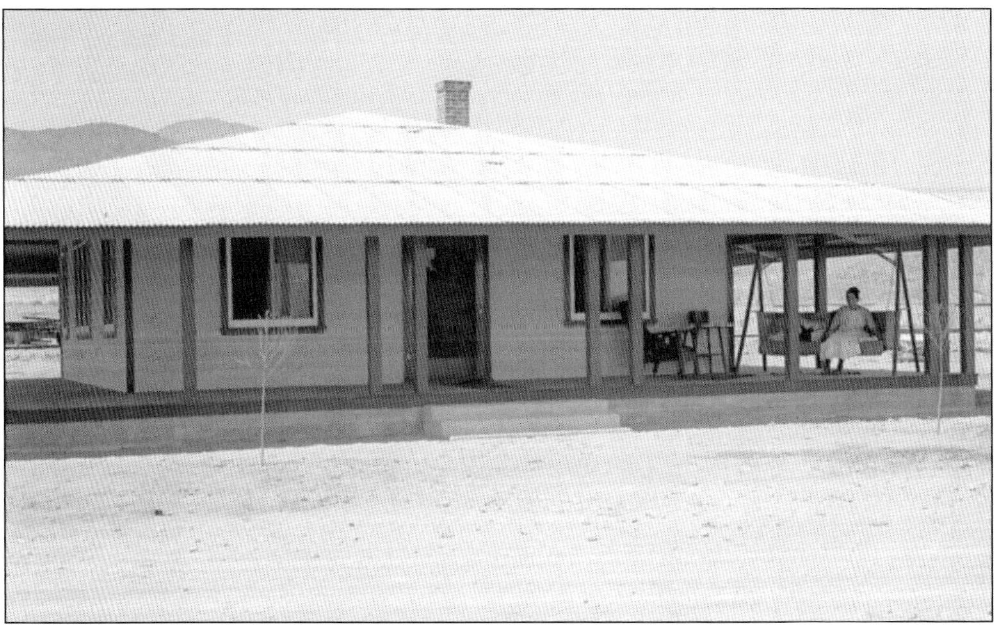

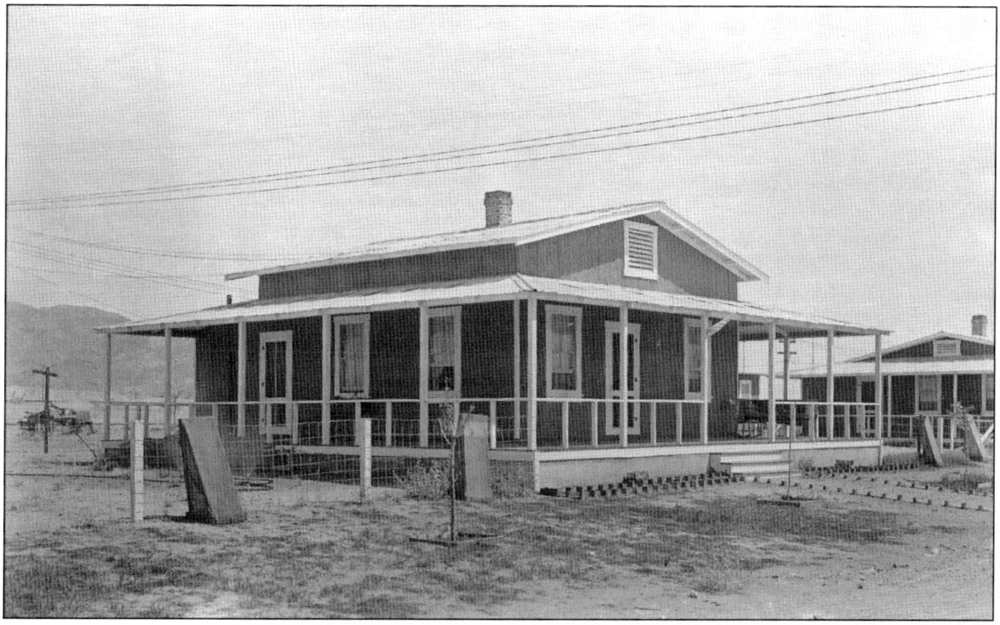

One house built on Magnolia Street also had a deep attic in addition to wide porches to keep even more of the sun's heat away from the living quarters. This was the only house built with this feature, so it probably did not help much against summer heat.

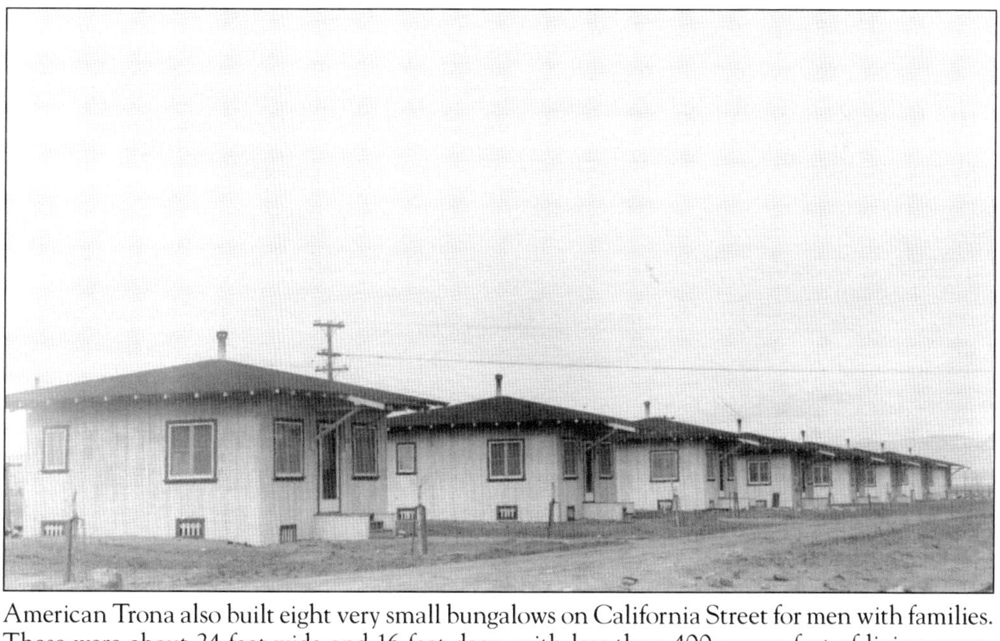

American Trona also built eight very small bungalows on California Street for men with families. These were about 24 feet wide and 16 feet deep, with less than 400 square feet of living space. Even though they had Murphy beds to save space, they must have been uncomfortably cramped. None remain today.

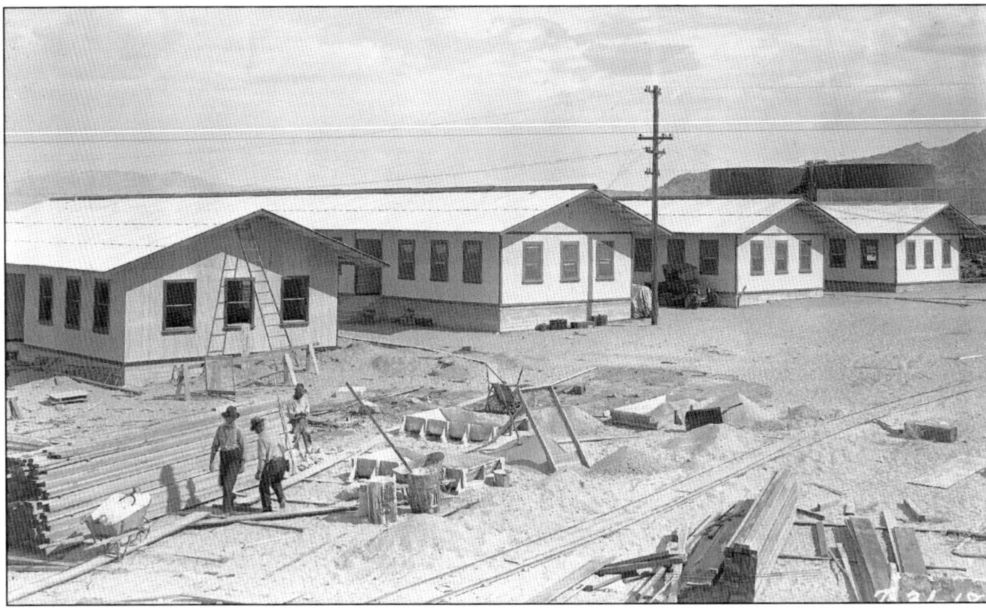

Even into the 1940s, most of the workers of American Trona Corporation, later AP&CC, were single and lived in one of the 15 bunkhouses owned by the company. The early bunkhouses were single story and contained about 20 rooms. Later, the company built two-story structures with 40 rooms. The rooms were typically 16 feet square and occupied by two men. They included beds and desks for each man and a wash basin. Restrooms and showers were shared by all. Dining was in the mess hall or coffee shop, also company-owned.

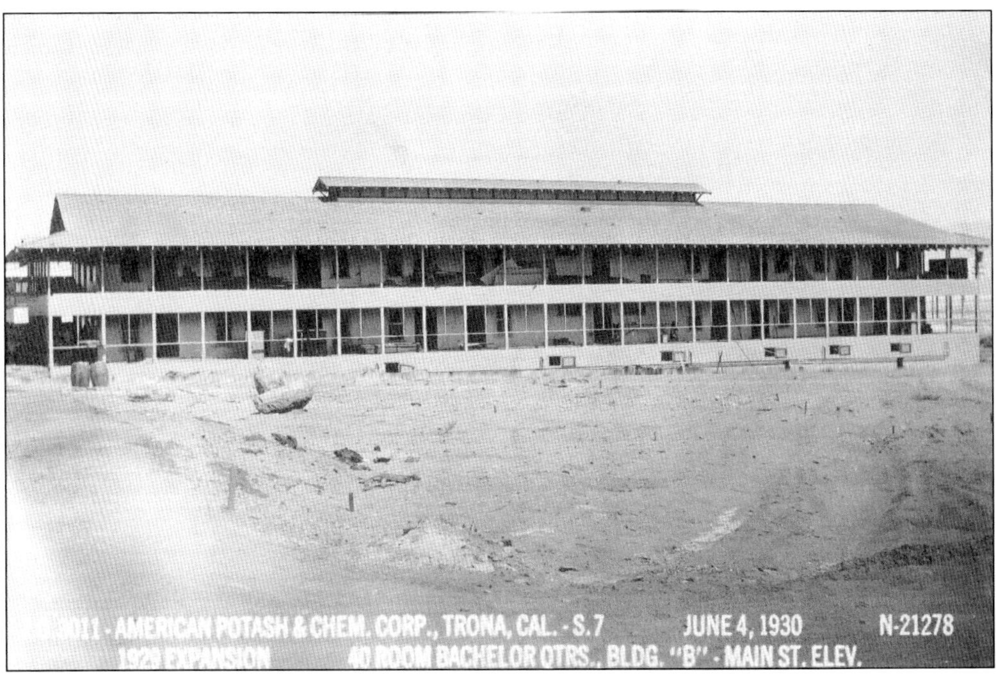

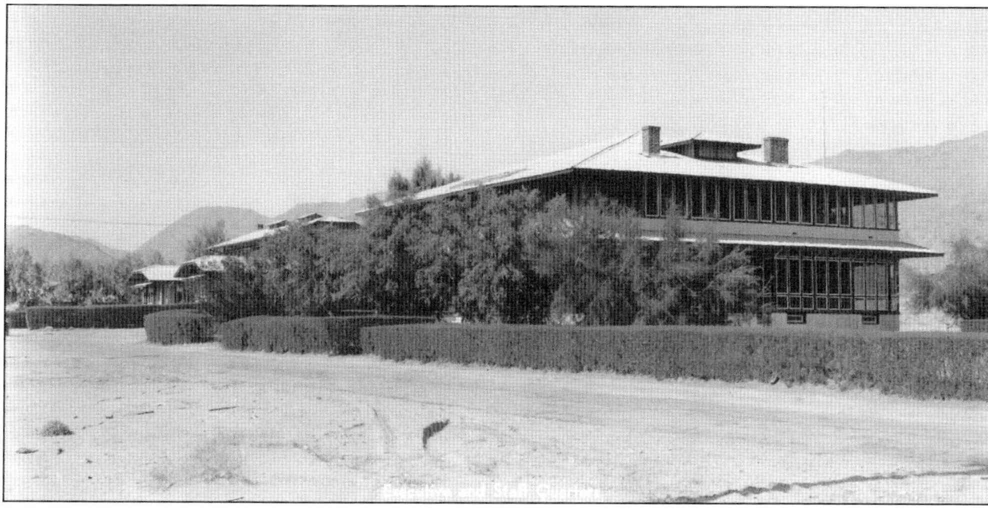

Executives and staff were provided with more luxurious quarters than the plant workers, with their rooms offering more space and privacy. Behind the staff quarters was the executive quarters building, with full-service rooms and a private kitchen run by a trained chef. The company also provided single women's quarters, largely occupied by the few teachers and nurses working for the company.

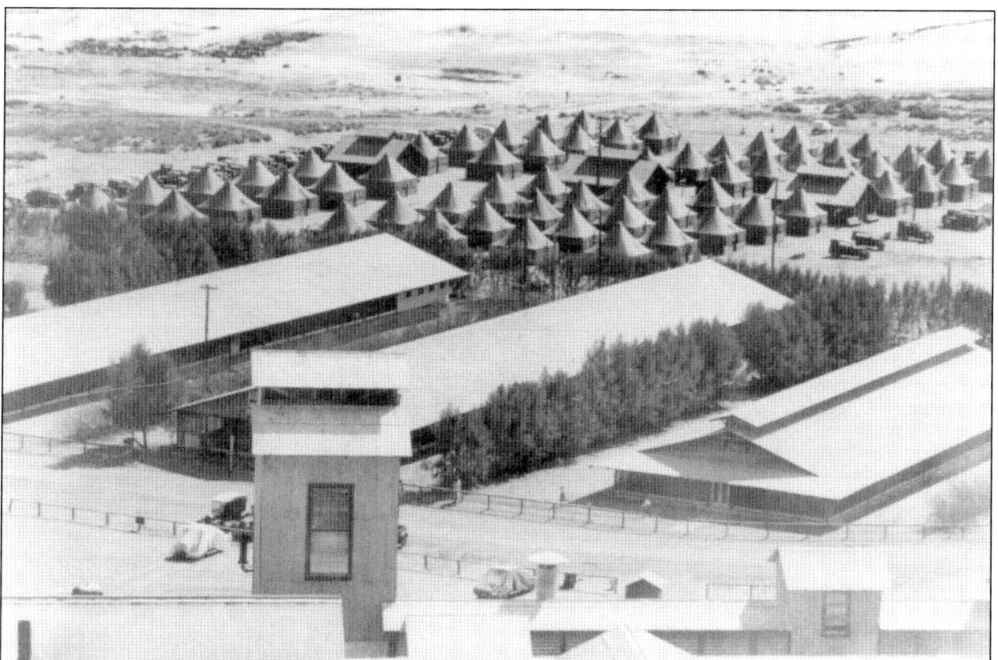

Throughout the 1929 expansion, which lasted until about 1935, construction workers lived in tents. These must have been unbearably hot during summer days, but they had the advantage of cooling more quickly in the evening than was possible in the bunkhouses. In winter, there was no relief from the subfreezing nighttime temperatures during December and January. As part of the 1929 expansion, AP&CC gradually added more family housing.

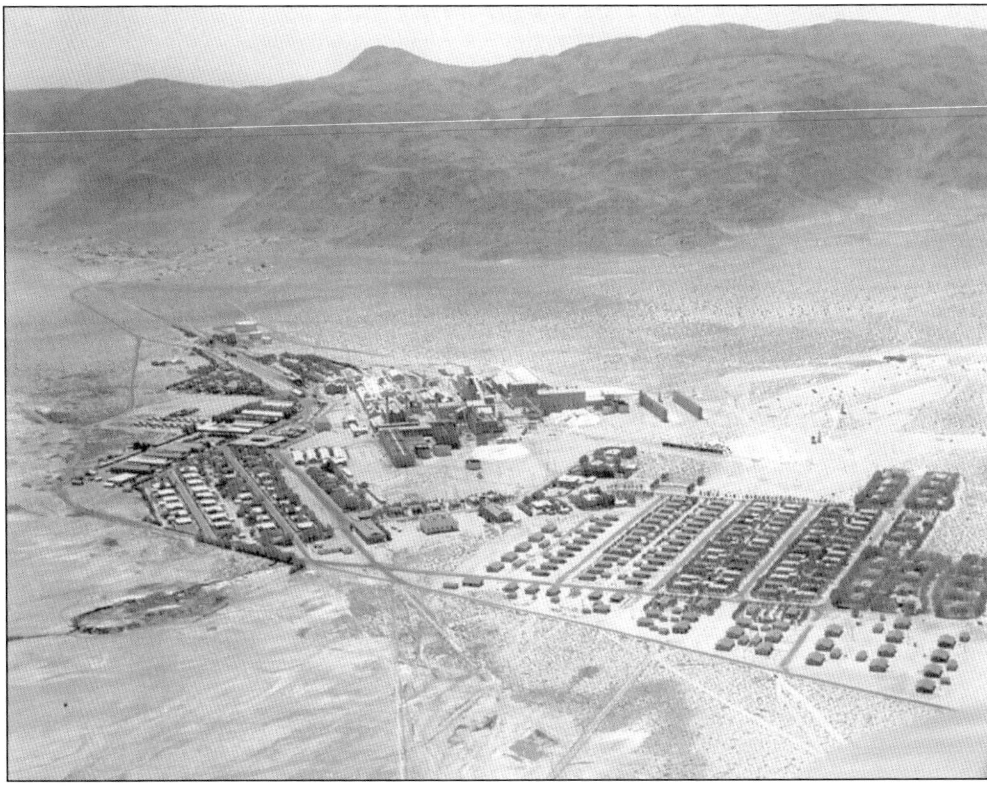

By the late 1930s, when this photograph was taken, the capacity of the Trona plant of AP&CC had more than doubled, and the town had grown to contain about 175 single-family homes. However, 15 bunkhouses remained and still provided the majority of the housing for employees.

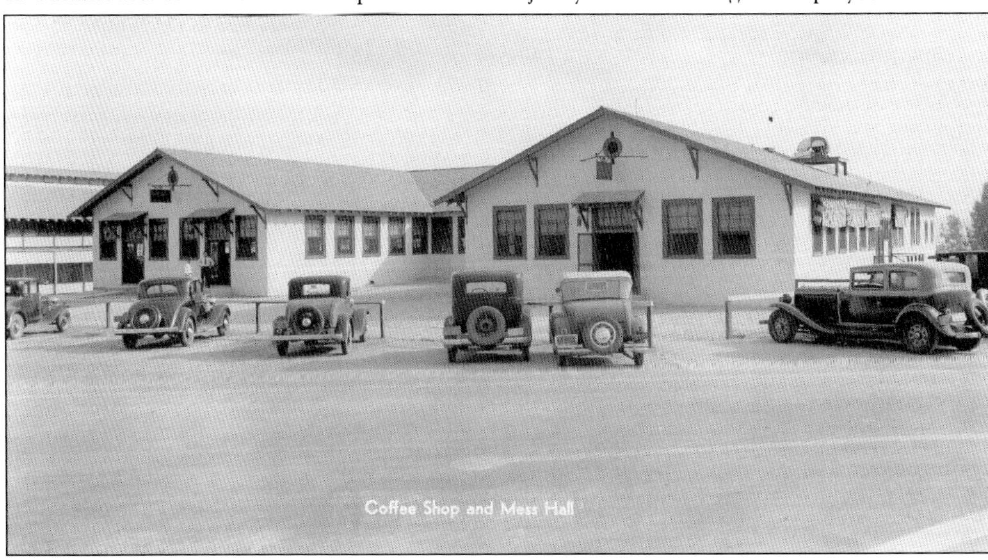

From when it was built during the 1929 expansion (original building shown) until it was destroyed by fire on October 19, 1950, the Trona Mess Hall and Trona Coffee Shop were the primary eating establishments for most employees of American Potash. The building was later expanded to enclose the central courtyard, and when Prohibition ended, this became a bar.

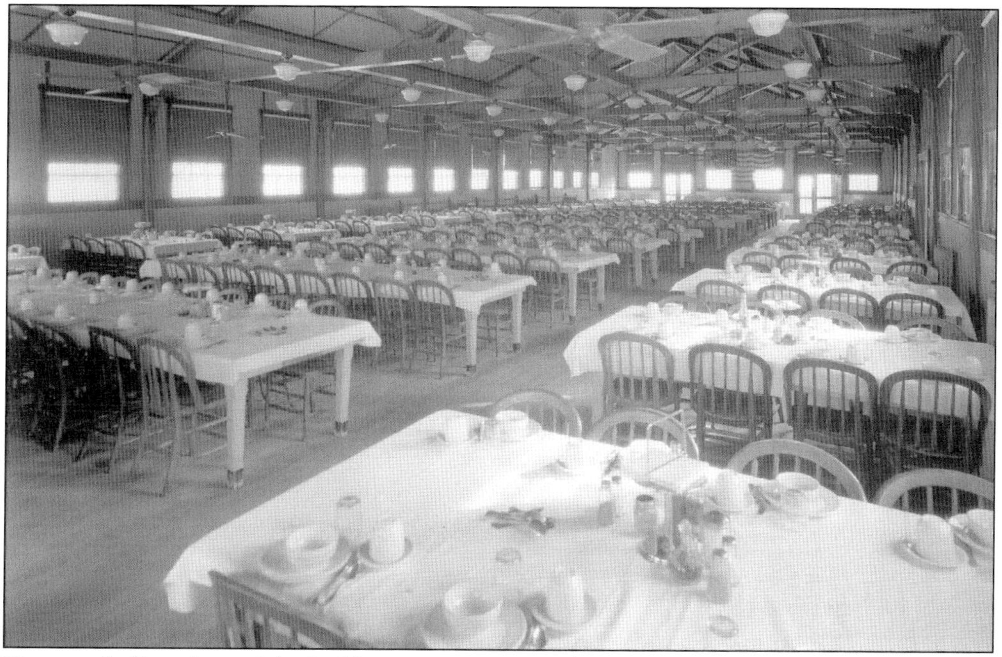

The mess hall was huge. It had table space to serve nearly 400 at one seating, close to the number of men on day shift. While they may not have always used tablecloths, they always used porcelain table service and metal utensils. Service was family style, with large bowls or trays of food being provided to each table.

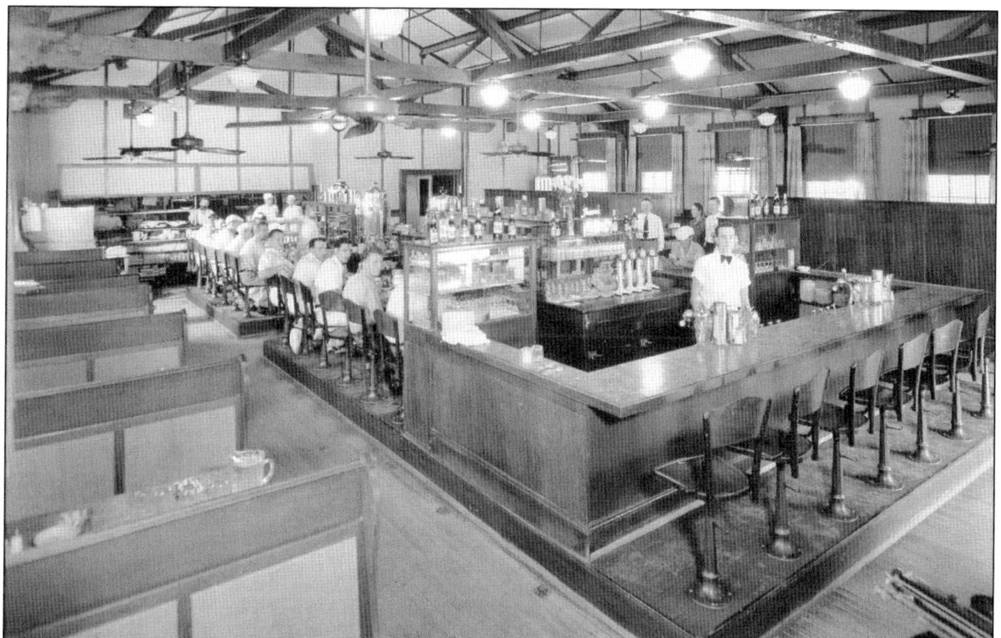

The coffee shop offered both counter and booth service with menus and waitresses. Where one was allowed to sit was determined by status in the company, and hourly workers were expected to eat in the mess hall. However, the soda fountain was open to all, and the soda jerk would mix an ice-cream malt to order.

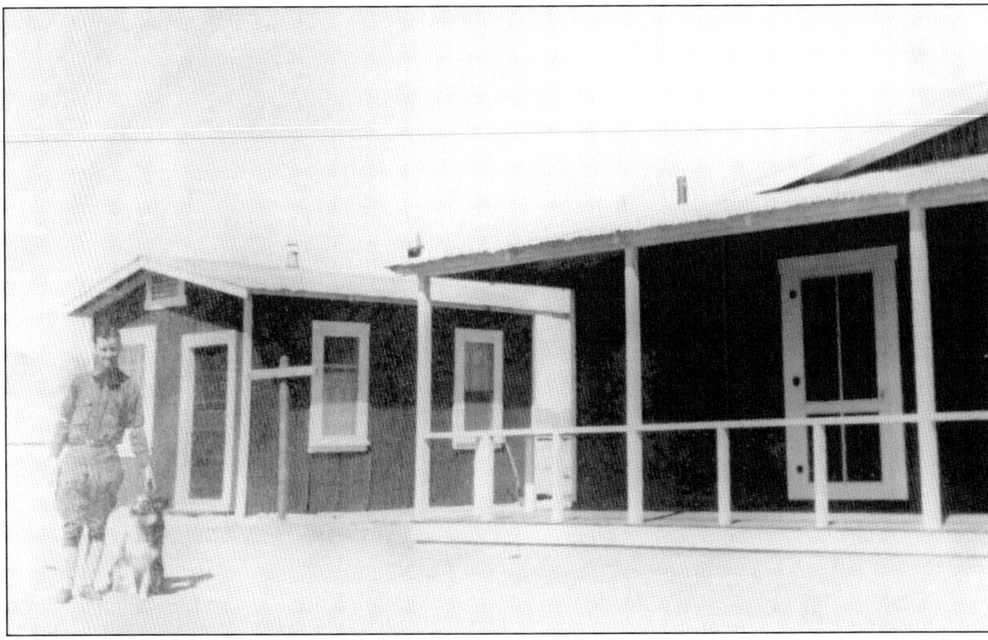

In September 1914, American Trona Corporation hired Dr. H.R. Evans as doctor. This 1916 photograph shows his medical office. In the clinic were a couple of beds for emergency use only. From a shelf in the waiting room, the skull of Joe "Hootch" Simpson grinned down. Hootch had the distinction of being lynched twice at Skidoo in 1908, first his actual lynching, then again for photographs.

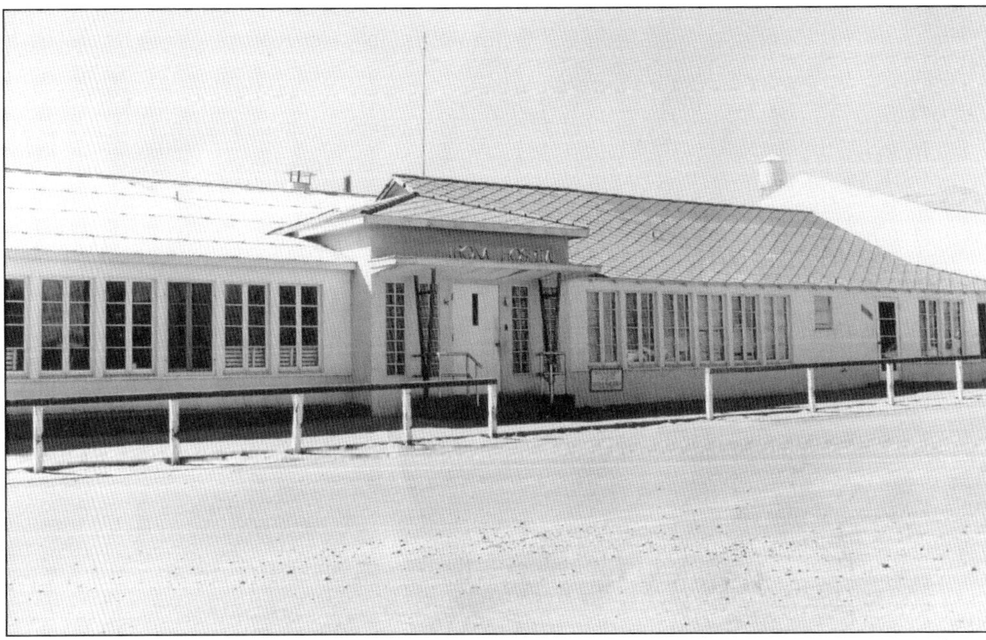

American Potash operated a fully staffed hospital with 12 beds. The company retained two doctors for the medical staff. They could treat most medical situations that might arise, from industrial injuries to the delivery of babies. As late as the late 1940s, it was the finest hospital within 100 miles.

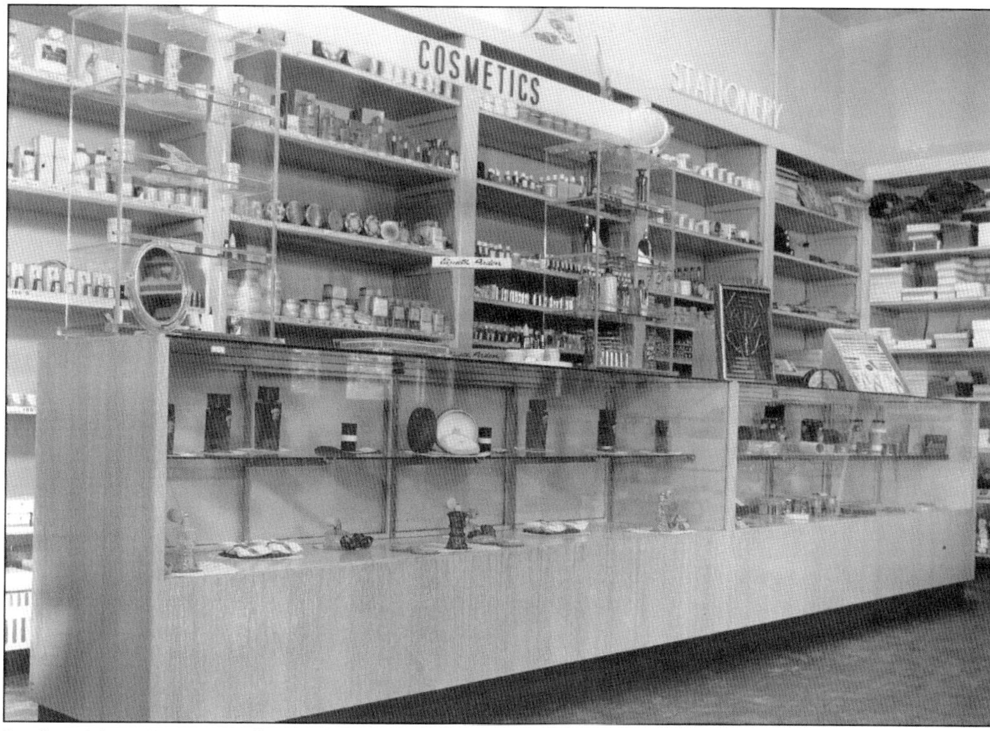

In the 1930s, Austin Hall was the heart of Trona. It housed nearly all of the commercial services that the community needed, including the butcher shop, grocery store, dry-goods store, soda fountain, drug tore, Trona Railroad, Western Union, telephone switchboard, barber shop, pool hall, San Bernardino County Library, and restrooms. The Austin Hall Pharmacy (below) sold not only drugs, but cosmetics, stationery, cameras and film, and even chemicals for developing photographs. All the stores did much of their business in Trona scrip, the money created by AP&CC. Only employees and school teachers were allowed to buy scrip, and every six months they would receive a rebate of the profits from those businesses trading in scrip, based on how much they bought. After 30 years, this rebate system ended on December 31, 1957.

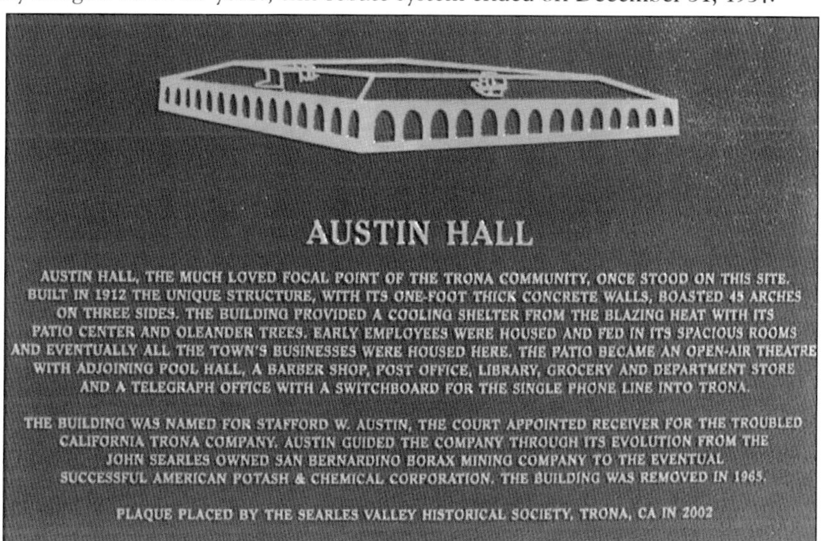

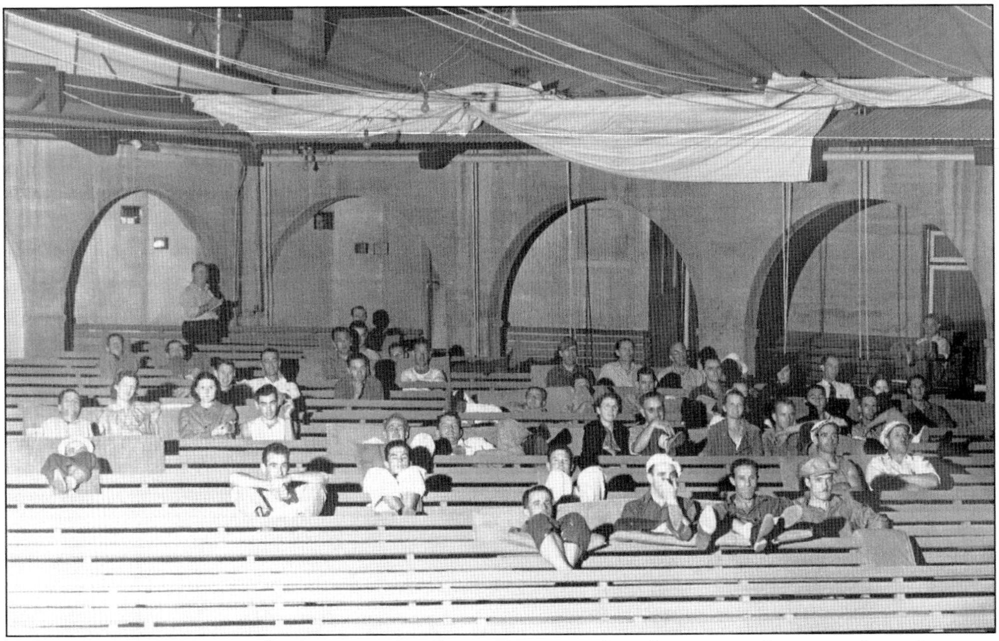

The center of Austin Hall was an open plaza. This served as the movie theater, where first-run movies were shown to both an evening crowd and at midnight for workers just going off shift (above). It was also the concert hall for the school band (below) and a place where local music and drama clubs could perform before an audience. For part of the day, it was just a pleasant place to relax with friends. It had a canvas cover, if needed, and pipes for plant steam beneath the seats so late-night movies in the winter could still be watched in relative comfort.

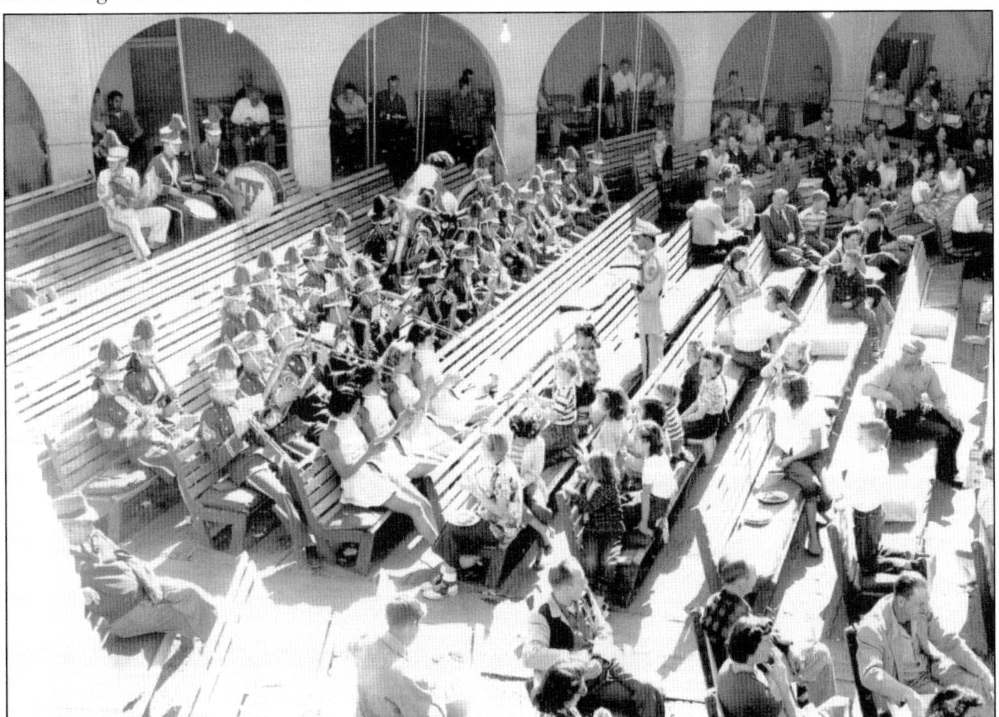

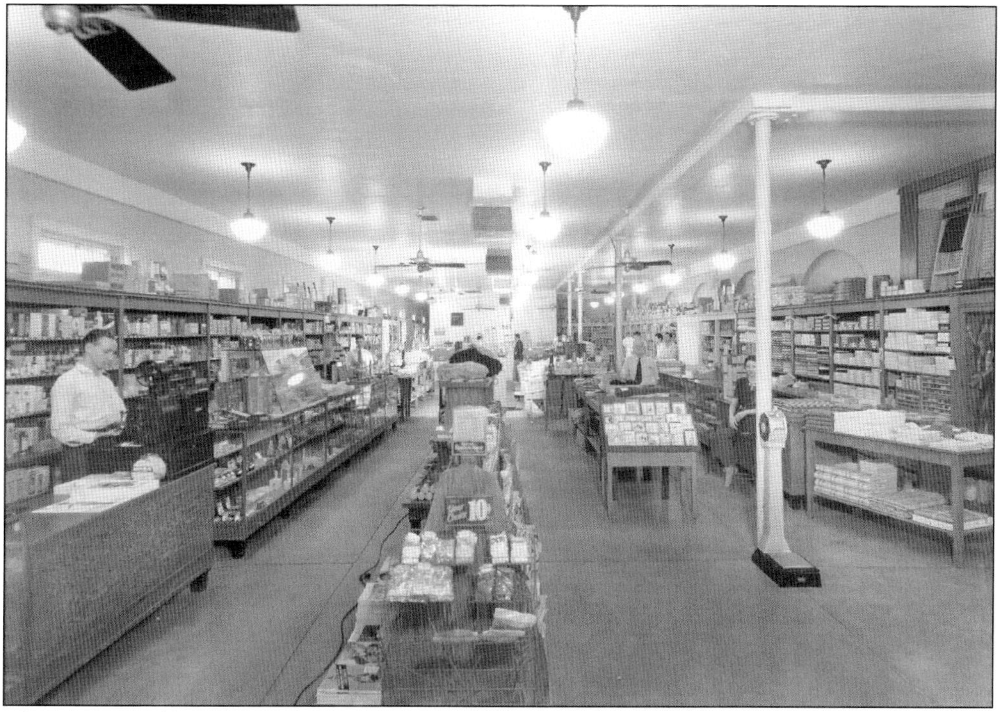

The Austin Hall Retail Store carried a very wide variety of dry goods, from bedding and sewing materials to watches, gift cards, clothes, and housewares.

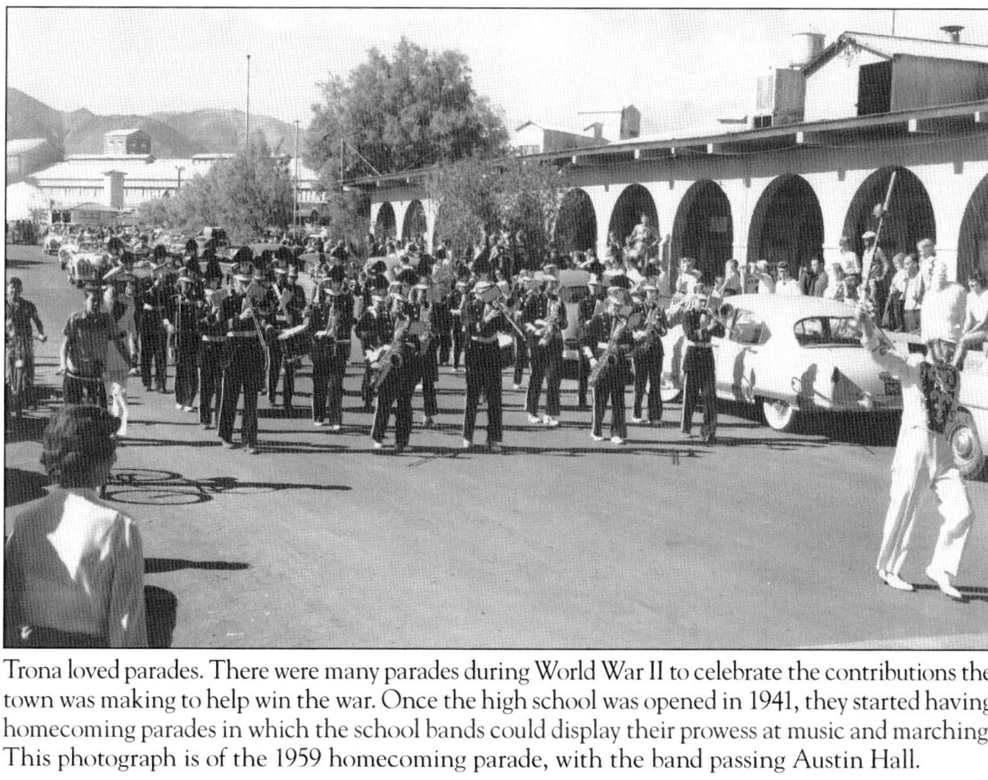

Trona loved parades. There were many parades during World War II to celebrate the contributions the town was making to help win the war. Once the high school was opened in 1941, they started having homecoming parades in which the school bands could display their prowess at music and marching. This photograph is of the 1959 homecoming parade, with the band passing Austin Hall.

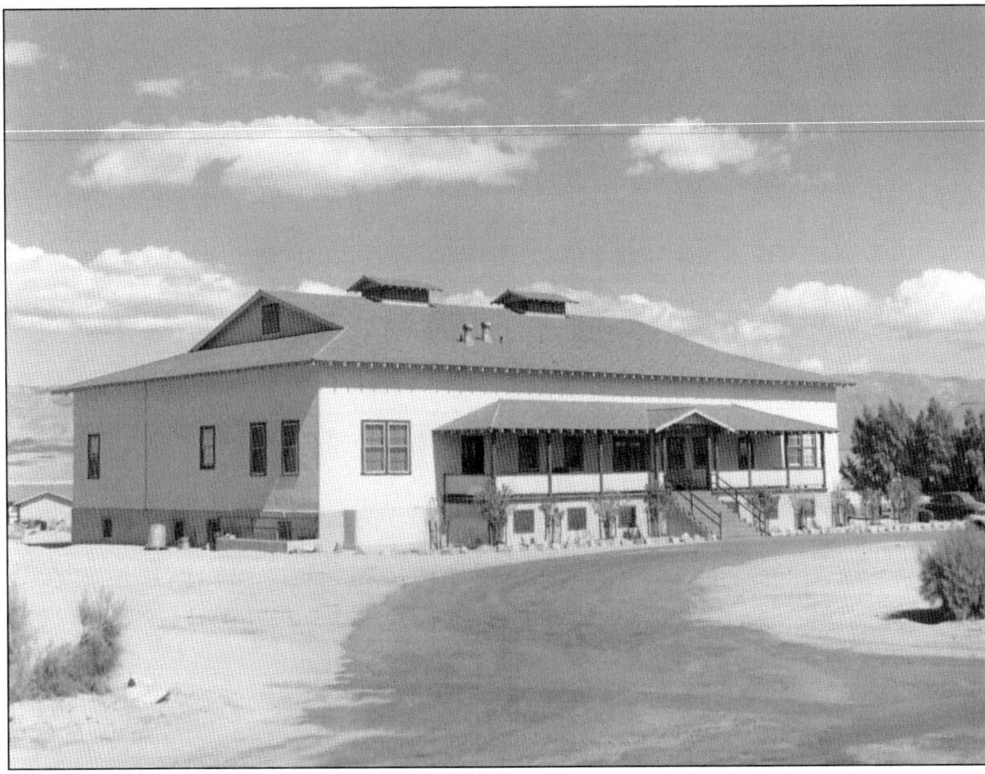

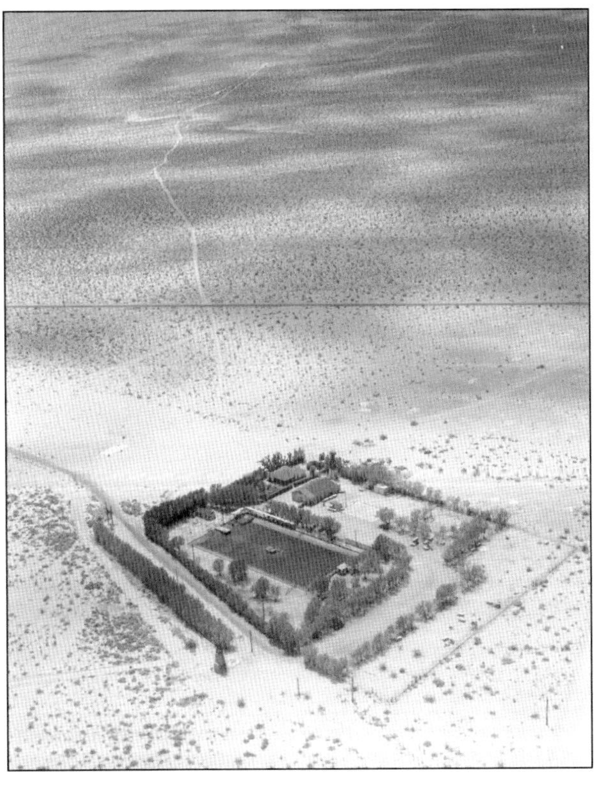

On July 16, 1937, AP&CC opened a recreation hall for employees. The main floor had a large ballroom dance floor, a stage with lighting and sound systems, a kitchen, and two lounges. The basement had a club room called Monte Carlo with a liquor bar and tables for gambling, a soft-drink fountain, pool tables, and even a four-lane bowling alley and combined archery and rifle range.

One of the most beloved places in Searles Valley was the Valley Wells Recreation Area. The highlight of the area was the large brackish-water reservoir that doubled as the second-largest swimming pool in California. The area eventually included tree-shaded picnic areas with tables and barbeques, a snack bar and recreation room, a concrete dance slab, shuffleboard, and lighted tennis courts.

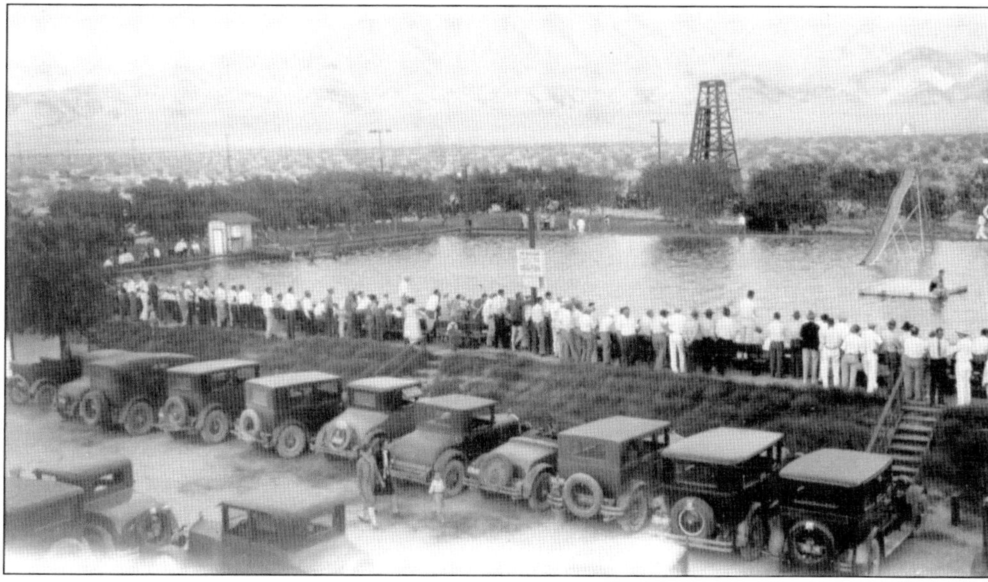

There were frequent company and community events held at Valley Wells, all centered on the pool, with many drawing large crowds of participants and spectators. During the summer, Valley Wells was used daily by many day-shift workers who would leave the plant and go directly to Valley Wells to cool down, swim and relax, and perhaps have dinner.

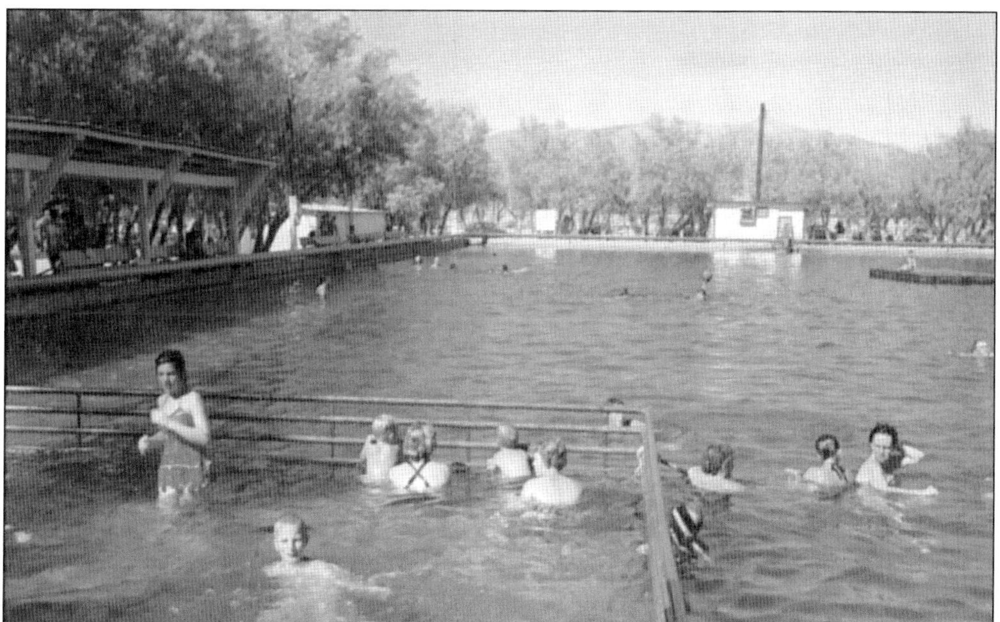

Every kid in Trona knew how to swim, much to the amazement of people living elsewhere. The school sponsored summer swimming lessons, and all the youngsters were more than eager to go to the pool for these classes. The classes were all taught by local volunteers. The pool also offered summer employment to many high school and college students as lifeguards.

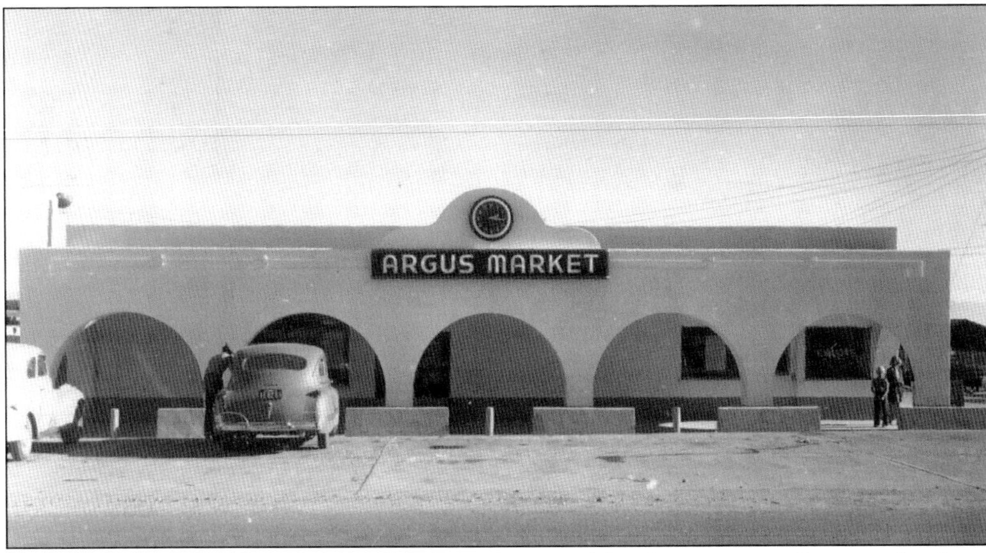

Trona had many grocery stores besides the one operated by the company. One was the Argus Market; the store shown in this photograph was built in 1942. The building adopted a façade similar to that of the company store in Austin Hall. It was owned by Henry "Hank" Heseman, who started the business in 1937 with a small produce stand.

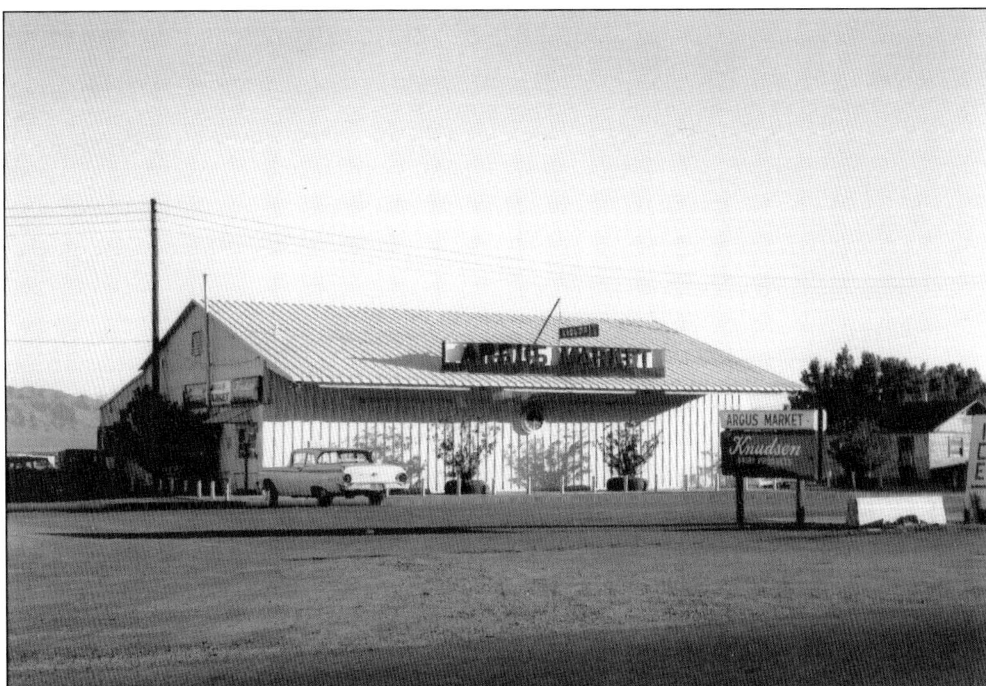

The original Argus Market building was replaced in 1953 with a new steel building on Trona Road, still in Argus. It was larger than the original Argus Market and was noted for its always-fresh produce and fine meats.

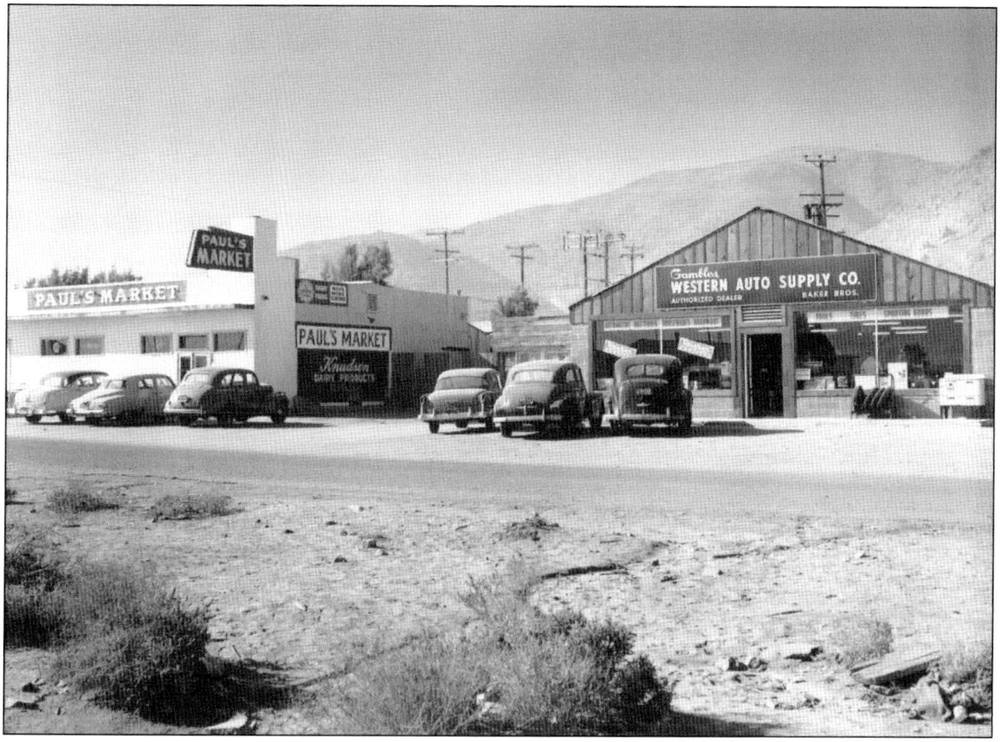

For a time, there was also a competing market in Argus, Paul's Market. It was on Third Street next to Gambles Western Auto Supply Co. store. Western Auto carried automobile parts as well as bicycles and camping gear. It also housed the Argus Post Office.

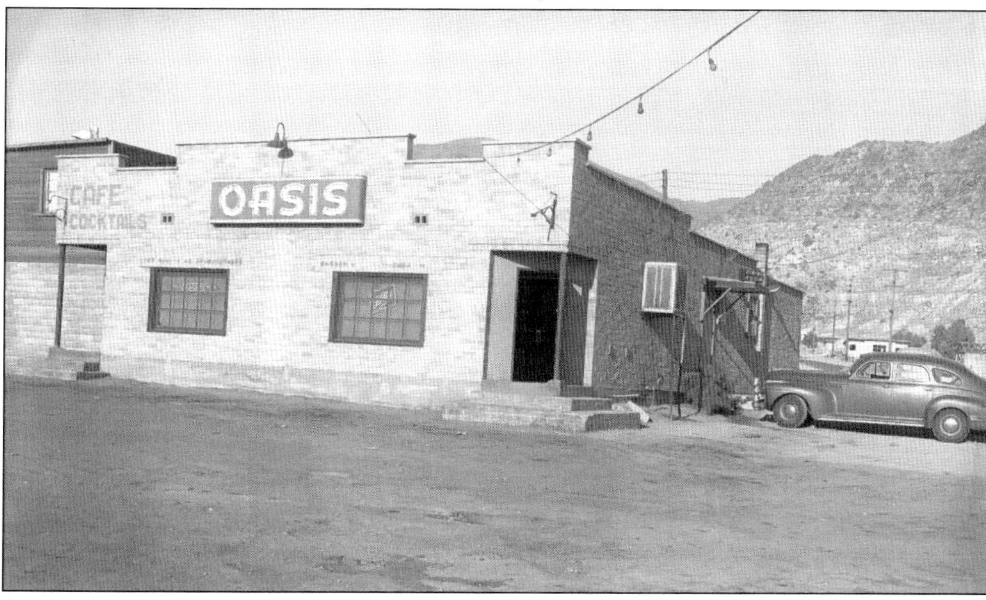

An oasis in the desert is a welcome sight. So it was for the residents in Searles Valley. Only in this case, the Oasis was a restaurant with a full-service bar located on Trona Road in Argus. One of their specialties was fine steaks. In the rear, they even had a banquet room to accommodate dinner meetings for larger groups.

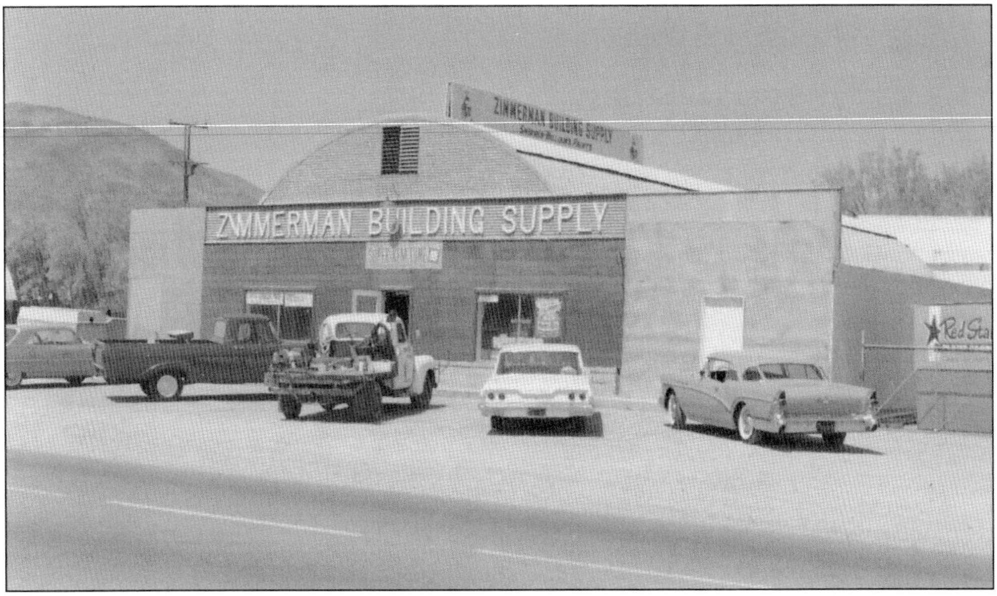

Zimmerman Building Supply carried a complete line of materials needed for either home construction or repair. It included items such as hardware, lumber, paint, tools, pipe, water heaters, furnaces, and coolers and even had fertilizer for gardens. Actually, they could provide nearly anything that was needed for the house.

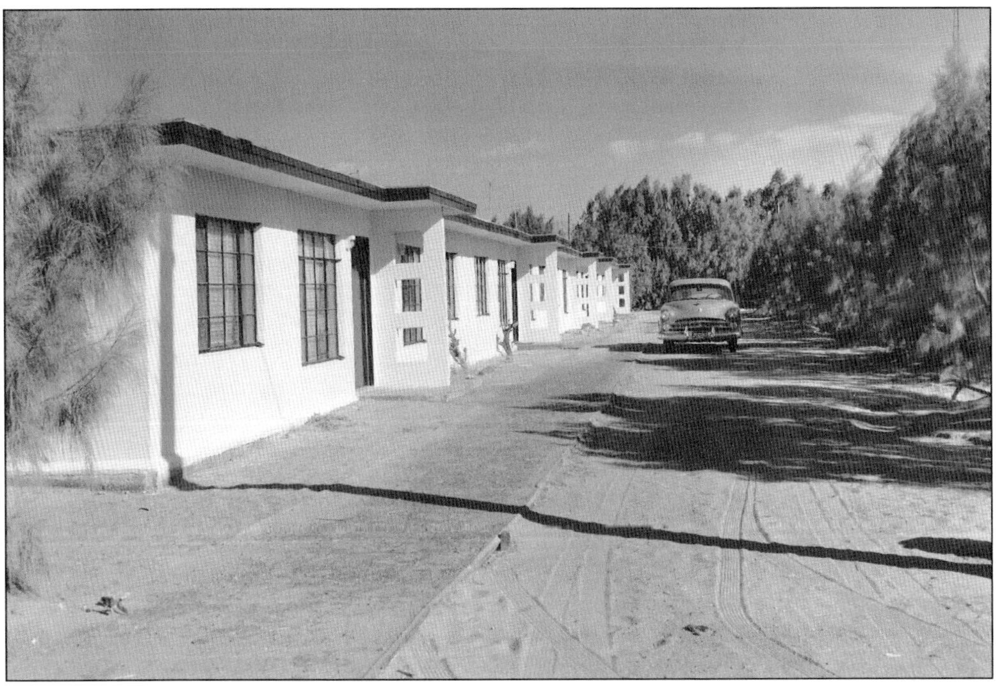

The end of World War II saw development of two apartment complexes by the company: the Fairway Apartments, named for their proximity to the Trona Golf Course, and the Wildrose Apartments, at the west end of Wildrose Street. These were all-concrete structures—walls, floor, and roof—although the Wildrose Apartments were built with pumice aggregate to allow nails to readily penetrate the walls.

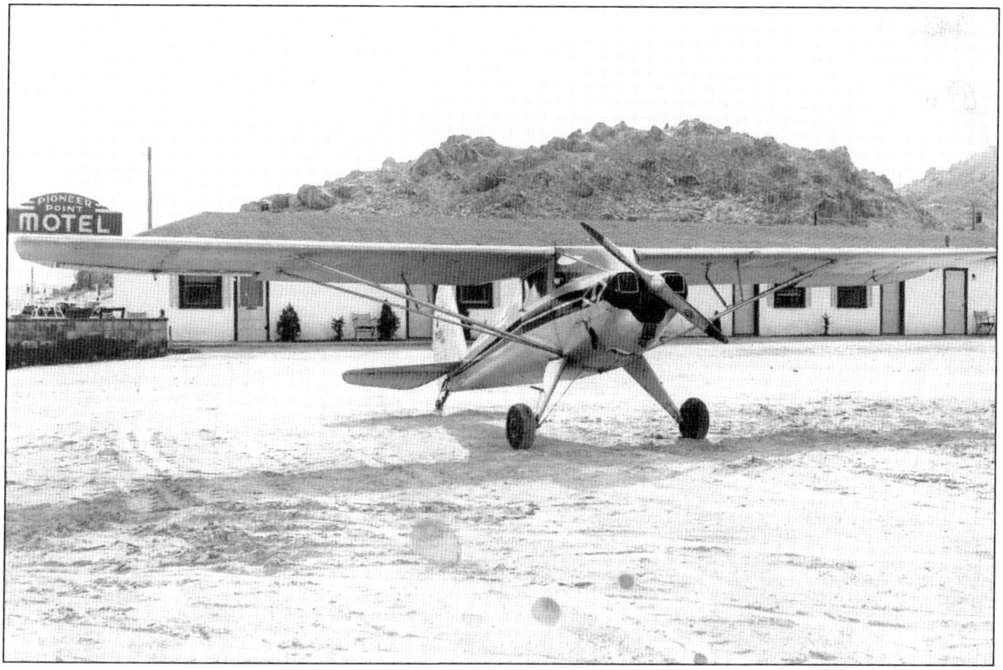

At one time, Searles Valley had two motels, Gabe's Argus Motel and the Pioneer Point Motel, shown in this 1948 photograph. Both offered basic accommodations in small rooms. However, the Pioneer Point Motel did have a small restaurant as part of its business.

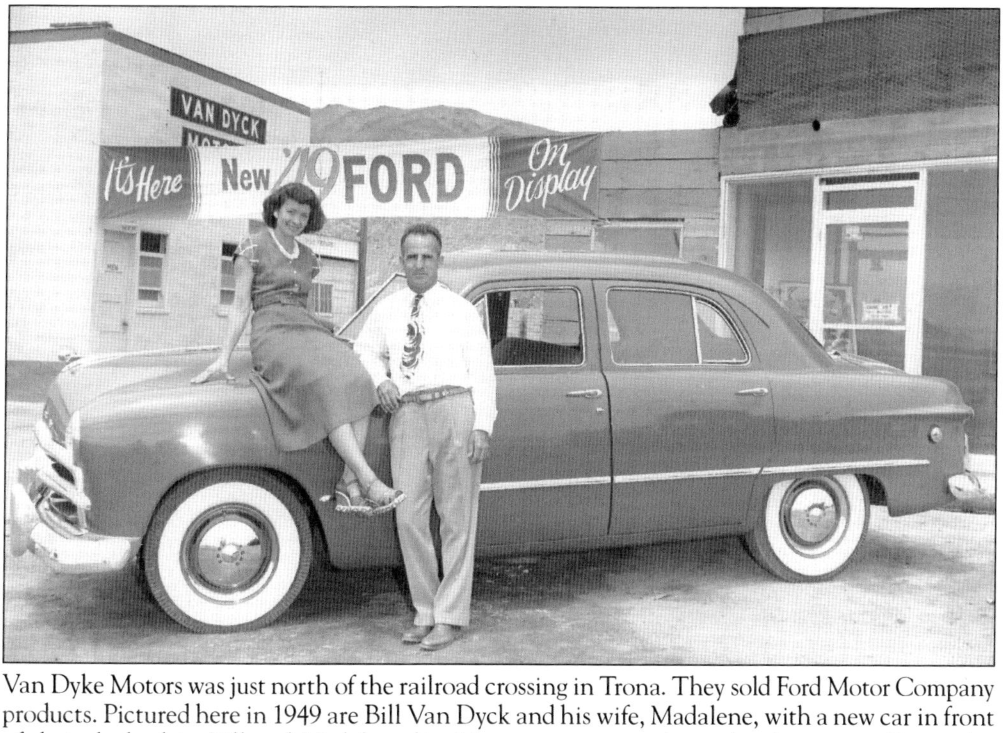

Van Dyke Motors was just north of the railroad crossing in Trona. They sold Ford Motor Company products. Pictured here in 1949 are Bill Van Dyck and his wife, Madalene, with a new car in front of their dealership. Bill and Madalene lived in an apartment above the showroom. Trona also had a Studebaker dealer, located in Pioneer Point.

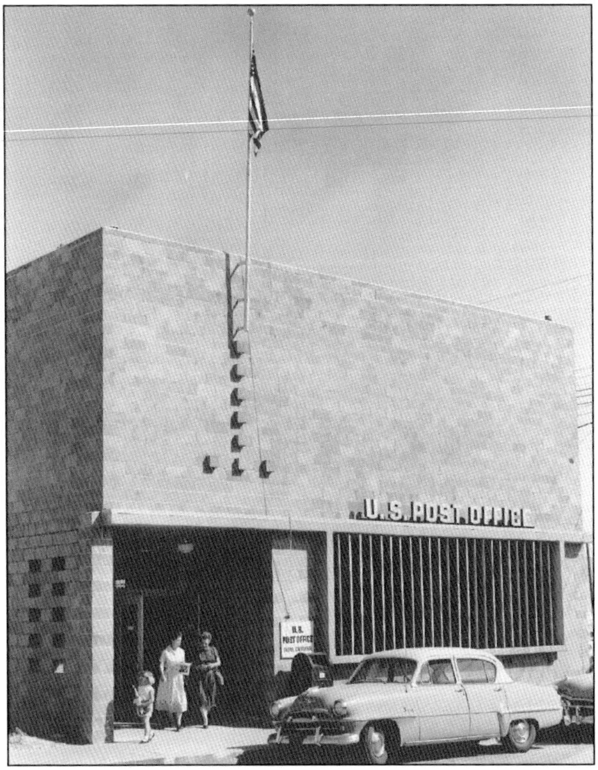

When the company decided to close Austin Hall in 1954, its occupants began seeking other quarters. When the Trona Masonic Lodge built a two-story building in 1955, the US Postal Service leased the ground floor for the Trona Post Office. This was before home delivery, so everyone checked their post-office box daily for mail. The last Austin Hall occupant, the pool hall, left in December 1961.

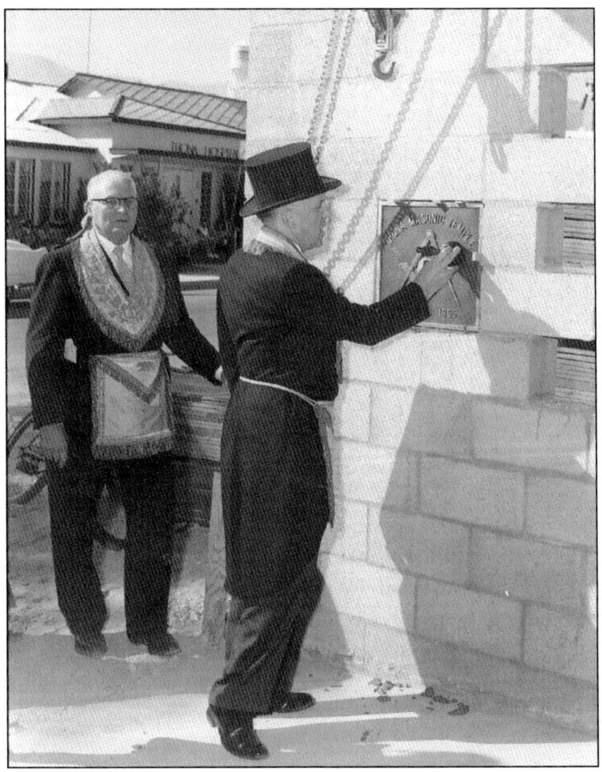

The Masonic lodge used the upper floor for its meetings and meetings of affiliated clubs Eastern Star, Job's Daughters, and DeMolay. The lodge dedicated its new building by placing a plaque at the foot of the steps leading up to the meeting hall.

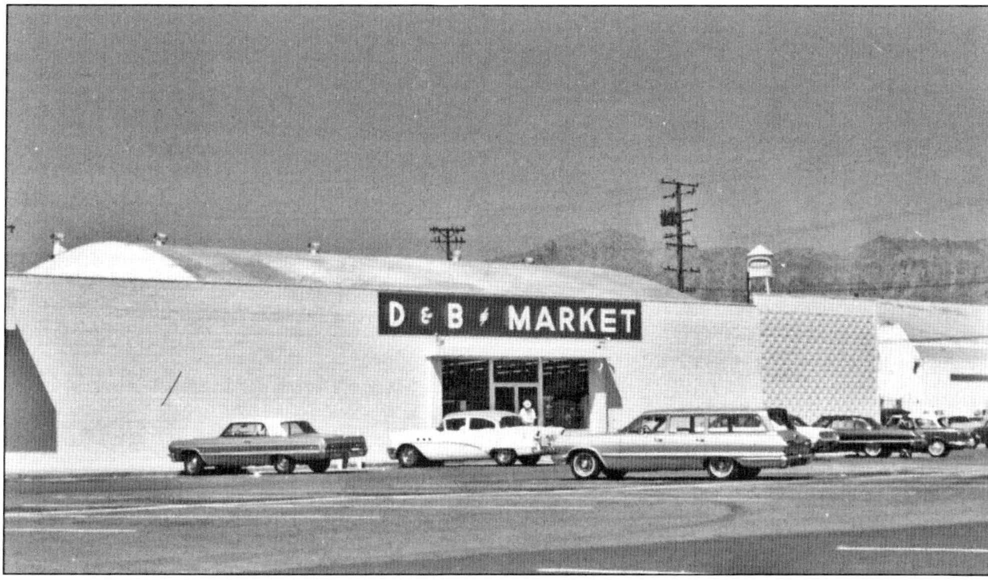

With the grocery in Austin Hall closing, a large new building was constructed, and this became Trona's first supermarket in September 1958 when the D&B Market opened. Dean Fairbank and Bertha Pope operated the market. It was a complete supermarket that included fresh produce and dairy products, all necessary dry staples, a well-stocked frozen-food section, and a butcher shop and fresh meat counter. The opening of D&B Department Store in May 1962 completed the Trona Shopping Center. Merchandise included home goods such as clothing, bedding, kitchen utensils, gift cards, and hardware. This section also housed Maury's Shoes.

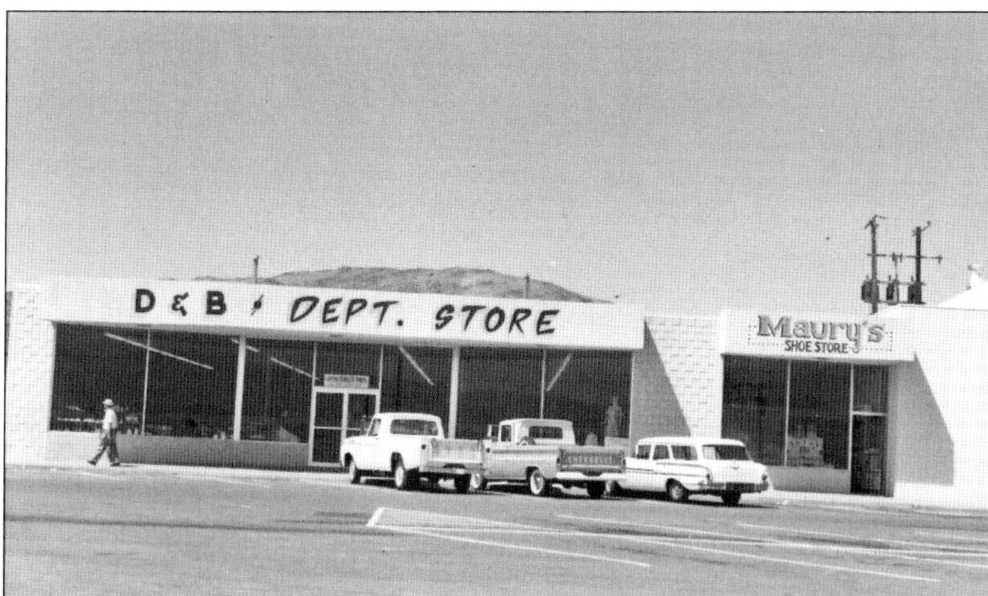

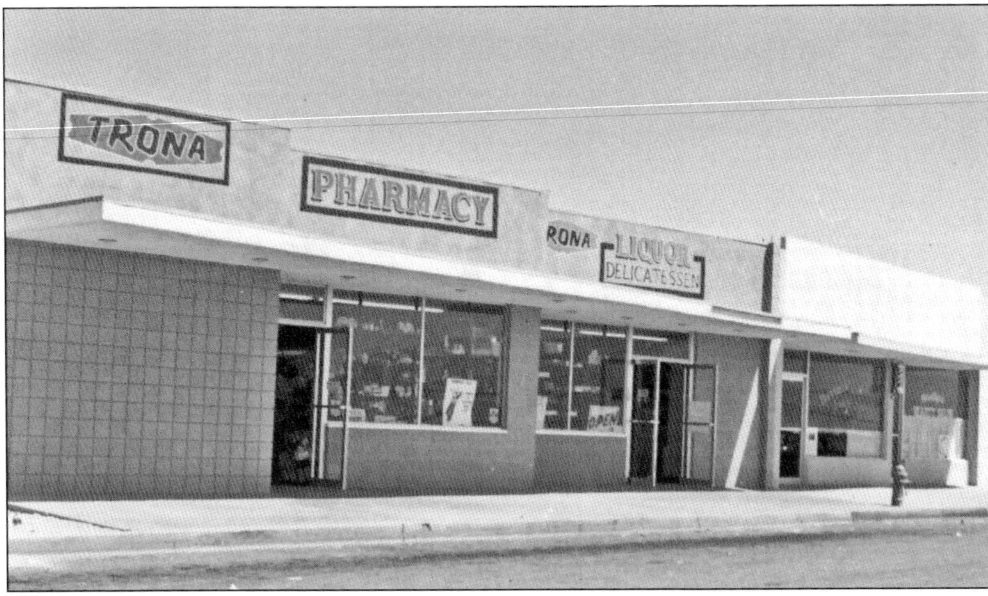

Around the corner from the department store and fronting on Trona Road were, from left to right, the Trona Pharmacy, Trona Liquor and Delicatessen, Virgil Trotter's Barber Shop, and Dorothy's Beauty Salon.

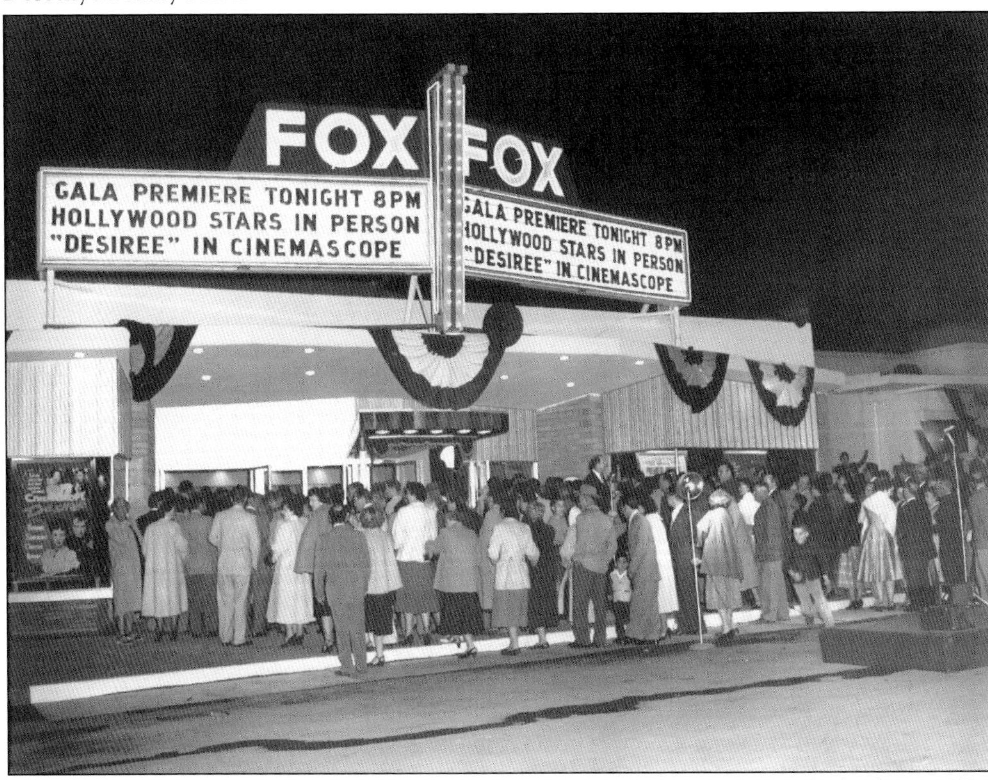

On November 18, 1954, the Fox Theater in Trona held a gala premiere with the house filled to capacity. Hollywood stars on hand included Edmond O'Brien, Rita Moreno, and Broderick Crawford. The new theater was across the street southeast of Austin Hall.

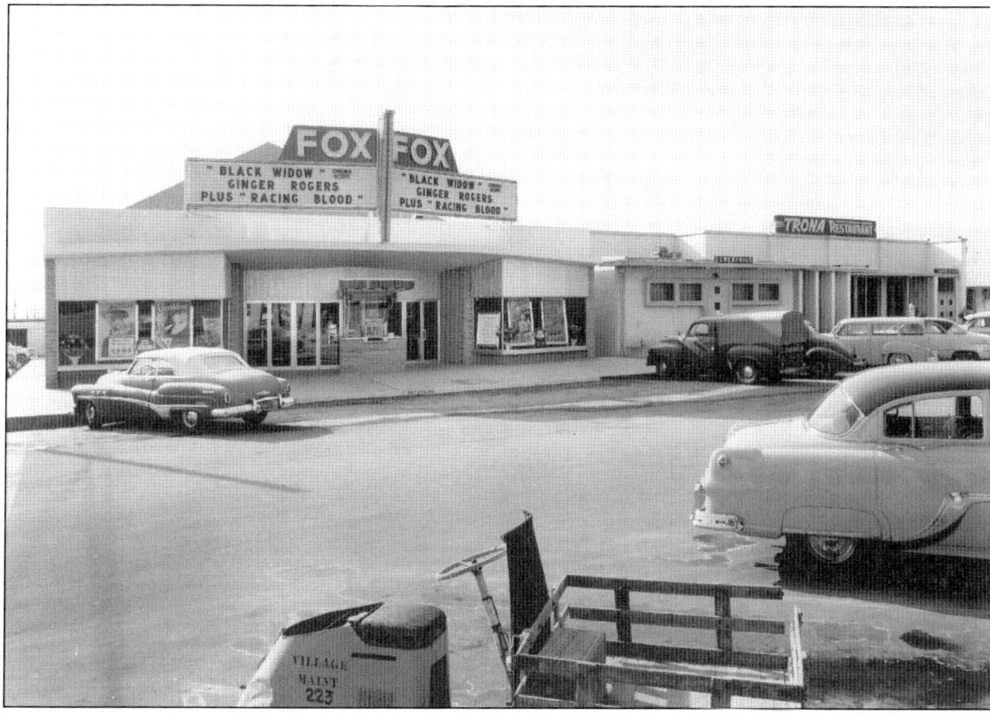

To the west of the new theater was the Sidewinder saloon, a favorite watering hole in Trona. West of the Sidewinder was the new Trona Restaurant. It was owned by George Lee and known widely for its outstanding Chinese cuisine.

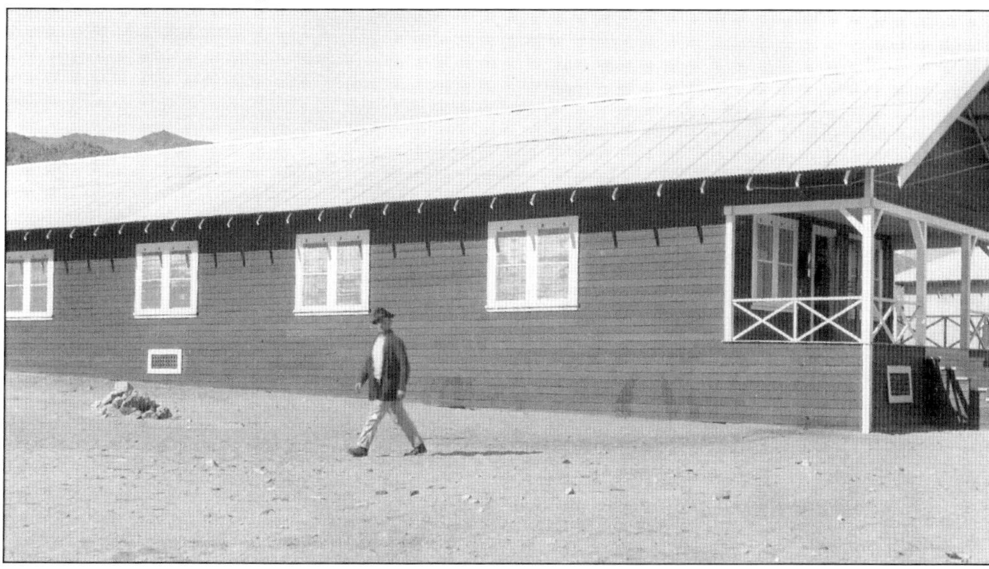

Partially because of its isolation, the people in Searles Valley entertained themselves away from work by forming a wide variety of clubs. One of the first was a social club, actually a secret society for men only, known as the Amalgamated Order of Billy Goats. Its purpose was to stir up desirable social activities among the men of Trona. One activity was an annual ball held at Billy Goat Hall in Borosolvay, beginning in 1928. The dress code for men was tuxedos, and women wore formals.

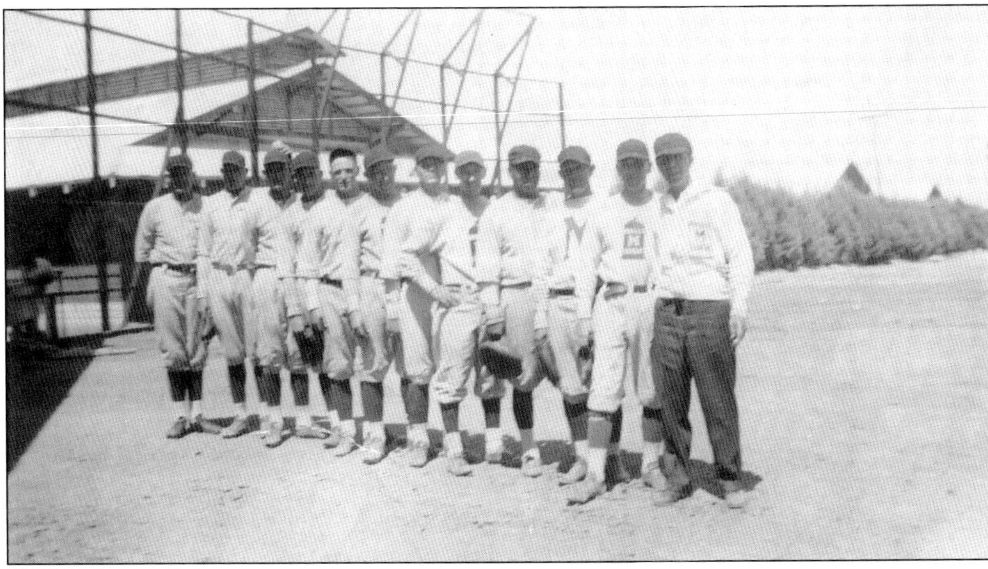

As early as 1918 and continuing into the 1940s, anyone who was a good baseball player could have a job working for American Potash if they agreed to also play on the company's Trona Tigers baseball team. They played teams from all over the desert area and consistently won most of their games. Pictured here are the 1920s Tigers and their ball field.

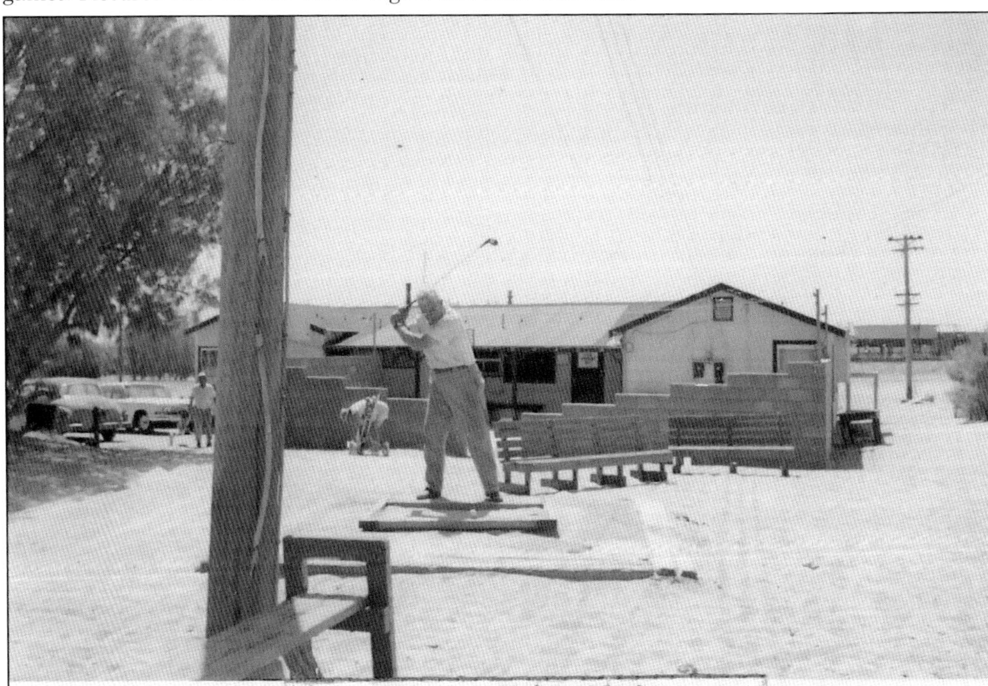

In 1926, the Trona Golf Club built a 5,500-yard 18-hole golf course. Because water was scarce, the course had no grass, and players followed Trona rules. These allowed every fairway shot to be teed; in the rough, one played the lie. Greens were oiled sand, and players raked them smooth before putting. Today, the golf course is at Valley Wells and has grass greens, although fairways are still sand with Trona rules.

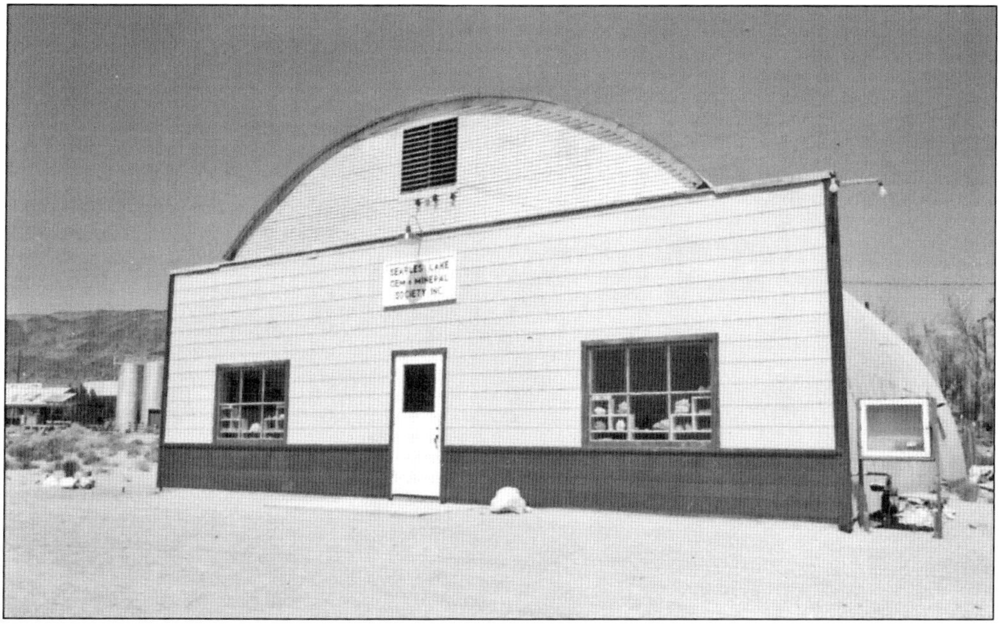

Another club, the Searles Lake Gem and Mineral Society, was a natural for Searles Valley because no vegetation hid the beautiful rocks. It was formed in 1941 by Ann Pipkin and continues today. One activity today is hosting the popular annual Gem-O-Rama gem show. Of course these are just three of the clubs and organizations in Trona; there were still 20 other clubs in 1975.

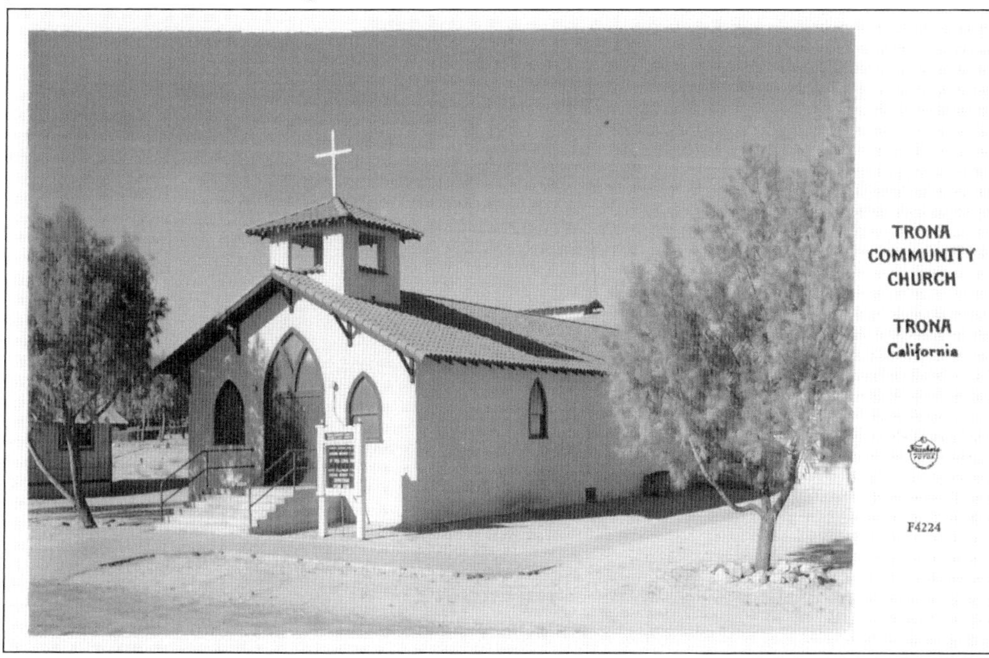

Initially, Searles Valley was home to few families but many single men here just to work. One consequence was several liquor establishments but no churches. As the company built employee housing, the men brought their families, and a need for churches arose. Today there are no public bars but eight active churches. The first congregation to meet was Methodist, starting in 1922 in the schoolhouse. They moved into their own building on September 24, 1939.

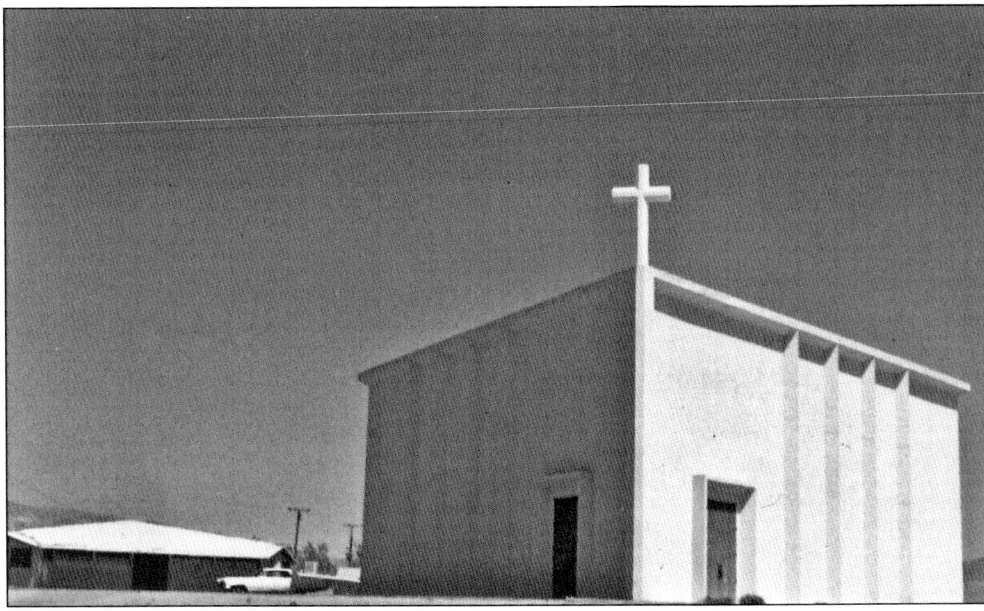

The Catholic congregation first met in homes in 1924, moved into Bunk House 8 for a period, and finally in 1958 moved into its architectural masterpiece, the large triangular building shown here. The building was designed by the local priest. Its three sides denote the Father, Son, and Holy Spirit.

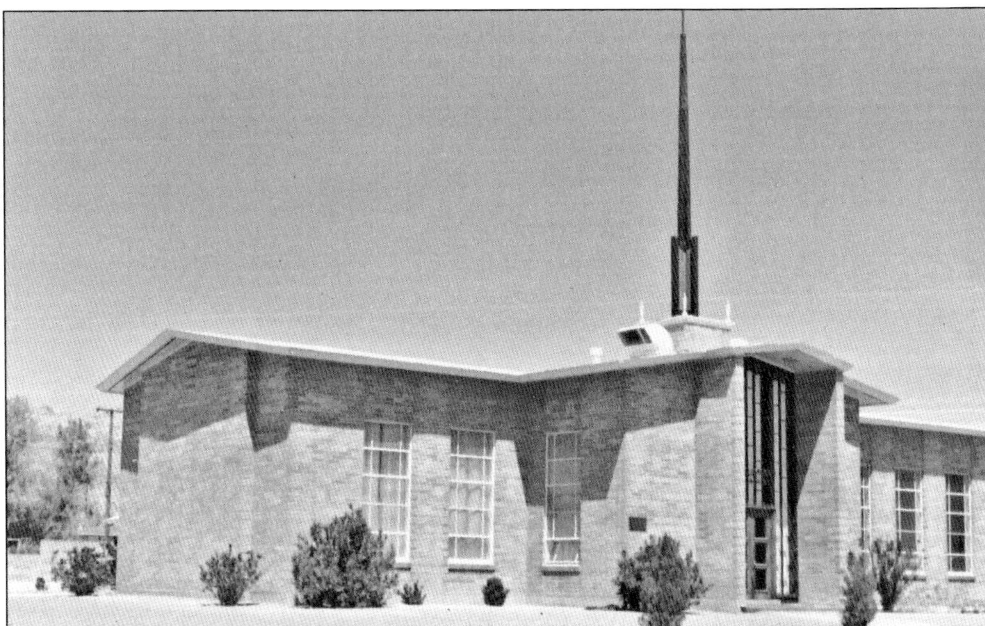

The Mormon congregation first organized in October 1940. As membership grew, they moved first into Billy Goat Hall at Borosolvay and then into the Trona Recreation Center. On November 27, 1960, they dedicated their new chapel, shown here.

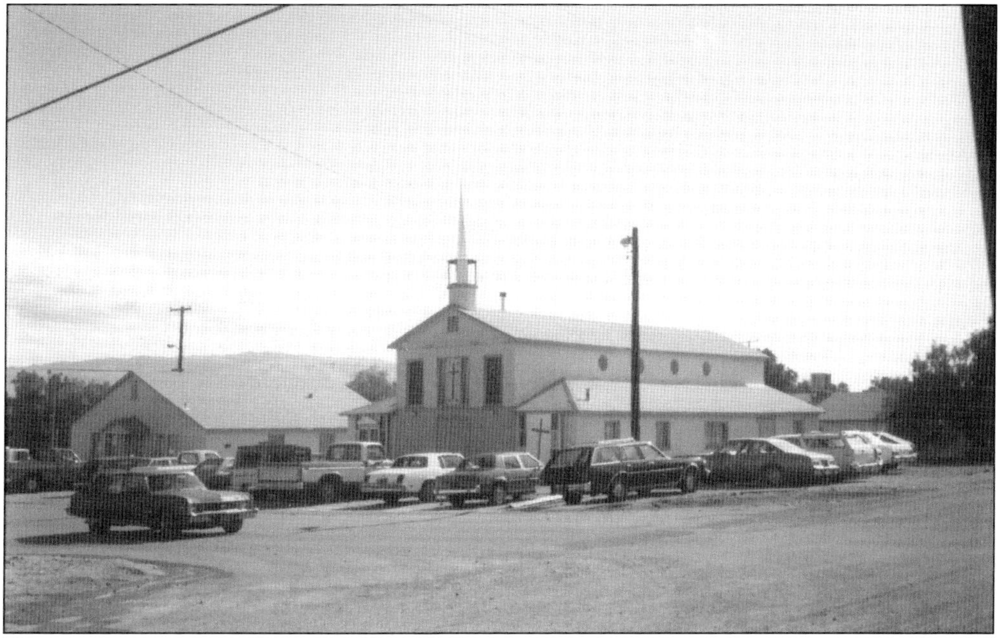

The congregation of the Four Square Church first met in early 1941 in a corrugated-metal garage. Construction of the present church began in 1947 using buildings from the World War II internment camp at Manzanar. The building was dedicated on October 27, 1949.

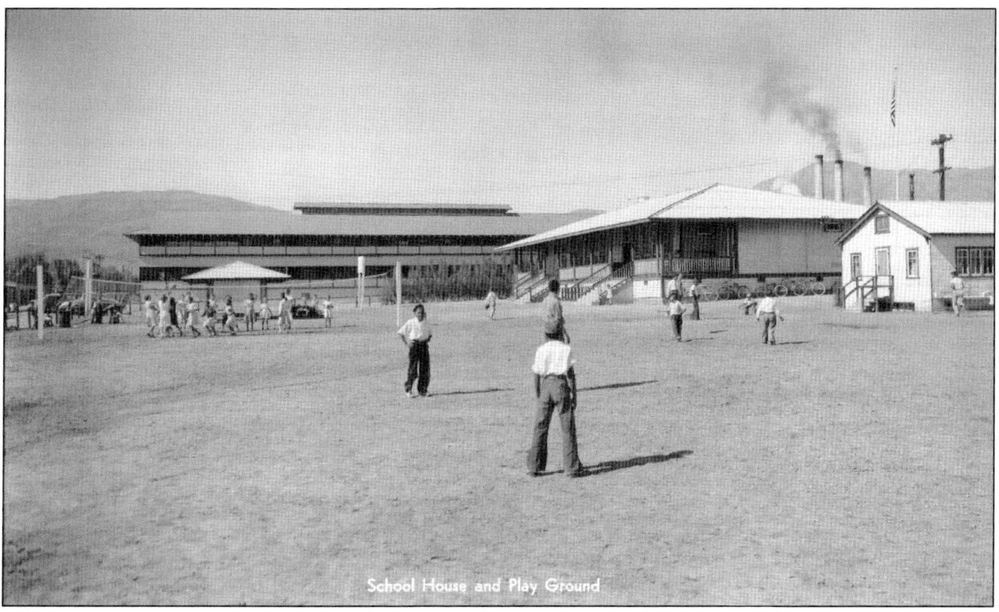

In 1918, American Trona Corporation built a new schoolhouse, again with just one room but with folding partitions in the center. It had wide porches, later enclosed as more space became necessary. The school served grades one through eight. The large field behind the building served as their playground. This building still stands and is just west of the building now owned by the Searles Lake Gem and Mineral Society.

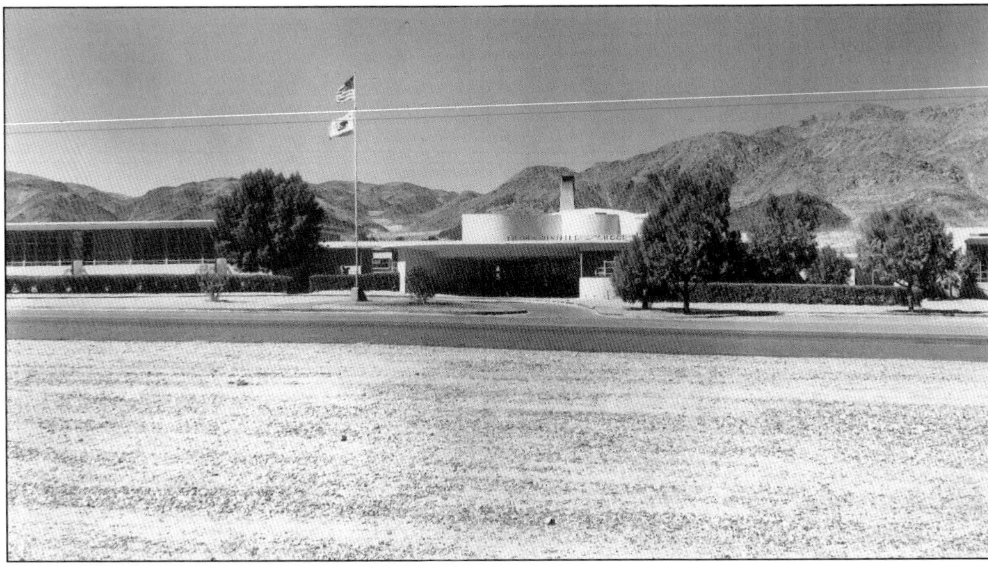

In 1939, the school added grades 9 and 10, using an AP&CC house on Magnolia Street for classrooms. Then, in September 1941, the school moved onto its new campus, which allowed it to include grades 1 through 12. Over the following years, a full-size gymnasium was added in 1951 and the Round School to the west that now contains the elementary school, in 1978.

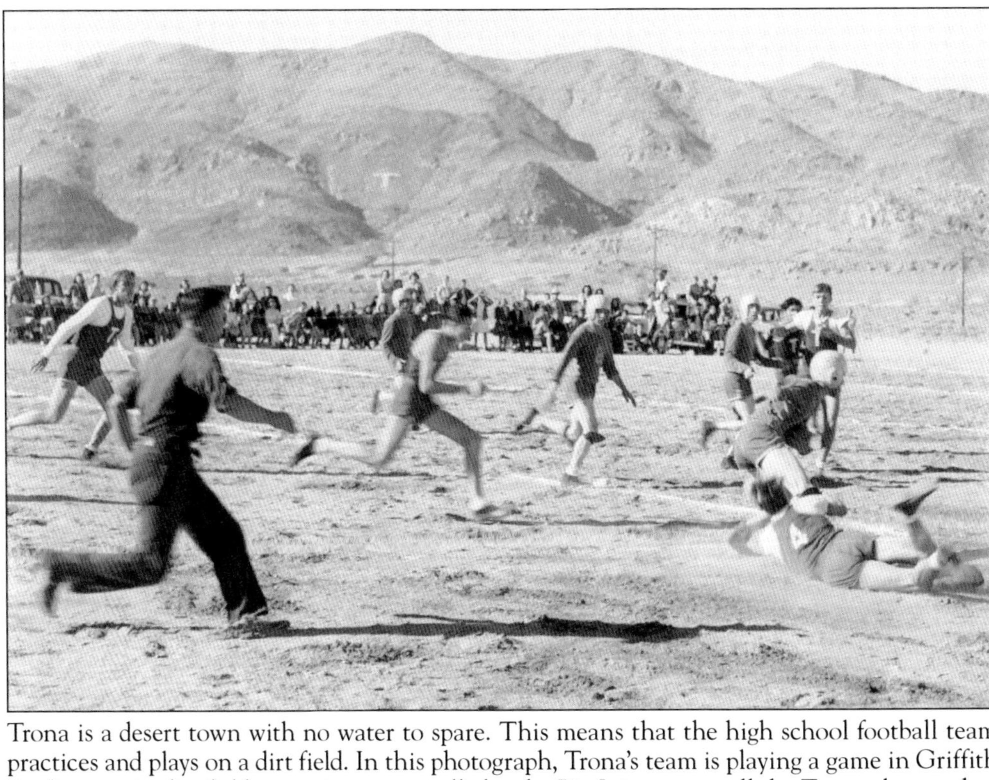

Trona is a desert town with no water to spare. This means that the high school football team practices and plays on a dirt field. In this photograph, Trona's team is playing a game in Griffith Stadium on its dirt field; opposing teams called it the Pit. It is easy to tell the Trona players; they are the ones without helmets. In those days, neither team wore padding or even long pants. The Trona T can be seen on the hills in the distance.

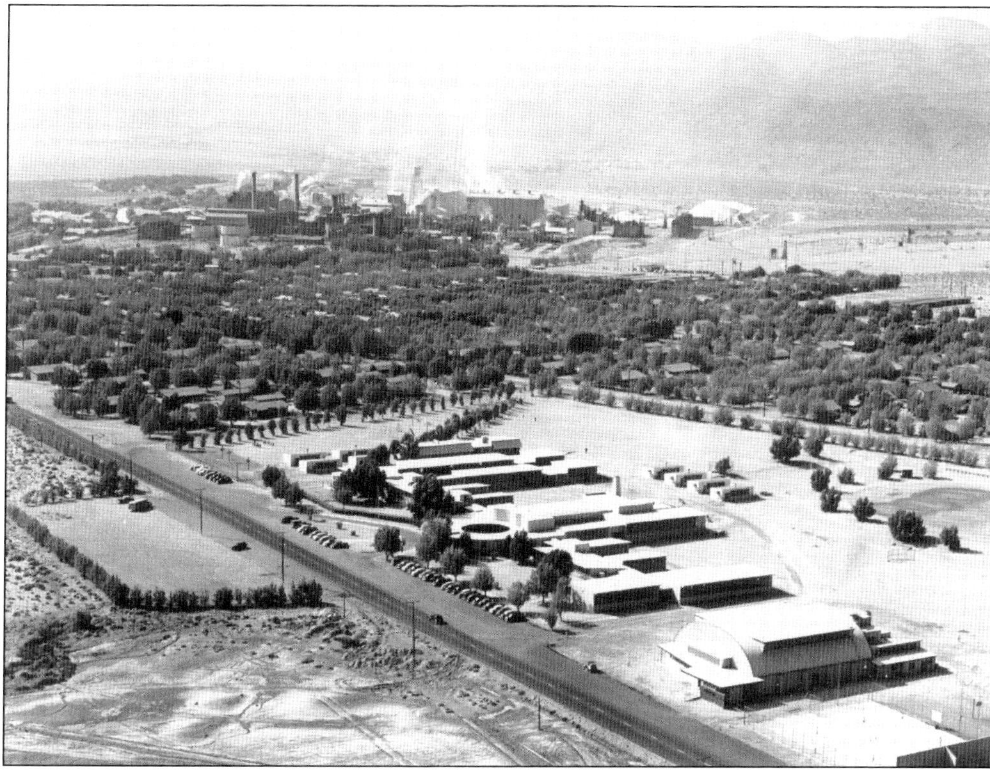

This 1950 aerial photograph provides a good view of the school, with the town and plant of American Potash behind. The elementary school was in the farther building, the gymnasium is the high rounded building in the foreground, and the high school is at center. The auditorium is located to the right of the round building at center left.

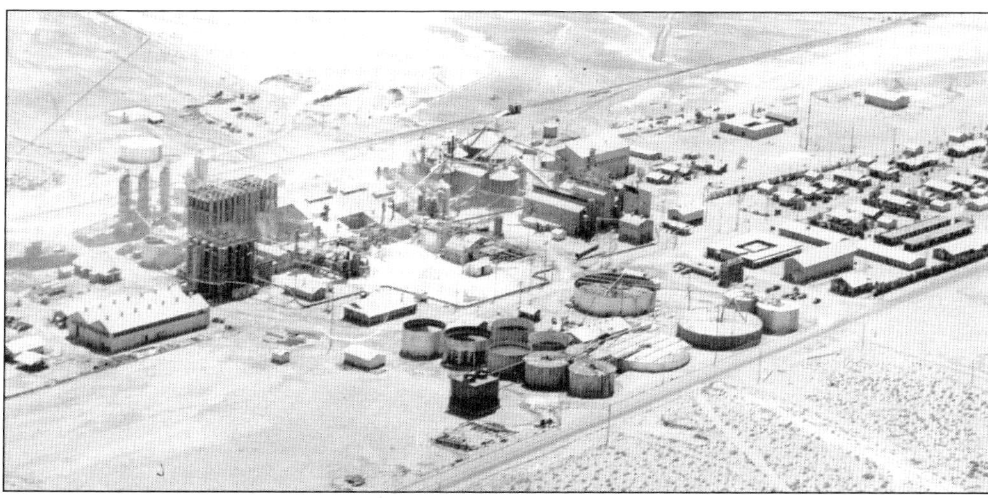

Although Trona was the largest community in Searles Valley, there were other smaller communities as well. At the plant of the West End Chemical Company, the employees lived in housing similar to that in Trona.

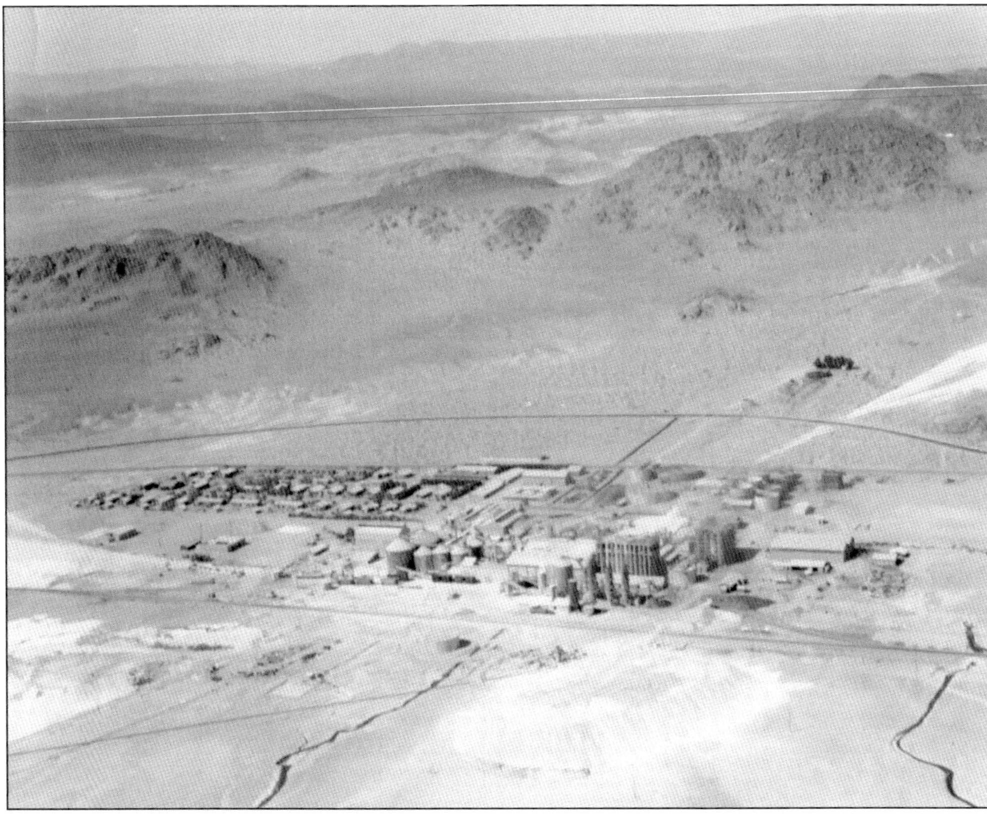

This 1940s photograph shows that the Westend community was composed of several dozen homes. Those who lived at Westend had to be an employee of the chemical plant.

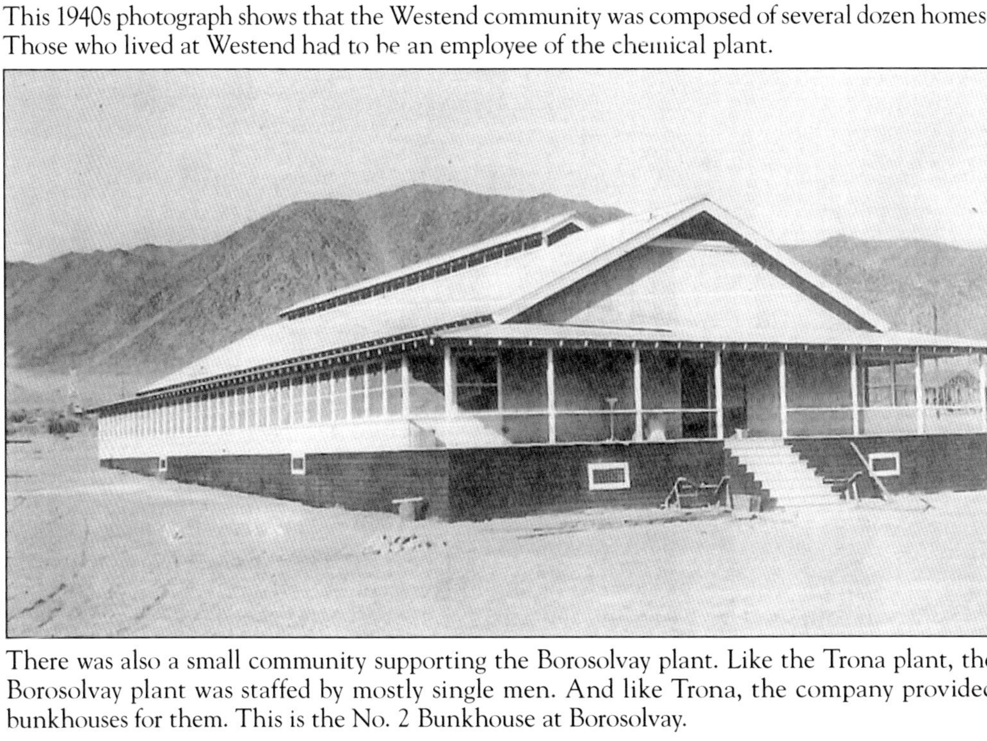

There was also a small community supporting the Borosolvay plant. Like the Trona plant, the Borosolvay plant was staffed by mostly single men. And like Trona, the company provided bunkhouses for them. This is the No. 2 Bunkhouse at Borosolvay.

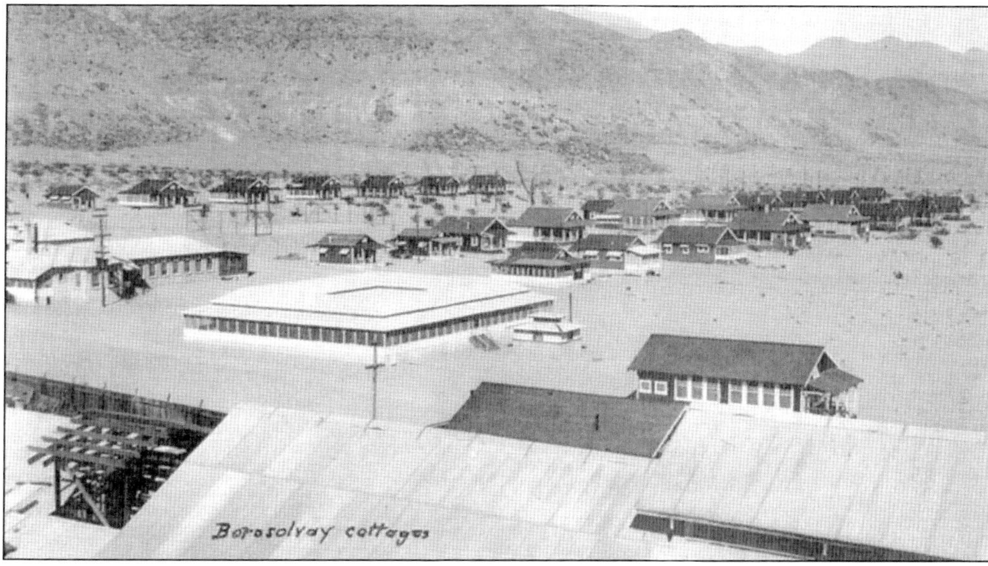

Even after the Borosolvay plant closed permanently on February 1, 1921, people continued to live in the Borosolvay housing. Many of these were married men with families who were unable to find suitable housing closer to their work at Trona or Westend. Borosolvay is pictured here during this period in the 1920s.

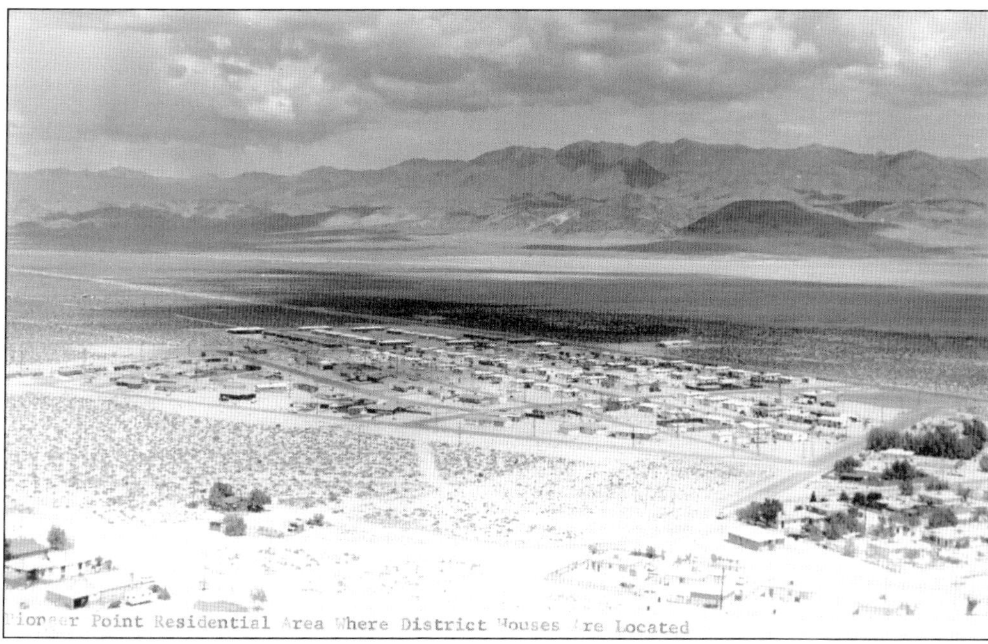

The largest housing area in Searles Valley today was originally called Point of Rocks, but today it is known as Pioneer Point, or simply the Point. This area is almost exclusively housing, with only two businesses and one church. Development of the Point began with individual ownership, but later, the Searles Valley Development Company, a subsidiary of American Potash, built houses to meet the demand it expected.

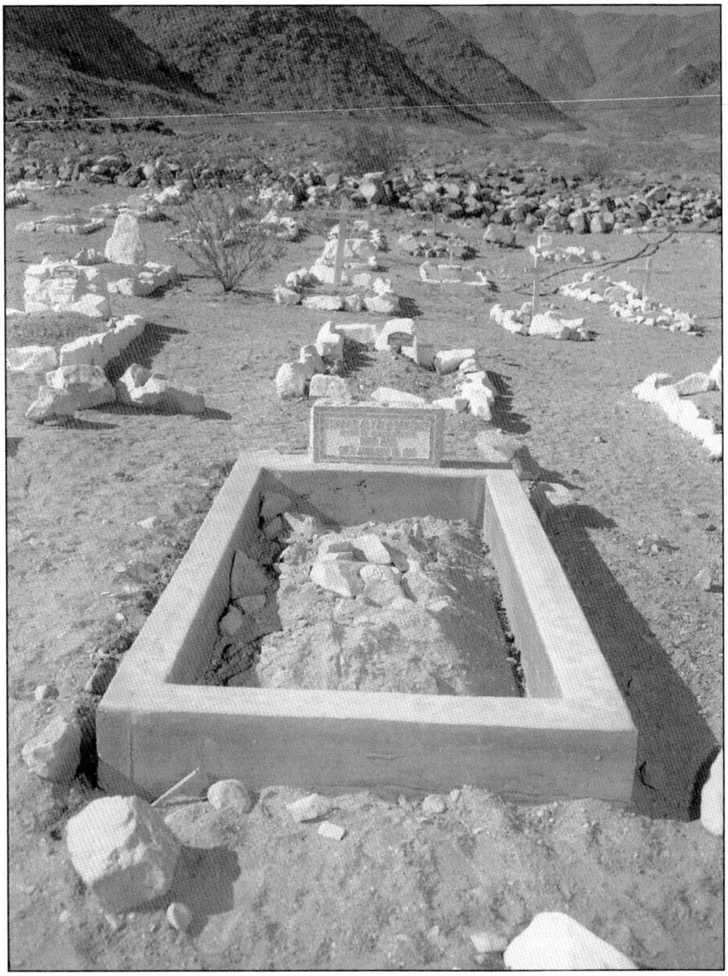

Searles Valley has two cemeteries. The oldest, pictured here, was on the south side of Argus. There are several noteworthy people buried here, among them Chris Wicht, "the most beloved saloon keeper in Ballarat."

The Rocket Research Institute was founded in 1943 to promote the study of rockets. Rockets carrying commemorative mail were fired from Inyo County north of Searles Lake, across the San Bernardino County line into the lake, from the late 1940s to the mid-1950s.

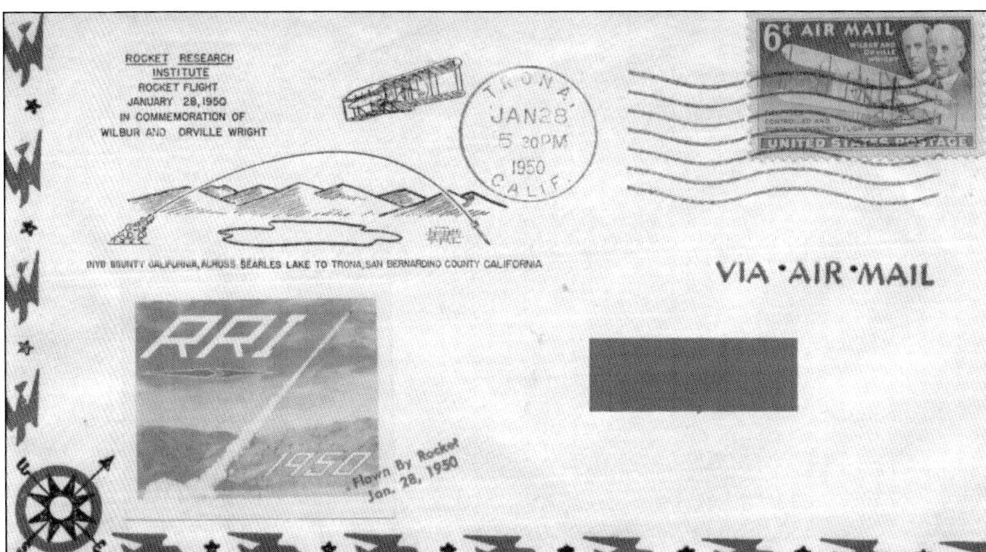

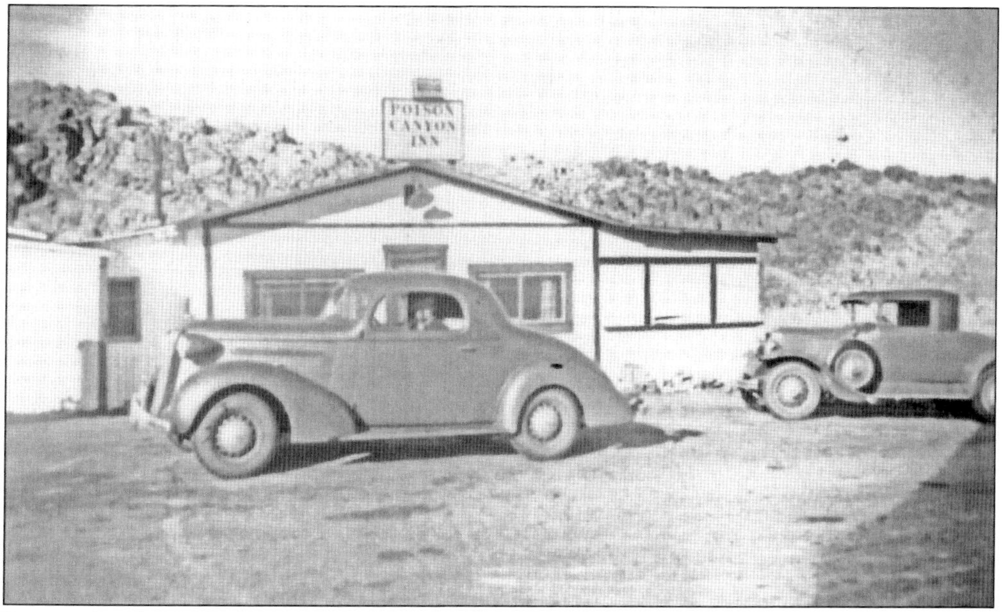

Because Searles Valley was remote, it received only sporadic enforcement of anti-liquor laws during Prohibition. Although the chemical companies could not sell alcohol, several bootleggers set up establishments to serve the considerable local demand. One establishment was the Poison Canyon Inn, located halfway through the canyon. Although the Poison Canyon Inn served food, the main attraction was beer brewed on site by the owner, Pat Patterson. His brother Tom Patterson operated another bar and gambling house known as Patterson's Place at a patented millsite north of Trona, next to the Nadeau Road (below). Sleeping quarters provided a place for travelers and gamblers such as Wyatt Earp. Later, the site became Poeville, named for Cecil Poe. Finally, Ezra King purchased the site, and it became known as the Lazy "K" Ranch.

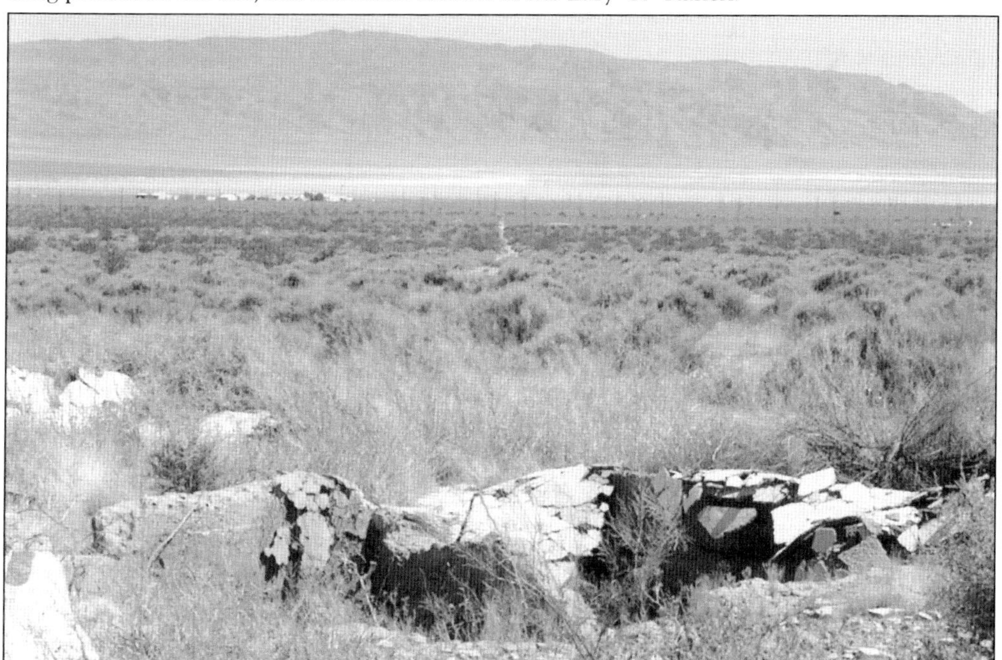

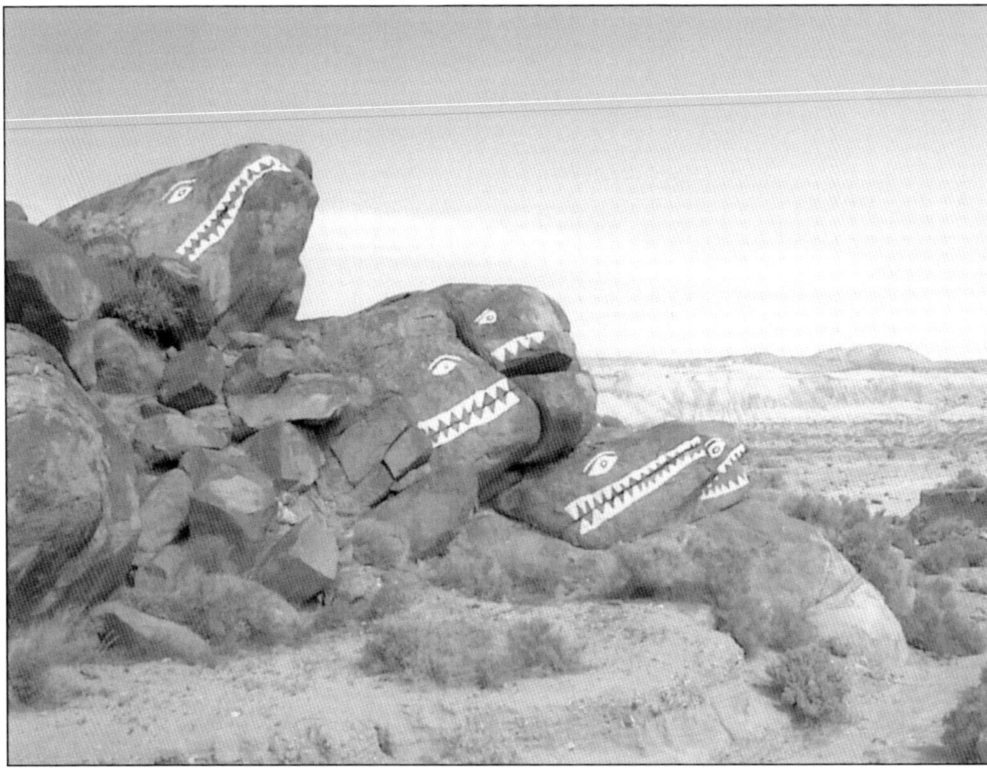

The road to Searles Valley passes through Poison Canyon. At the canyon's eastern end, the road passes Fish Head Rocks, first called the Whale Heads. This unusual formation was first painted in 1934 by Joe Fox and continues to be renewed when sun and wind causes the paint to flake off.

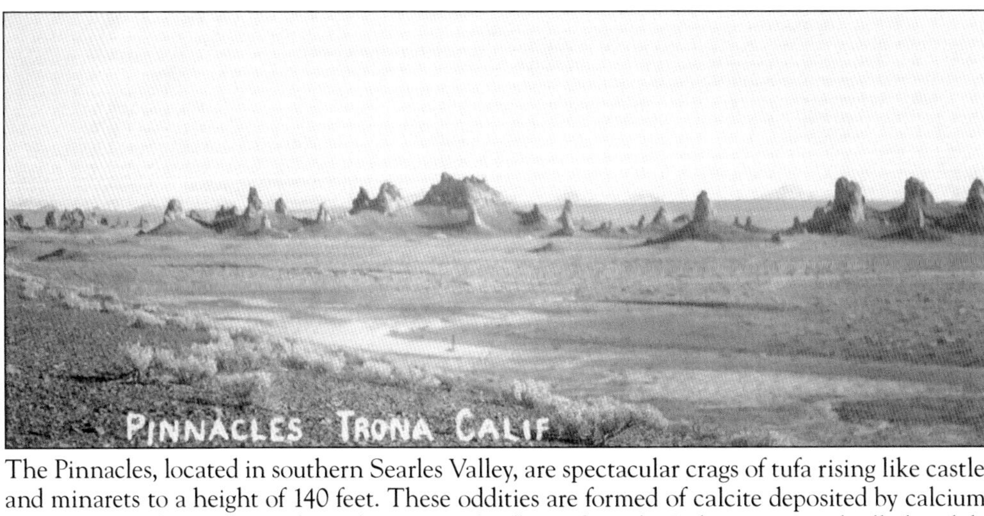

The Pinnacles, located in southern Searles Valley, are spectacular crags of tufa rising like castles and minarets to a height of 140 feet. These oddities are formed of calcite deposited by calcium-bearing groundwater rising through seeps in the floor of Searles Lake to mix with alkaline lake water. It is now a National Natural Landmark. For more than 50 years, the Pinnacles have been a favorite location for movie productions and television commercials.

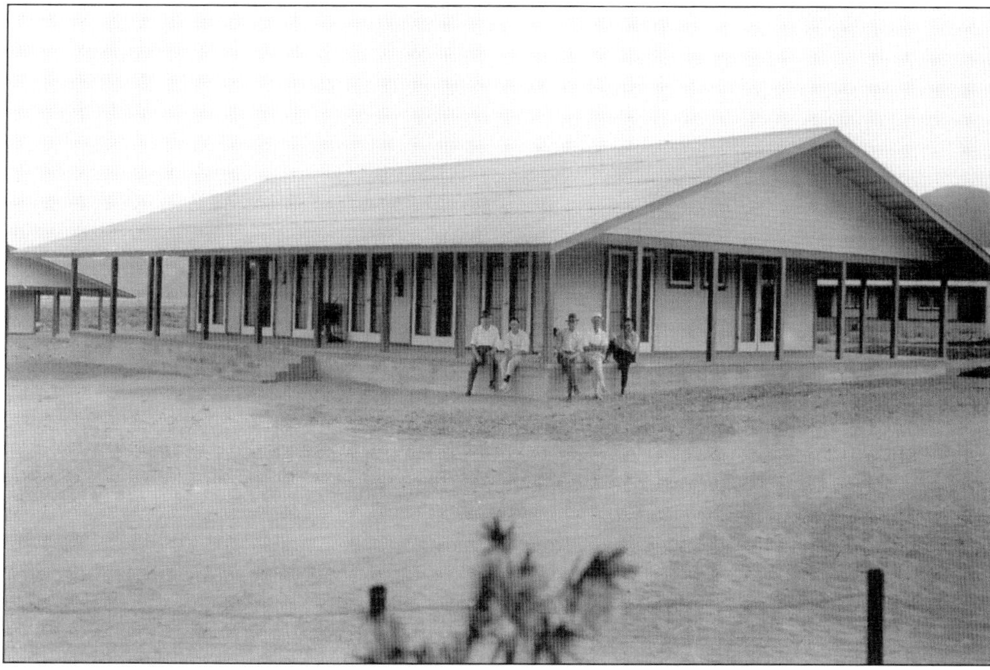

In 1916, American Trona Corporation constructed a guesthouse for visiting owners, managers, and engineers. The photograph above shows how it looked shortly after it was finished. Each room could hold a bed and table and had a small side room with a shower, wash basin, and toilet. Below is the same building today, only now it is the Old Guest House Museum of the Searles Valley Historical Society. The society also owns five other historic properties in Searles Valley and a large archive of historical photographs and printed materials. These provided much of the material in this book.

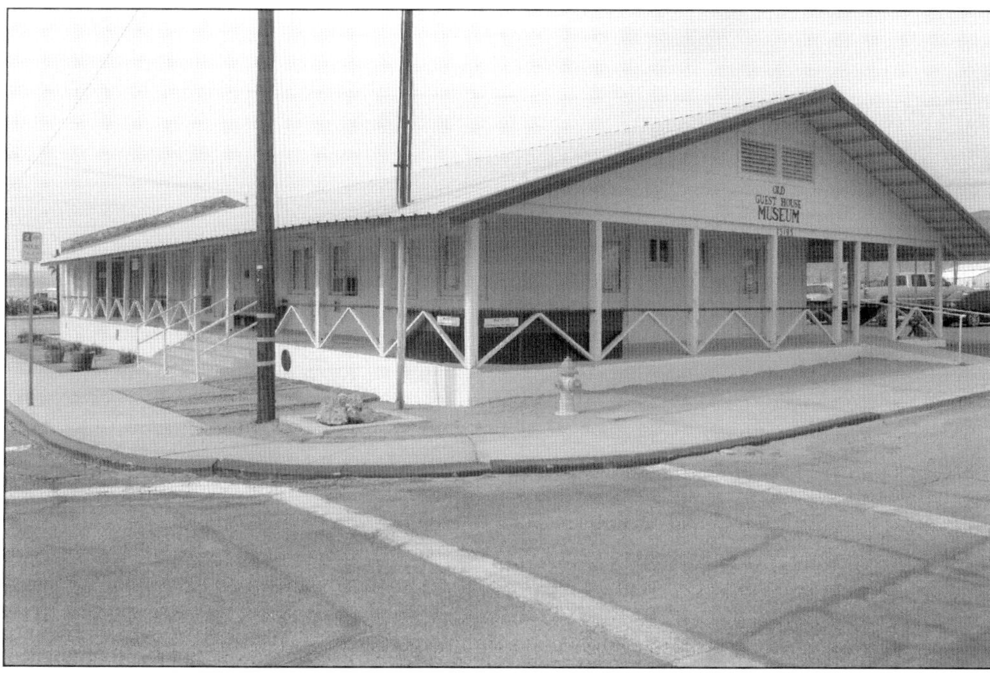